YOUNG X-MEN

Recently, the X-Men fought a war to save the life of the first mutant born since M-Day.
The X-Men, led by Cyclops, won the war and the baby was sent to the future for
her safety. But one of the casualties was Professor Xavier, the founder of the X-Men.
With Xavier gone, and his dream seemingly dead with him, Cyclops disbanded
the X-Men and the mutants scattered across the globe.

FINAL GENESIS

Writer: Marc Guggenheim
Pencils: Yanick Paquette

NO LONGER
PROPERTY OF PPLD

Inks: Ray Snyder with Kris Justice (Issue #3)
Colors: Rob Schwager
Letters: Dave Sharpe
Covers: Terry Dodson & Rachel Dodson
Assistant Editors: Daniel Ketchum & Will Panzo
Editor: Nick Lowe

Dedicated to Stéphane Peru

Collection Editor: Jennifer Grünwald • **Editorial Assistant:** Alex Starbuck
Assistant Editors: Cory Levine & John Denning • **Editor, Special Projects:** Mark D. Beazley
Senior Editor, Special Projects: Jeff Youngquist • **Senior Vice President of Sales:** David Gabriel
Production Spring Hoteling

Editor an Buckley

PIKES PEAK LIBRARY DISTRICT

181186255

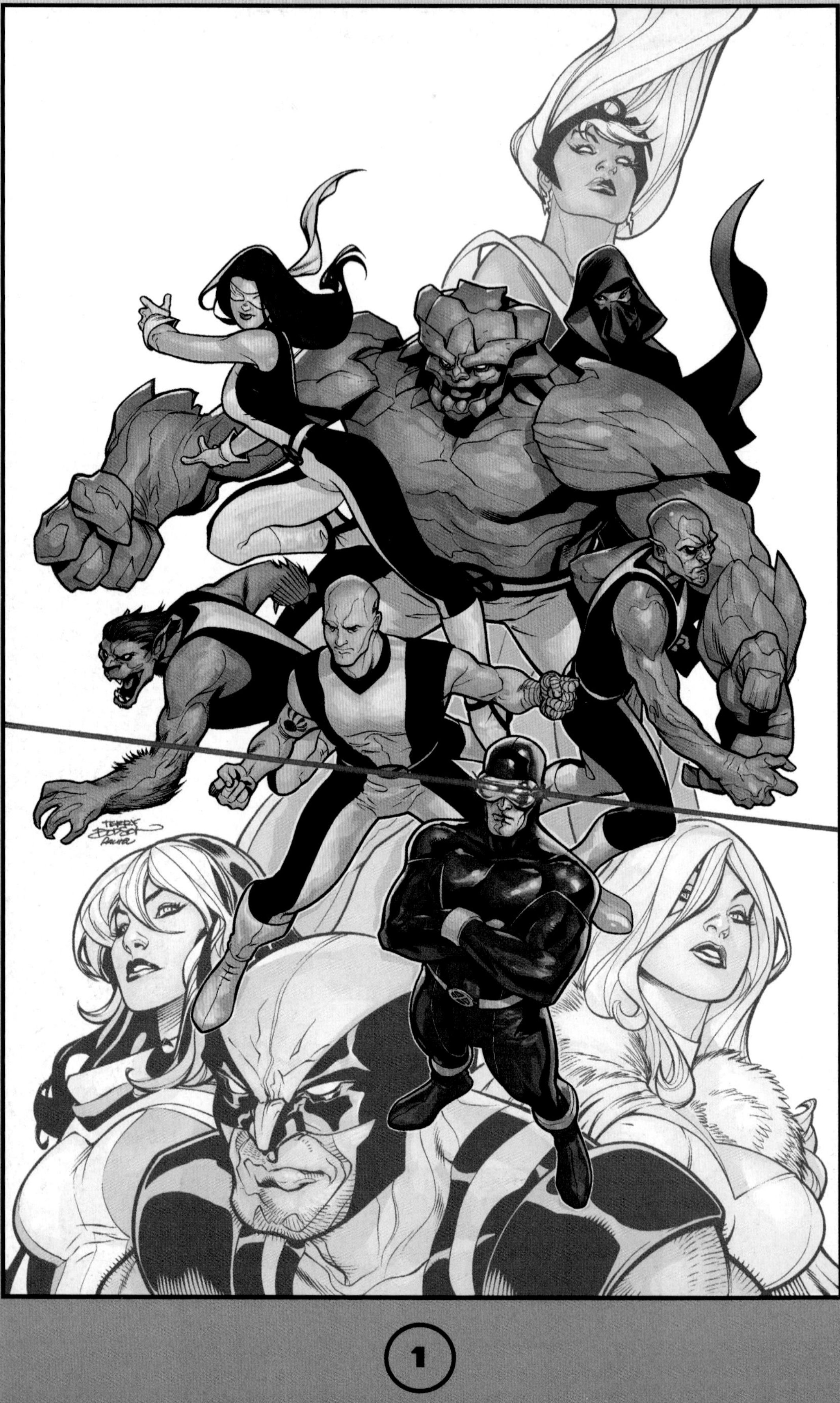

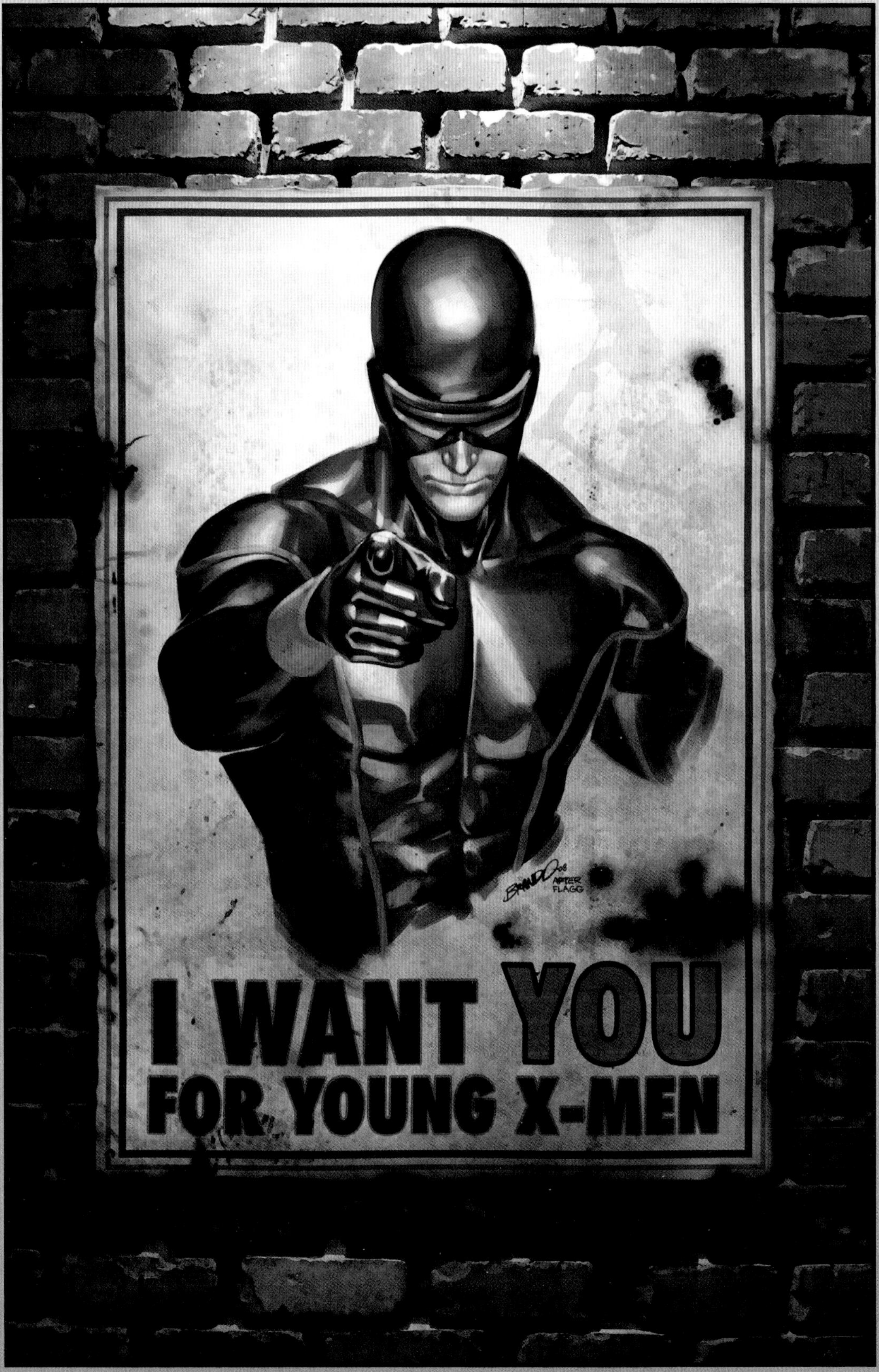
I WANT YOU
FOR YOUNG X-MEN
BRANDO '08 AFTER FLAGG

1

Variant Cover by Brandon Peterson

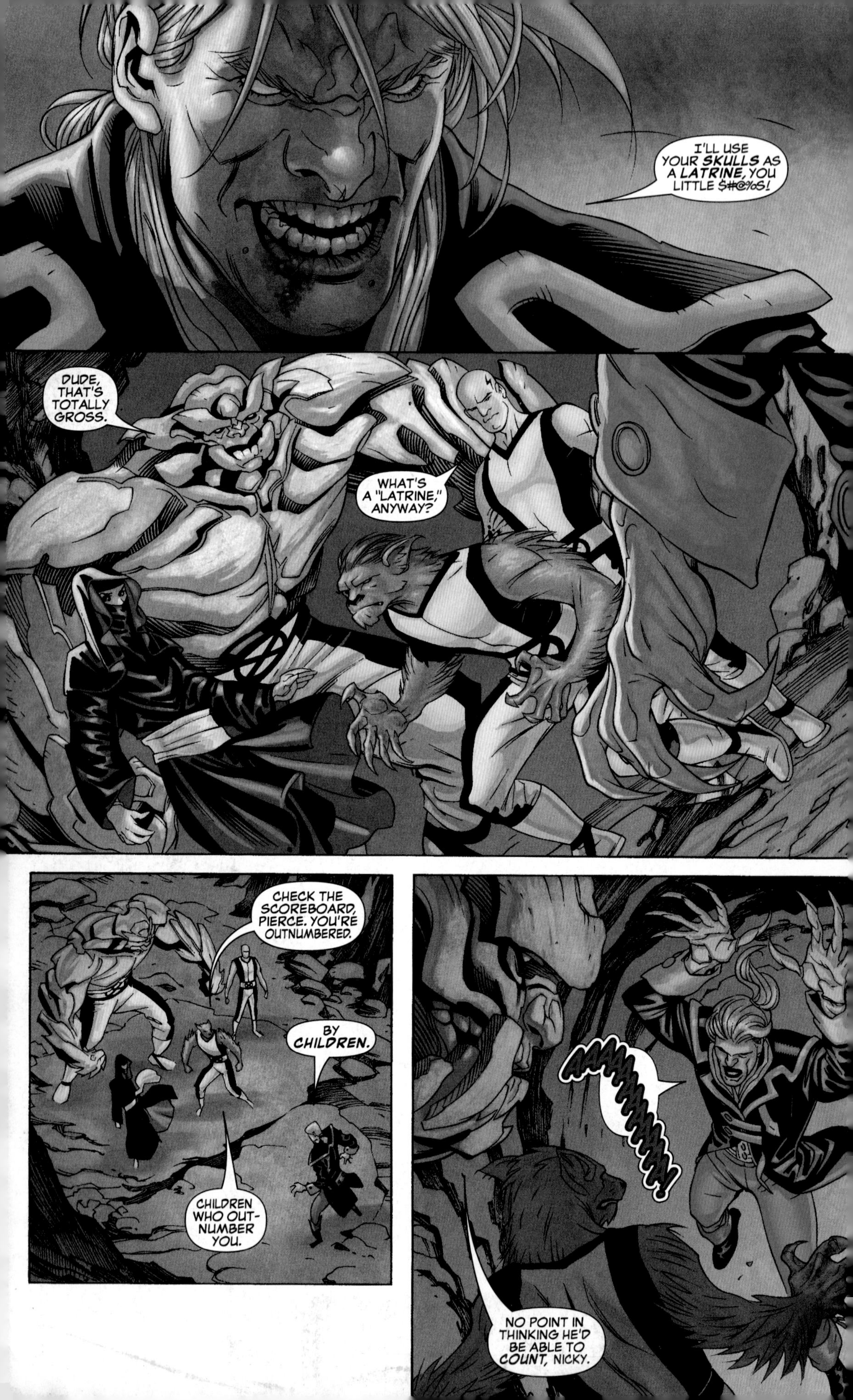
I'LL USE YOUR SKULLS AS A LATRINE, YOU LITTLE $#@%S!
DUDE, THAT'S TOTALLY GROSS.
WHAT'S A "LATRINE," ANYWAY?
CHECK THE SCOREBOARD, PIERCE. YOU'RE OUTNUMBERED.
BY CHILDREN.
CHILDREN WHO OUT-NUMBER YOU.
AAAAAAAAAAH!
NO POINT IN THINKING HE'D BE ABLE TO COUNT, NICKY.

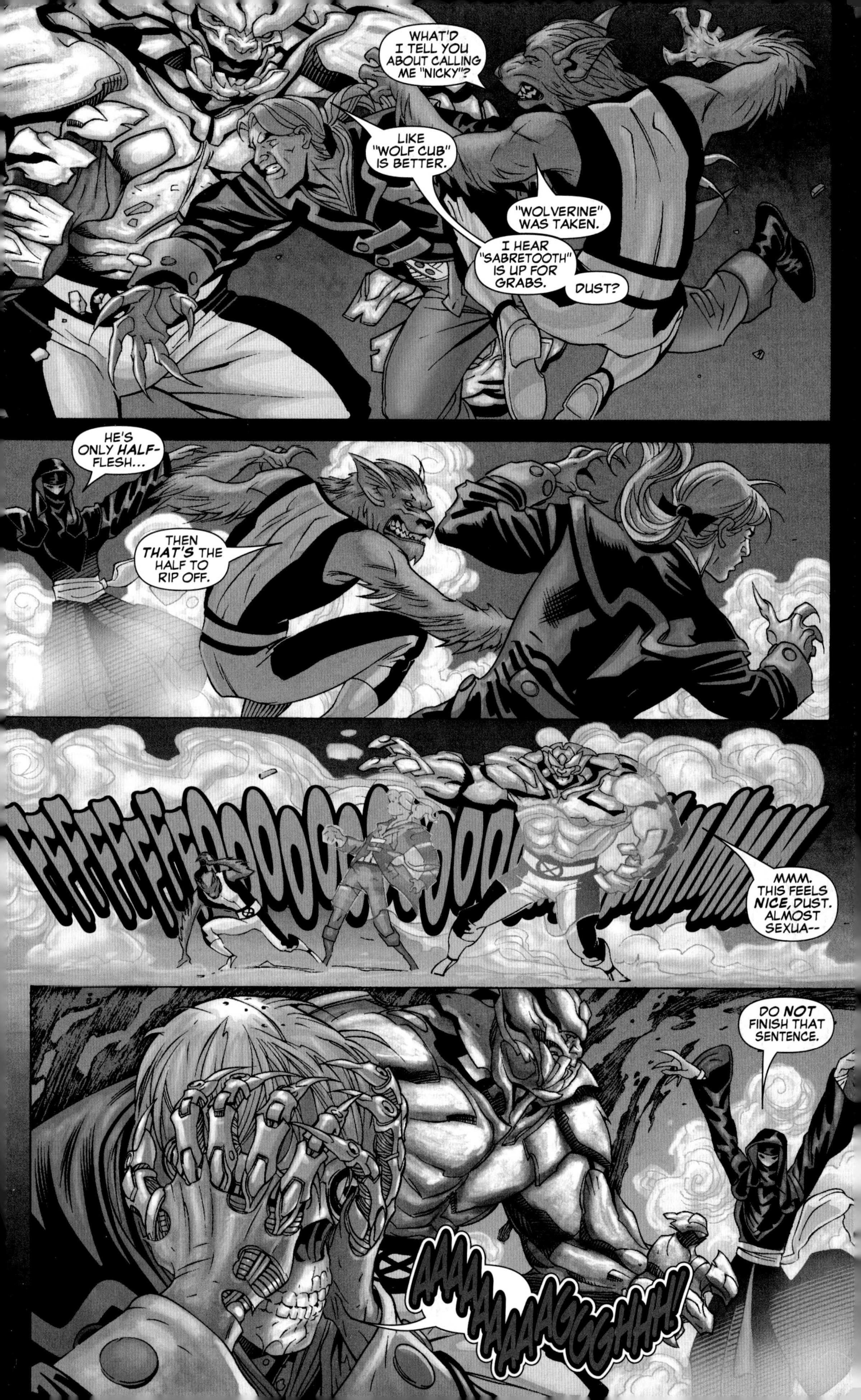
WHAT'D I TELL YOU ABOUT CALLING ME "NICKY"?
LIKE "WOLF CUB" IS BETTER.
"WOLVERINE" WAS TAKEN.
I HEAR "SABRETOOTH" IS UP FOR GRABS.
DUST?
HE'S ONLY HALF-FLESH...
THEN THAT'S THE HALF TO RIP OFF.
FFFFFFOOOOOOOOOOO
MMM. THIS FEELS NICE, DUST. ALMOST SEXUA--
DO NOT FINISH THAT SENTENCE.
AAAAAAAAAGGGHHH!

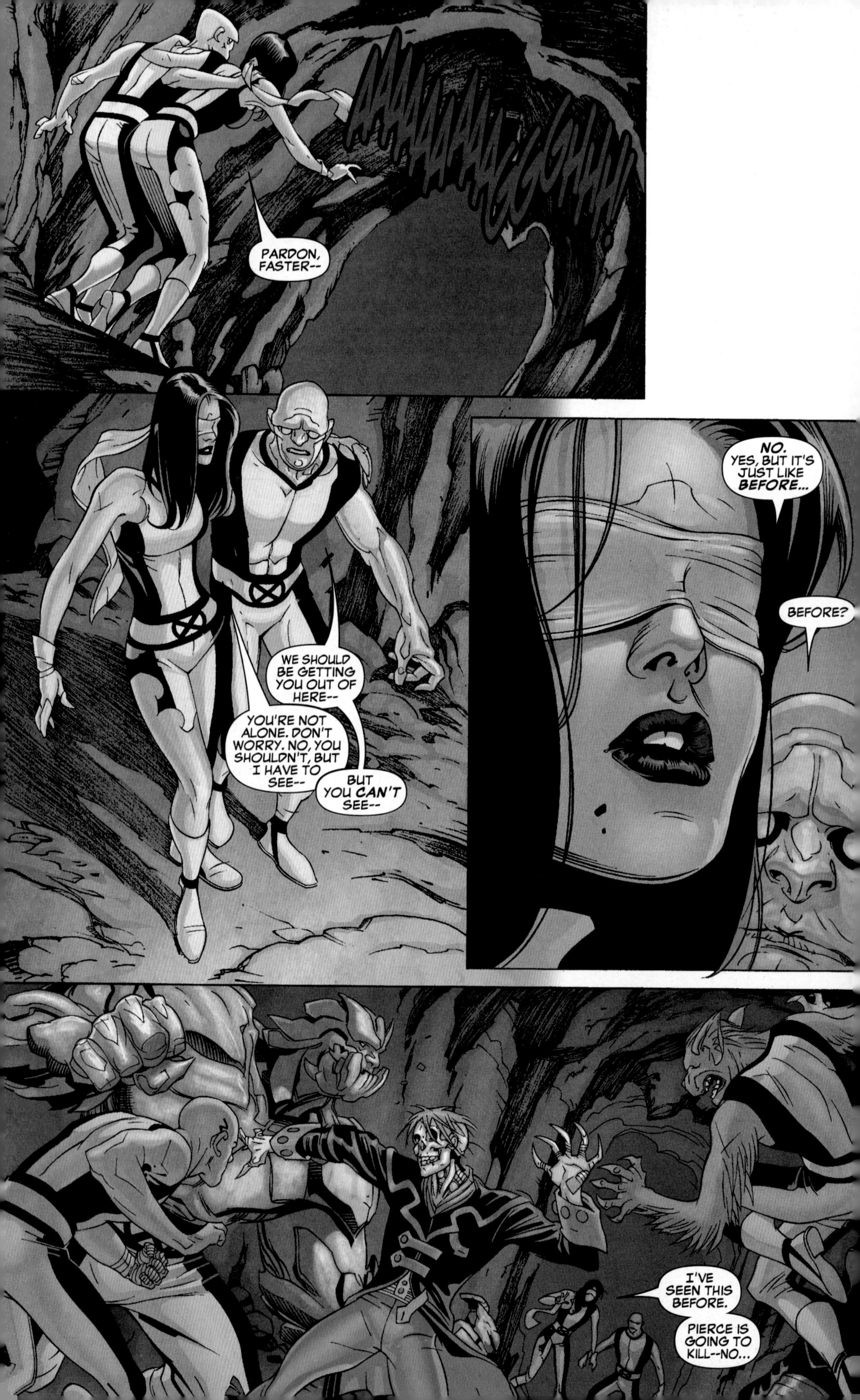
PARDON, FASTER--
WE SHOULD BE GETTING YOU OUT OF HERE--
YOU'RE NOT ALONE. DON'T WORRY. NO, YOU SHOULDN'T, BUT I HAVE TO SEE--
BUT YOU **CAN'T** SEE--
NO. YES, BUT IT'S JUST LIKE ***BEFORE...***
BEFORE?
I'VE SEEN THIS BEFORE.
PIERCE IS GOING TO KILL--NO...

SHAROOOM!

ACK--!

NO!

NNNNNNNNNNNOOOOOOOOOOOOOOOOOOOOOO!

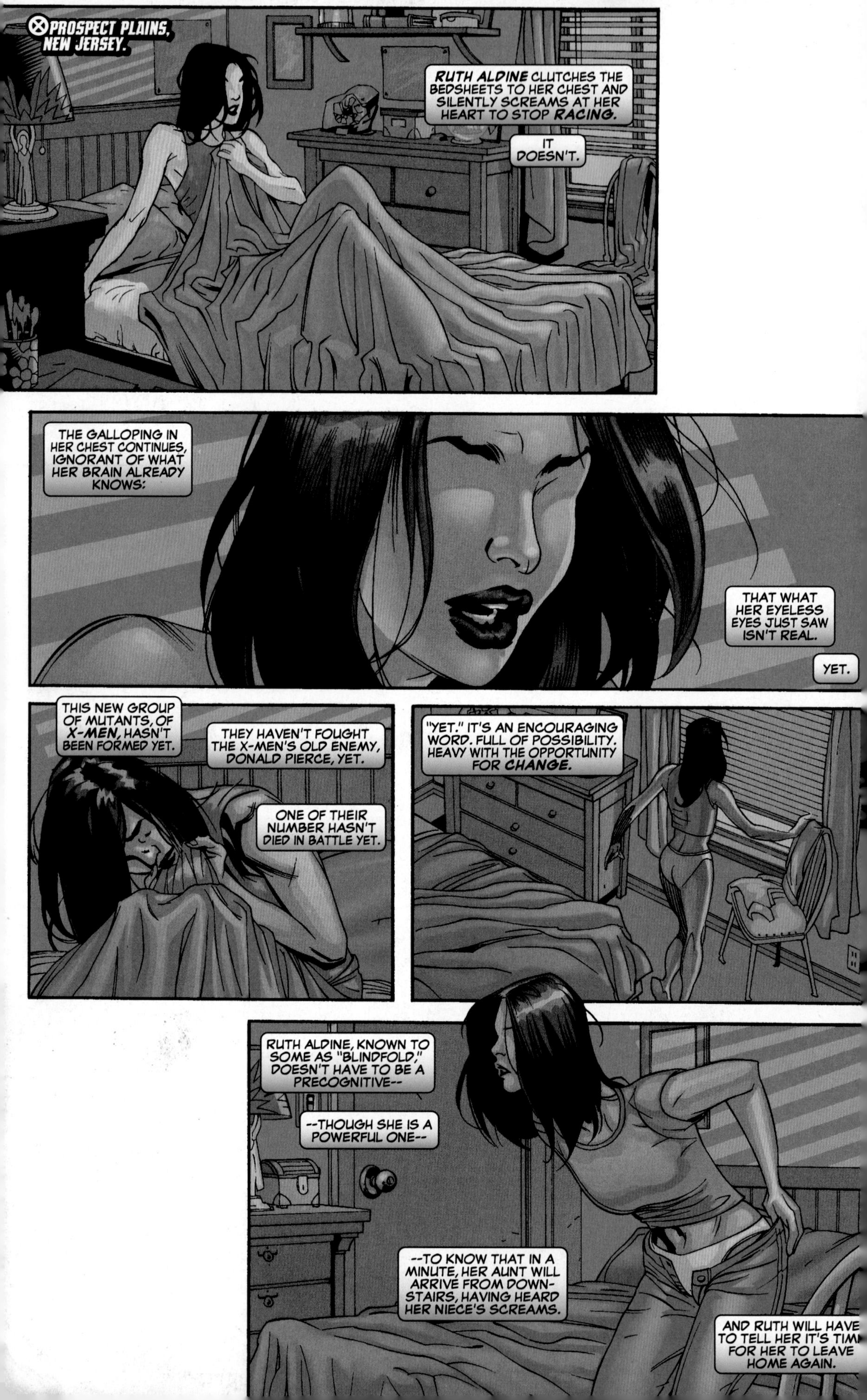
PROSPECT PLAINS, NEW JERSEY.
RUTH ALDINE CLUTCHES THE BEDSHEETS TO HER CHEST AND SILENTLY SCREAMS AT HER HEART TO STOP RACING.
IT DOESN'T.
THE GALLOPING IN HER CHEST CONTINUES, IGNORANT OF WHAT HER BRAIN ALREADY KNOWS:
THAT WHAT HER EYELESS EYES JUST SAW ISN'T REAL.
YET.
THIS NEW GROUP OF MUTANTS, OF X-MEN, HASN'T BEEN FORMED YET.
THEY HAVEN'T FOUGHT THE X-MEN'S OLD ENEMY, DONALD PIERCE, YET.
ONE OF THEIR NUMBER HASN'T DIED IN BATTLE YET.
"YET." IT'S AN ENCOURAGING WORD. FULL OF POSSIBILITY. HEAVY WITH THE OPPORTUNITY FOR CHANGE.
RUTH ALDINE, KNOWN TO SOME AS "BLINDFOLD," DOESN'T HAVE TO BE A PRECOGNITIVE--
--THOUGH SHE IS A POWERFUL ONE--
--TO KNOW THAT IN A MINUTE, HER AUNT WILL ARRIVE FROM DOWN-STAIRS, HAVING HEARD HER NIECE'S SCREAMS.
AND RUTH WILL HAVE TO TELL HER IT'S TIM FOR HER TO LEAVE HOME AGAIN.

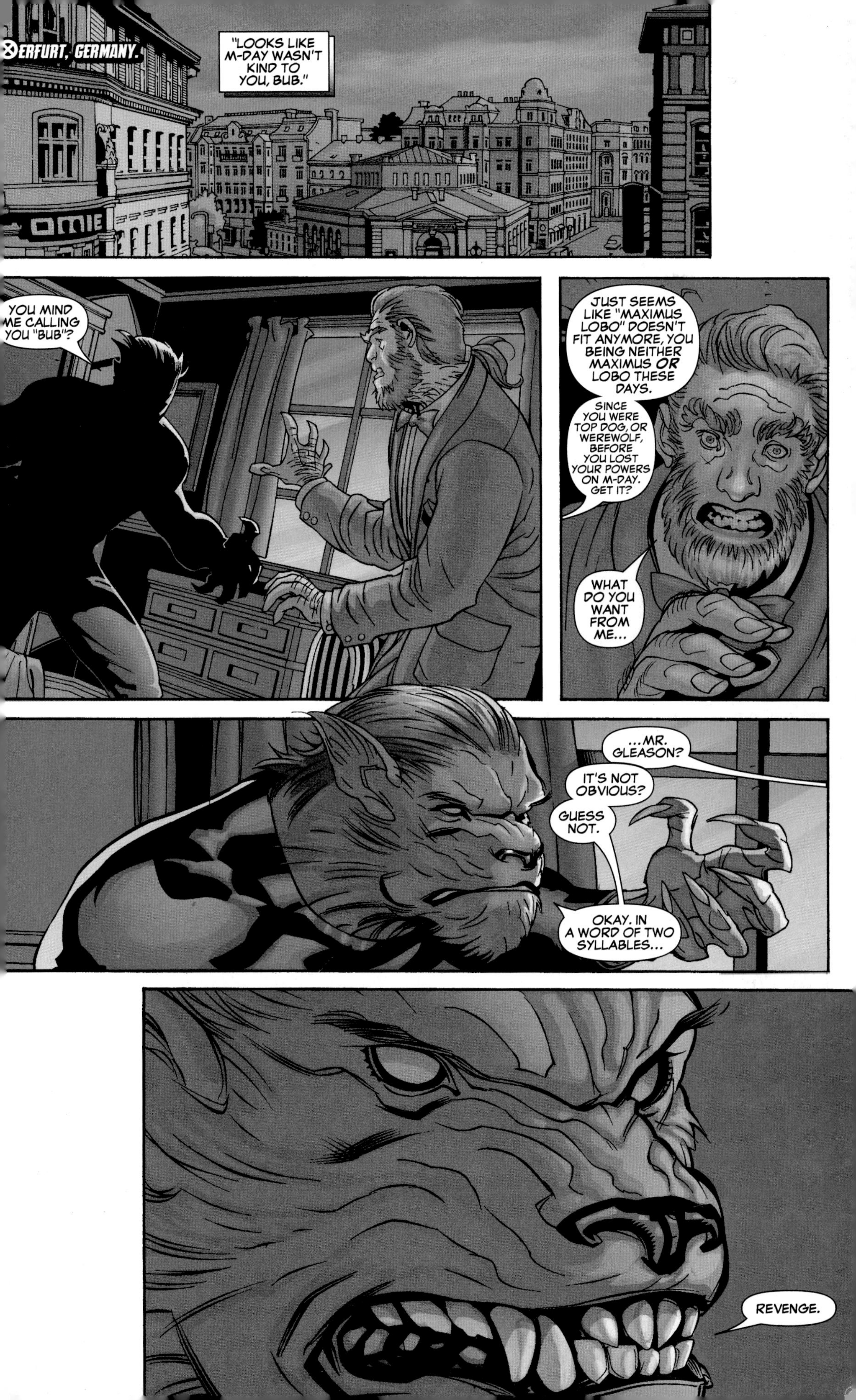
ERFURT, GERMANY.
"LOOKS LIKE M-DAY WASN'T KIND TO YOU, BUB."
YOU MIND ME CALLING YOU "BUB"?
JUST SEEMS LIKE "MAXIMUS LOBO" DOESN'T FIT ANYMORE, YOU BEING NEITHER MAXIMUS OR LOBO THESE DAYS.
SINCE YOU WERE TOP DOG, OR WEREWOLF, BEFORE YOU LOST YOUR POWERS ON M-DAY. GET IT?
WHAT DO YOU WANT FROM ME...
...MR. GLEASON?
IT'S NOT OBVIOUS?
GUESS NOT.
OKAY. IN A WORD OF TWO SYLLABLES...
REVENGE.

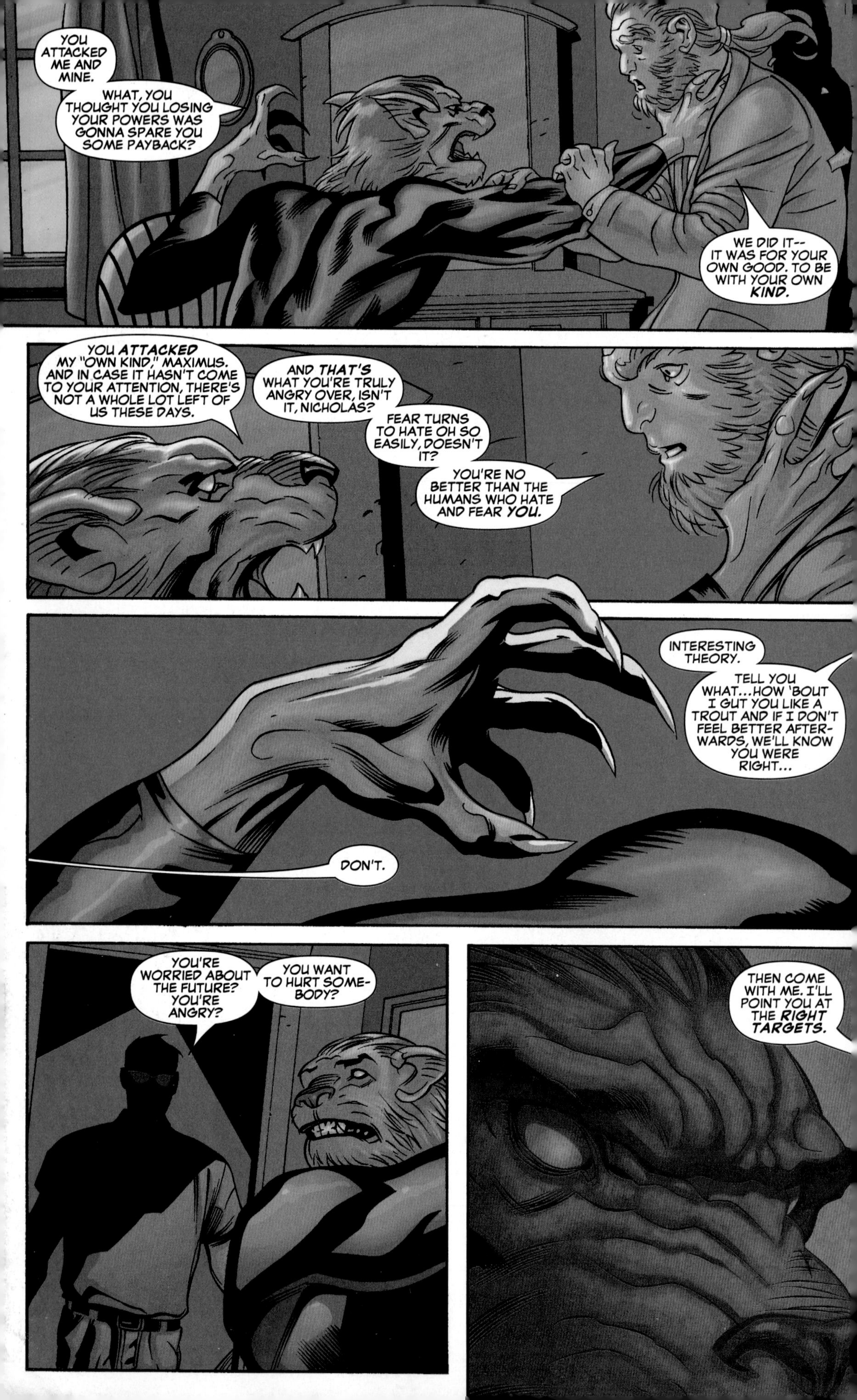
YOU ATTACKED ME AND MINE.
WHAT, YOU THOUGHT YOU LOSING YOUR POWERS WAS GONNA SPARE YOU SOME PAYBACK?
WE DID IT-- IT WAS FOR YOUR OWN GOOD. TO BE WITH YOUR OWN KIND.
YOU ATTACKED MY "OWN KIND," MAXIMUS. AND IN CASE IT HASN'T COME TO YOUR ATTENTION, THERE'S NOT A WHOLE LOT LEFT OF US THESE DAYS.
AND THAT'S WHAT YOU'RE TRULY ANGRY OVER, ISN'T IT, NICHOLAS?
FEAR TURNS TO HATE OH SO EASILY, DOESN'T IT?
YOU'RE NO BETTER THAN THE HUMANS WHO HATE AND FEAR YOU.
INTERESTING THEORY.
TELL YOU WHAT...HOW 'BOUT I GUT YOU LIKE A TROUT AND IF I DON'T FEEL BETTER AFTER-WARDS, WE'LL KNOW YOU WERE RIGHT...
DON'T.
YOU'RE WORRIED ABOUT THE FUTURE? YOU'RE ANGRY?
YOU WANT TO HURT SOME-BODY?
THEN COME WITH ME. I'LL POINT YOU AT THE RIGHT TARGETS.

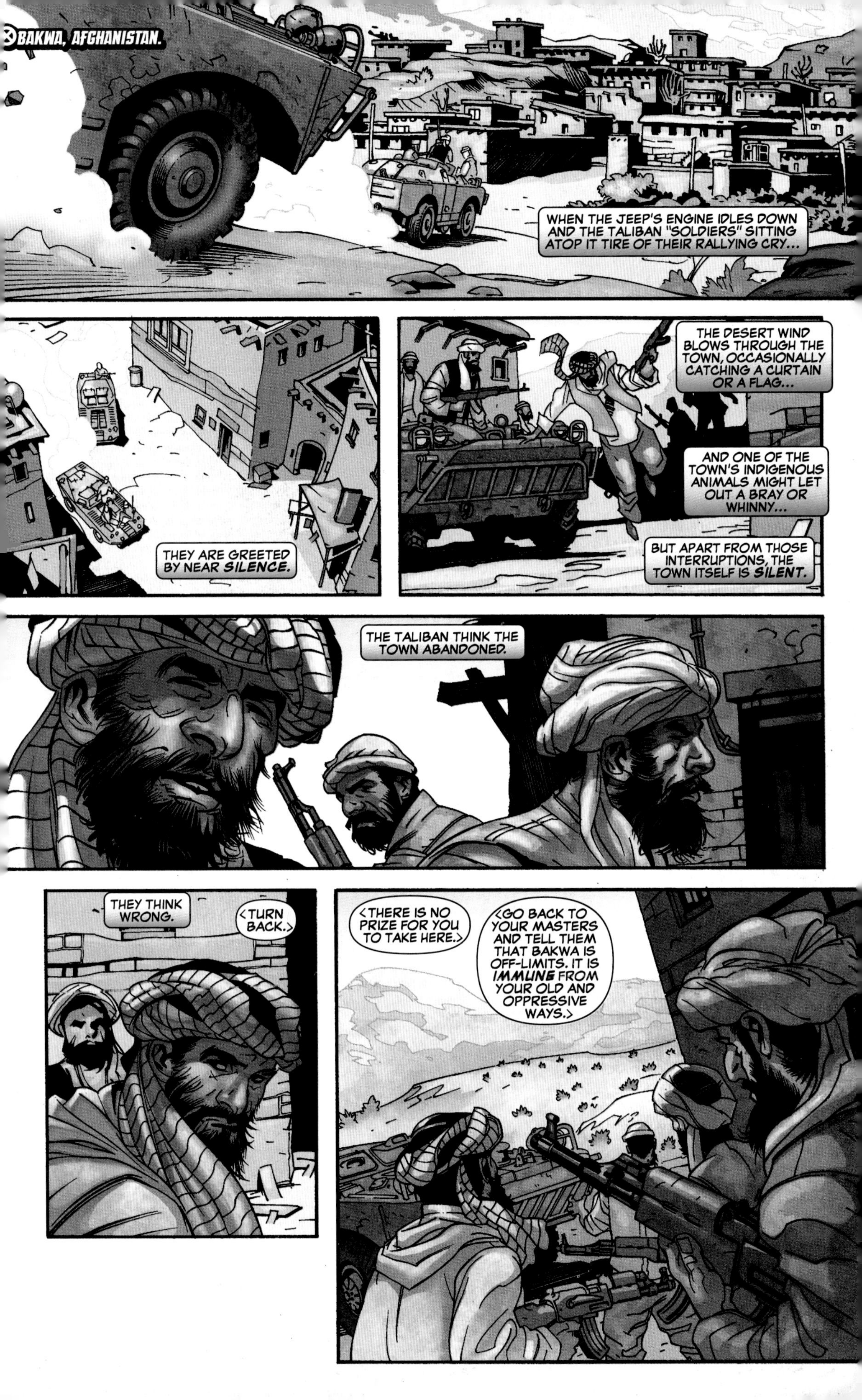
BAKWA, AFGHANISTAN.
WHEN THE JEEP'S ENGINE IDLES DOWN AND THE TALIBAN "SOLDIERS" SITTING ATOP IT TIRE OF THEIR RALLYING CRY...
THEY ARE GREETED BY NEAR SILENCE.
THE DESERT WIND BLOWS THROUGH THE TOWN, OCCASIONALLY CATCHING A CURTAIN OR A FLAG...
AND ONE OF THE TOWN'S INDIGENOUS ANIMALS MIGHT LET OUT A BRAY OR WHINNY...
BUT APART FROM THOSE INTERRUPTIONS, THE TOWN ITSELF IS SILENT.
THE TALIBAN THINK THE TOWN ABANDONED.
THEY THINK WRONG.
<TURN BACK.>
<THERE IS NO PRIZE FOR YOU TO TAKE HERE.>
<GO BACK TO YOUR MASTERS AND TELL THEM THAT BAKWA IS OFF-LIMITS. IT IS IMMUNE FROM YOUR OLD AND OPPRESSIVE WAYS.>

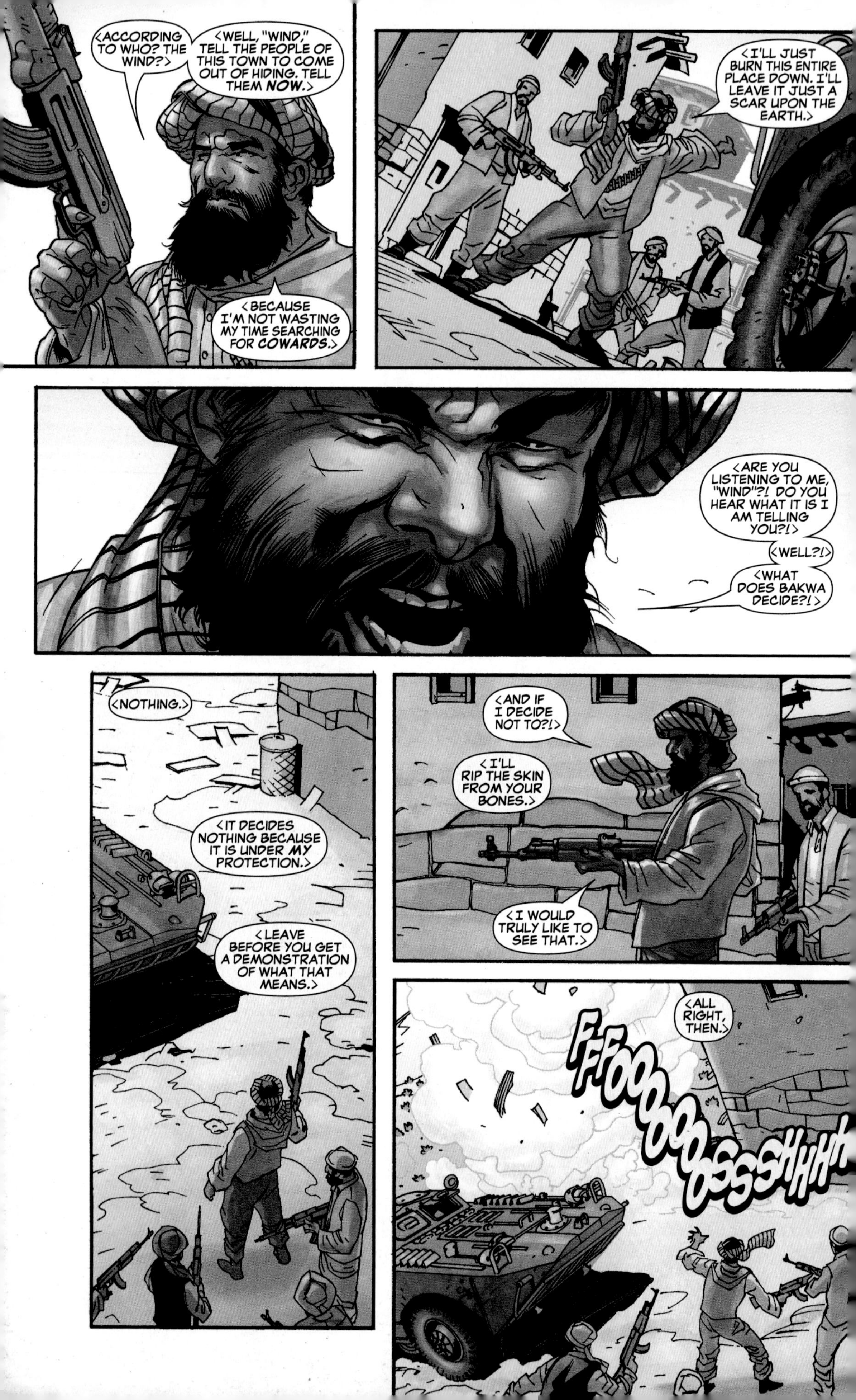
<ACCORDING TO WHO? THE WIND?>
<WELL, "WIND," TELL THE PEOPLE OF THIS TOWN TO COME OUT OF HIDING. TELL THEM **NOW**.>
<BECAUSE I'M NOT WASTING MY TIME SEARCHING FOR **COWARDS**.>
<I'LL JUST BURN THIS ENTIRE PLACE DOWN. I'LL LEAVE IT JUST A SCAR UPON THE EARTH.>
<ARE YOU LISTENING TO ME, "WIND"?! DO YOU HEAR WHAT IT IS I AM TELLING YOU?!>
<WELL?!>
<WHAT DOES BAKWA DECIDE?!>
<NOTHING.>
<IT DECIDES NOTHING BECAUSE IT IS UNDER **MY** PROTECTION.>
<LEAVE BEFORE YOU GET A DEMONSTRATION OF WHAT THAT MEANS.>
<AND IF I DECIDE NOT TO?!>
<I'LL RIP THE SKIN FROM YOUR BONES.>
<I WOULD TRULY LIKE TO SEE THAT.>
<ALL RIGHT, THEN.>
FFOOOOOOOSSSSHHHH

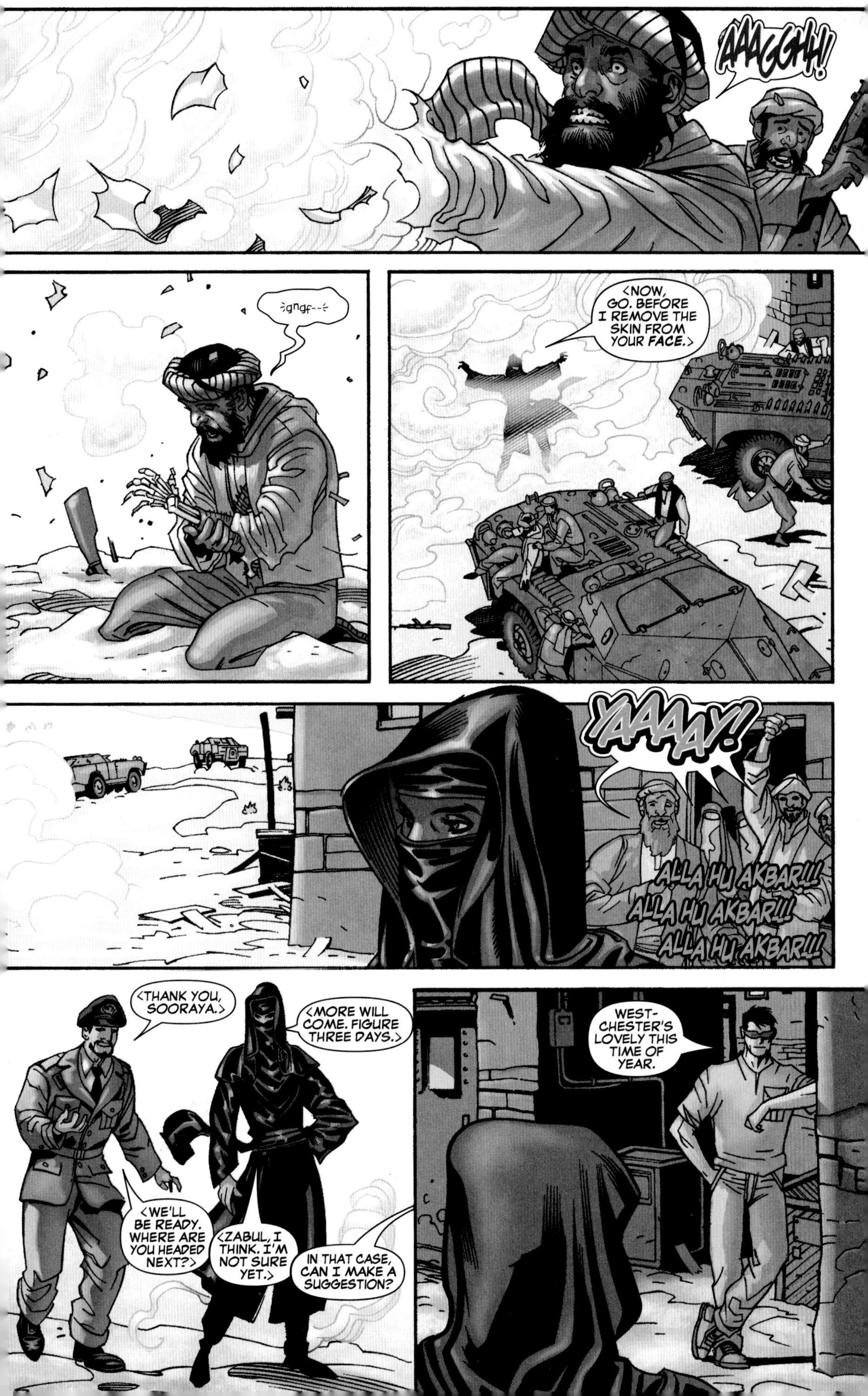

AAAGGHH!
gngf--
<NOW, GO. BEFORE I REMOVE THE SKIN FROM YOUR FACE.>
YAAAAY!
ALLA HU AKBAR!!!
ALLA HU AKBAR!!!
ALLA HU AKBAR!!!
<THANK YOU, SOORAYA.>
<MORE WILL COME. FIGURE THREE DAYS.>
<WE'LL BE READY. WHERE ARE YOU HEADED NEXT?>
<ZABUL, I THINK. I'M NOT SURE YET.>
IN THAT CASE, CAN I MAKE A SUGGESTION?
WEST-CHESTER'S LOVELY THIS TIME OF YEAR.

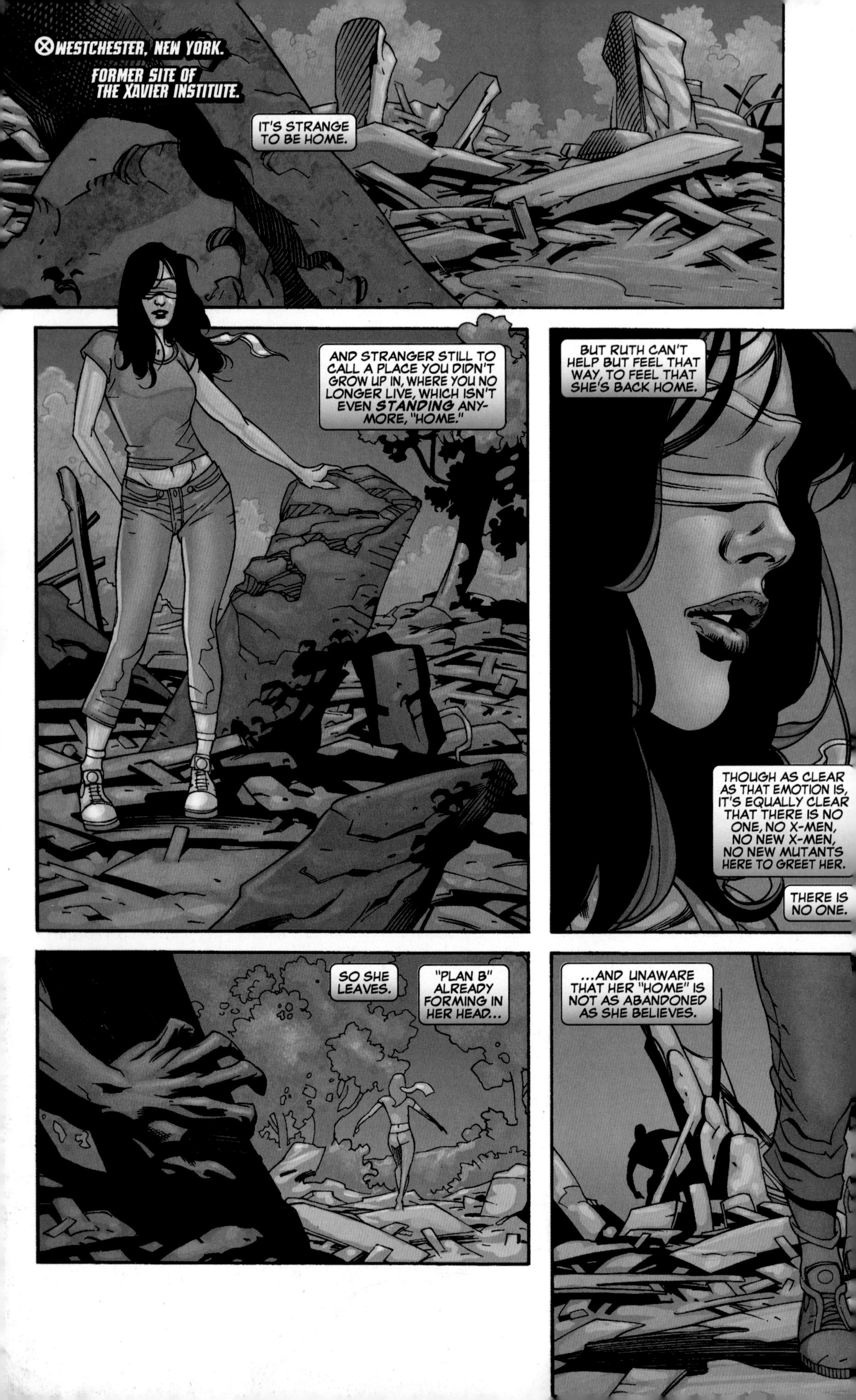
WESTCHESTER, NEW YORK.
FORMER SITE OF THE XAVIER INSTITUTE.
IT'S STRANGE TO BE HOME.
AND STRANGER STILL TO CALL A PLACE YOU DIDN'T GROW UP IN, WHERE YOU NO LONGER LIVE, WHICH ISN'T EVEN STANDING ANYMORE, "HOME."
BUT RUTH CAN'T HELP BUT FEEL THAT WAY, TO FEEL THAT SHE'S BACK HOME.
THOUGH AS CLEAR AS THAT EMOTION IS, IT'S EQUALLY CLEAR THAT THERE IS NO ONE, NO X-MEN, NO NEW X-MEN, NO NEW MUTANTS HERE TO GREET HER.
THERE IS NO ONE.
SO SHE LEAVES.
"PLAN B" ALREADY FORMING IN HER HEAD...
...AND UNAWARE THAT HER "HOME" IS NOT AS ABANDONED AS SHE BELIEVES.

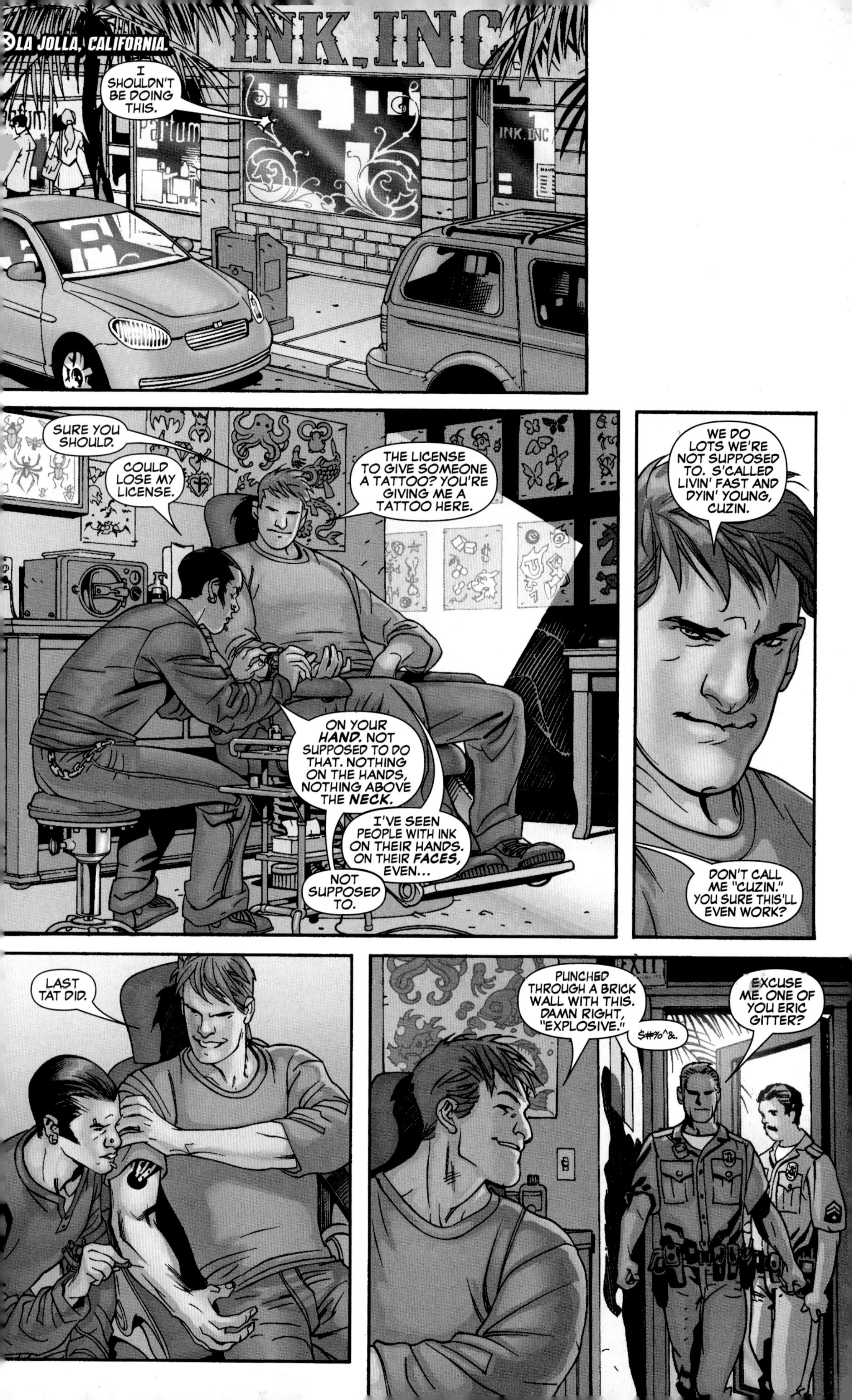
LA JOLLA, CALIFORNIA.
INK, INC
I SHOULDN'T BE DOING THIS.
SURE YOU SHOULD.
COULD LOSE MY LICENSE.
THE LICENSE TO GIVE SOMEONE A TATTOO? YOU'RE GIVING ME A TATTOO HERE.
ON YOUR HAND. NOT SUPPOSED TO DO THAT. NOTHING ON THE HANDS, NOTHING ABOVE THE NECK.
I'VE SEEN PEOPLE WITH INK ON THEIR HANDS. ON THEIR FACES, EVEN...
NOT SUPPOSED TO.
WE DO LOTS WE'RE NOT SUPPOSED TO. S'CALLED LIVIN' FAST AND DYIN' YOUNG, CUZIN.
DON'T CALL ME "CUZIN." YOU SURE THIS'LL EVEN WORK?
LAST TAT DID.
PUNCHED THROUGH A BRICK WALL WITH THIS. DAMN RIGHT, "EXPLOSIVE."
$#%^&.
EXCUSE ME. ONE OF YOU ERIC GITTER?

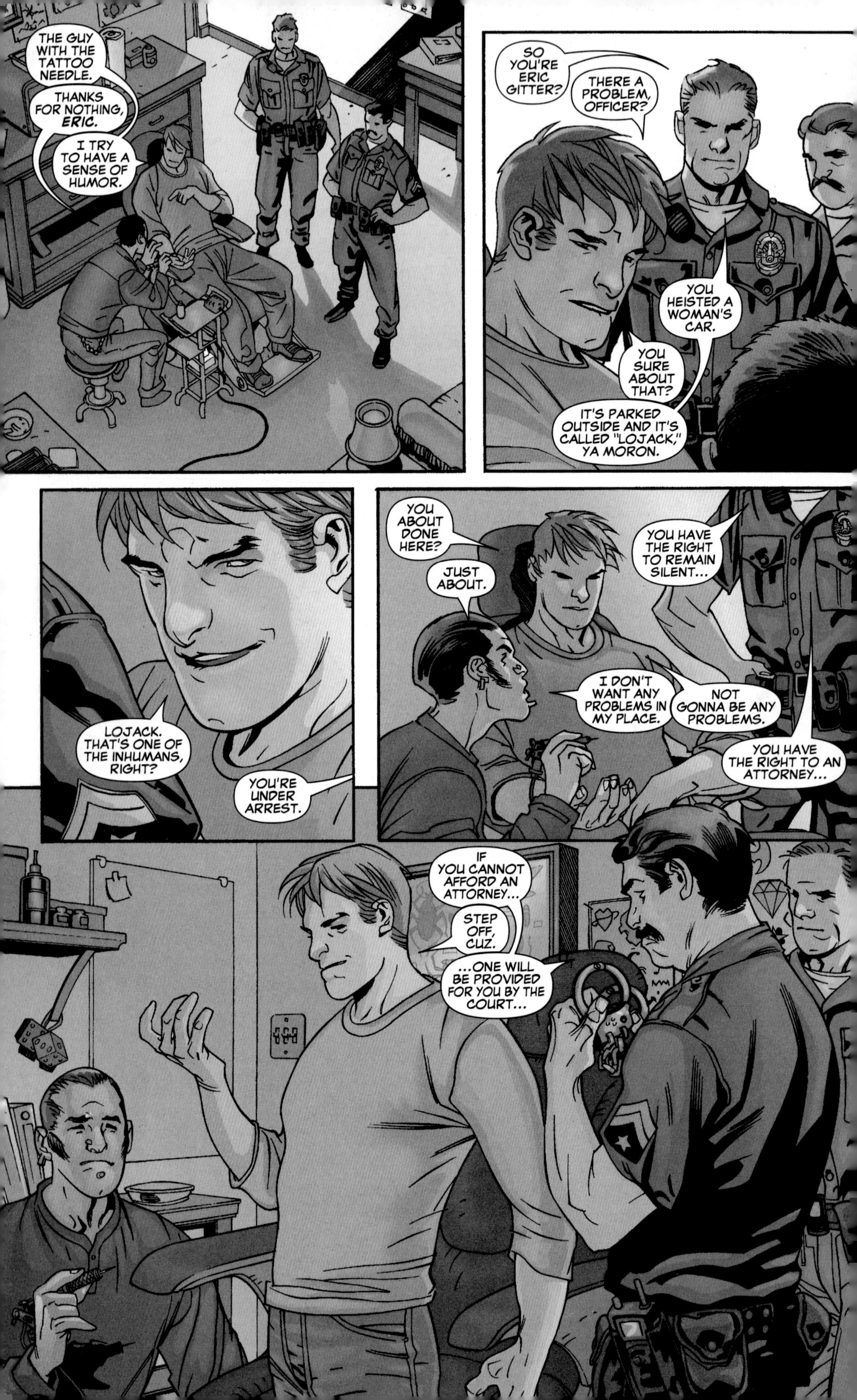
THE GUY WITH THE TATTOO NEEDLE.
THANKS FOR NOTHING, ERIC.
I TRY TO HAVE A SENSE OF HUMOR.
SO YOU'RE ERIC GITTER?
THERE A PROBLEM, OFFICER?
YOU HEISTED A WOMAN'S CAR.
YOU SURE ABOUT THAT?
IT'S PARKED OUTSIDE AND IT'S CALLED "LOJACK," YA MORON.
LOJACK. THAT'S ONE OF THE INHUMANS, RIGHT?
YOU'RE UNDER ARREST.
YOU ABOUT DONE HERE?
JUST ABOUT.
YOU HAVE THE RIGHT TO REMAIN SILENT...
I DON'T WANT ANY PROBLEMS IN MY PLACE.
NOT GONNA BE ANY PROBLEMS.
YOU HAVE THE RIGHT TO AN ATTORNEY...
IF YOU CANNOT AFFORD AN ATTORNEY...
STEP OFF, CUZ.
...ONE WILL BE PROVIDED FOR YOU BY THE COURT...

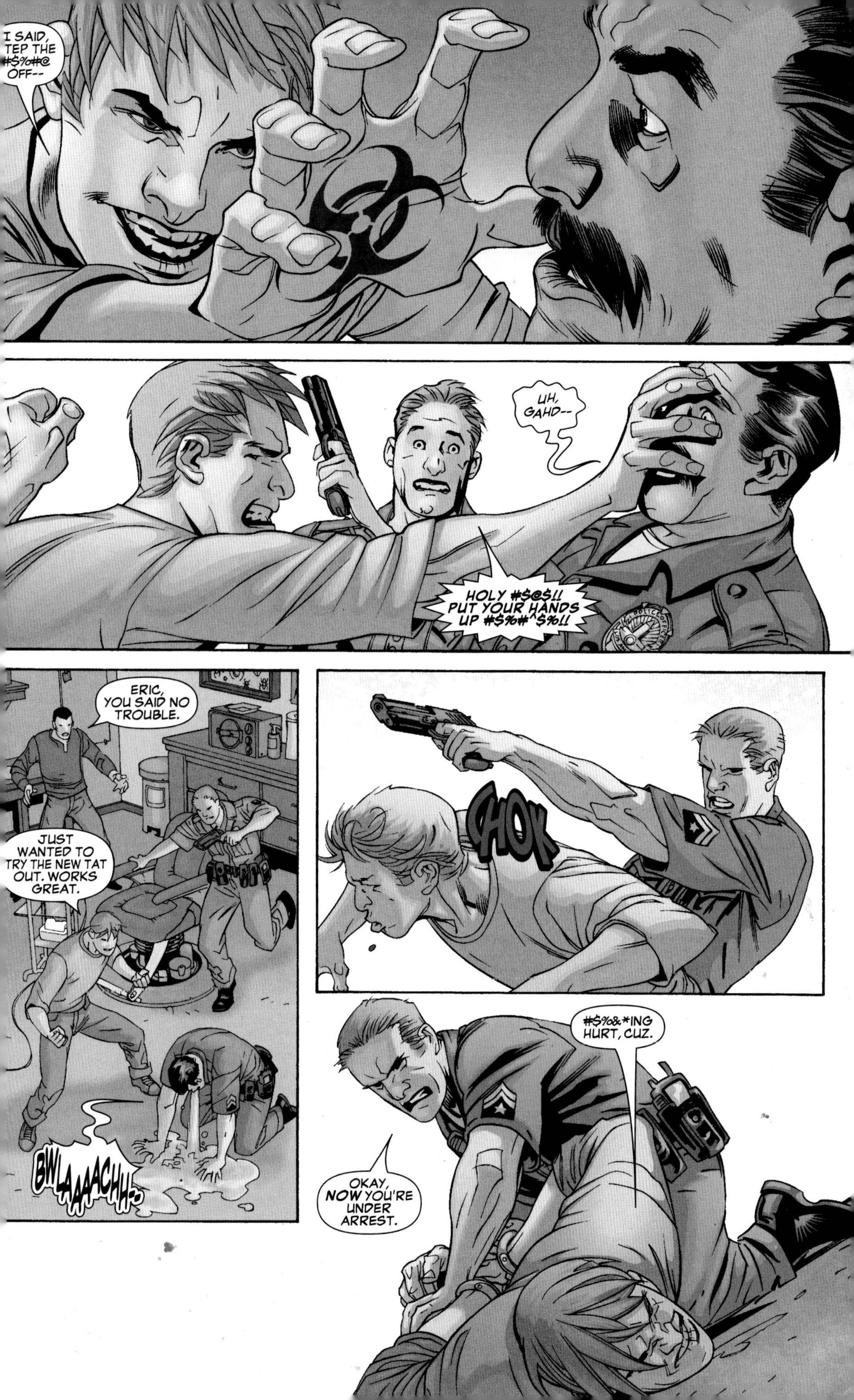
I SAID, TEP THE #$%#@ OFF--
UH, GAHD--
HOLY #$@$!! PUT YOUR HANDS UP #$%#^$%!!
ERIC, YOU SAID NO TROUBLE.
JUST WANTED TO TRY THE NEW TAT OUT. WORKS GREAT.
BWLAAAACHH
CHOK
#$%&*ING HURT, CUZ.
OKAY, NOW YOU'RE UNDER ARREST.

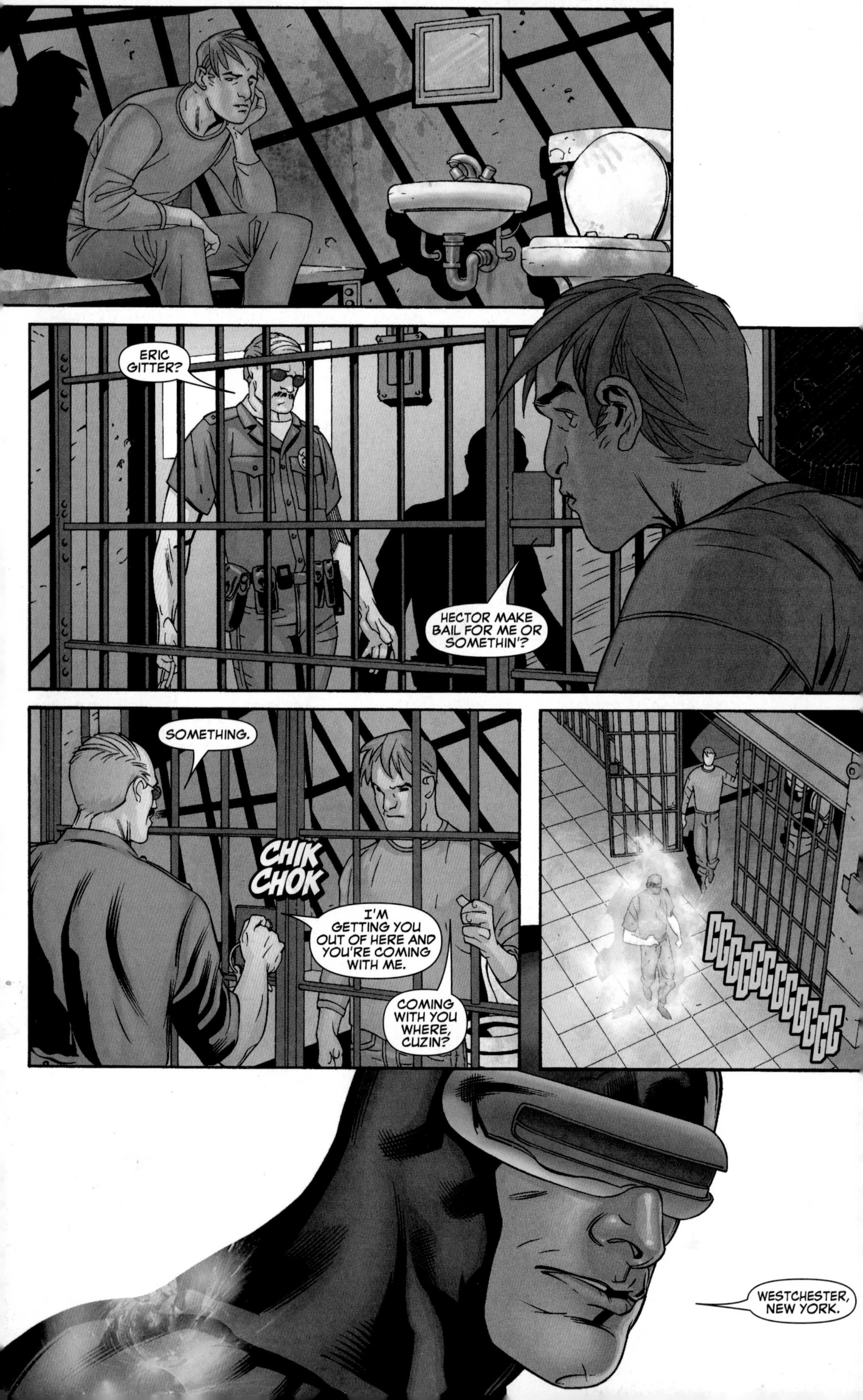
ERIC GITTER?
HECTOR MAKE BAIL FOR ME OR SOMETHIN'?
SOMETHING.
CHIK CHOK
I'M GETTING YOU OUT OF HERE AND YOU'RE COMING WITH ME.
COMING WITH YOU WHERE, CUZIN?
CCCCCCCCCCCC
WESTCHESTER, NEW YORK.

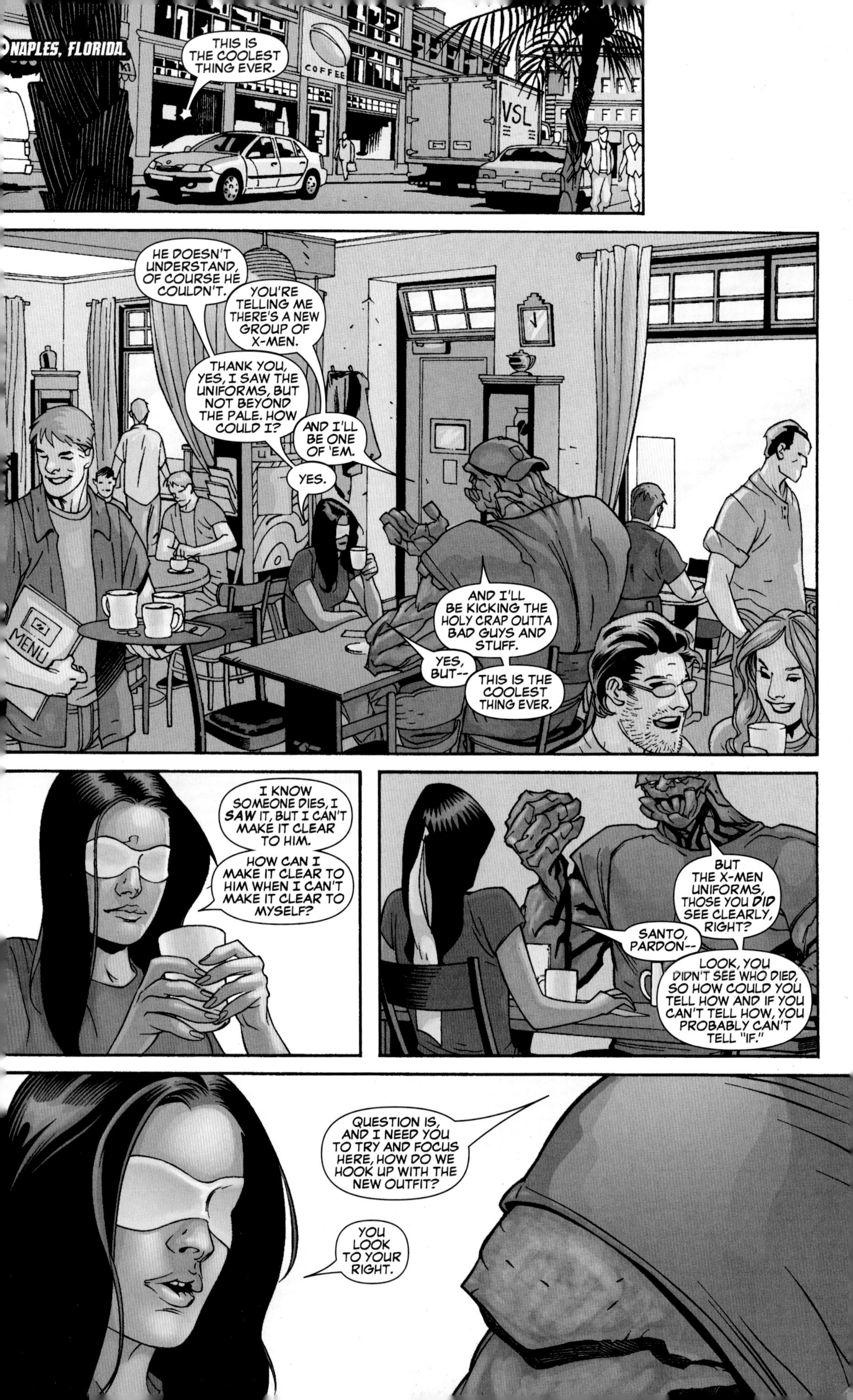
NAPLES, FLORIDA.
THIS IS THE COOLEST THING EVER.
HE DOESN'T UNDERSTAND, OF COURSE HE COULDN'T.
YOU'RE TELLING ME THERE'S A NEW GROUP OF X-MEN.
THANK YOU, YES, I SAW THE UNIFORMS, BUT NOT BEYOND THE PALE. HOW COULD I?
AND I'LL BE ONE OF 'EM.
YES.
AND I'LL BE KICKING THE HOLY CRAP OUTTA BAD GUYS AND STUFF.
YES, BUT--
THIS IS THE COOLEST THING EVER.
MENU
I KNOW SOMEONE DIES, I SAW IT, BUT I CAN'T MAKE IT CLEAR TO HIM.
HOW CAN I MAKE IT CLEAR TO HIM WHEN I CAN'T MAKE IT CLEAR TO MYSELF?
BUT THE X-MEN UNIFORMS, THOSE YOU DID SEE CLEARLY, RIGHT?
SANTO, PARDON--
LOOK, YOU DIDN'T SEE WHO DIED, SO HOW COULD YOU TELL HOW AND IF YOU CAN'T TELL HOW, YOU PROBABLY CAN'T TELL "IF."
QUESTION IS, AND I NEED YOU TO TRY AND FOCUS HERE, HOW DO WE HOOK UP WITH THE NEW OUTFIT?
YOU LOOK TO YOUR RIGHT.

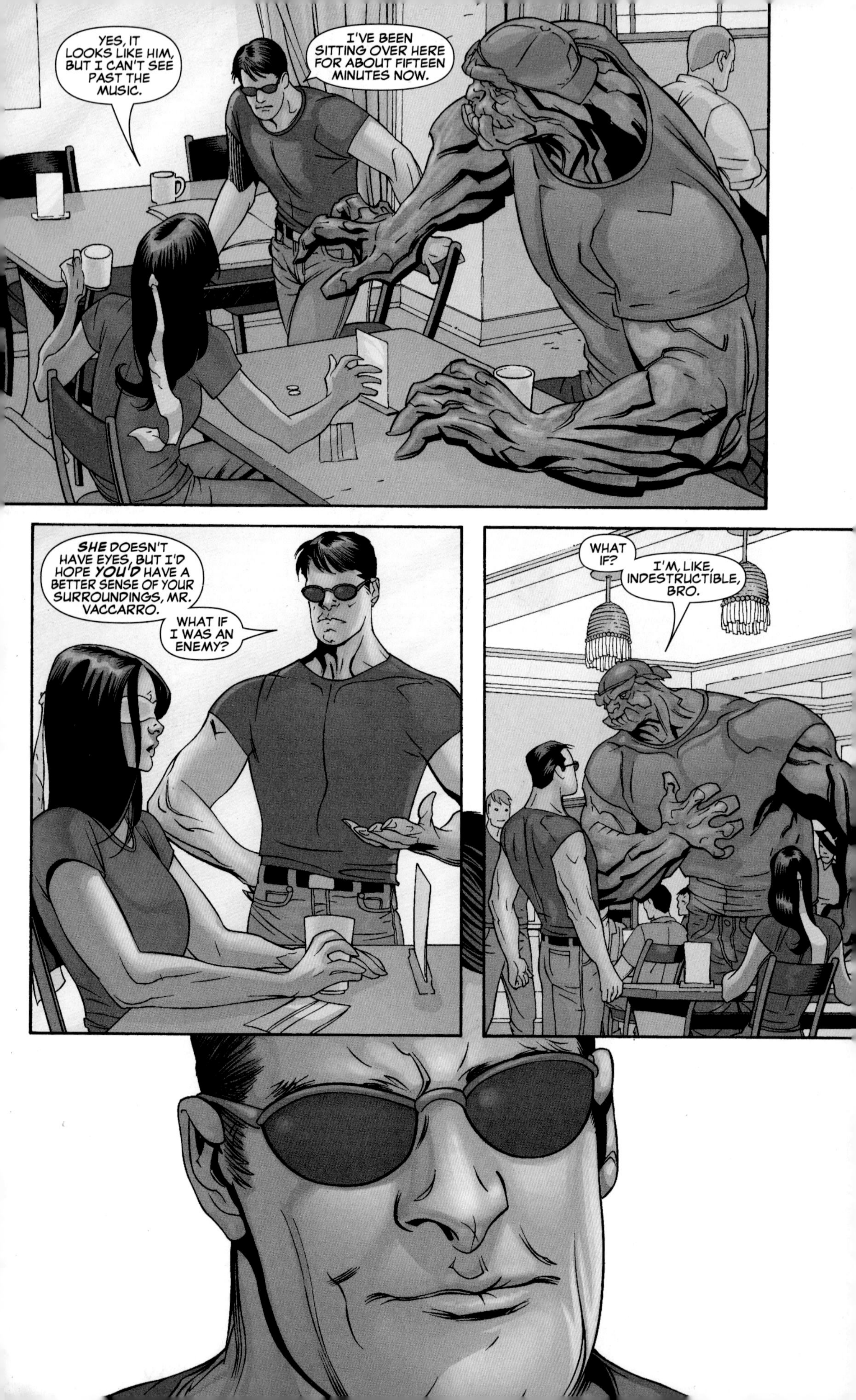
YES, IT LOOKS LIKE HIM, BUT I CAN'T SEE PAST THE MUSIC.
I'VE BEEN SITTING OVER HERE FOR ABOUT FIFTEEN MINUTES NOW.
SHE DOESN'T HAVE EYES, BUT I'D HOPE YOU'D HAVE A BETTER SENSE OF YOUR SURROUNDINGS, MR. VACCARRO.
WHAT IF I WAS AN ENEMY?
WHAT IF?
I'M, LIKE, INDESTRUCTIBLE, BRO.

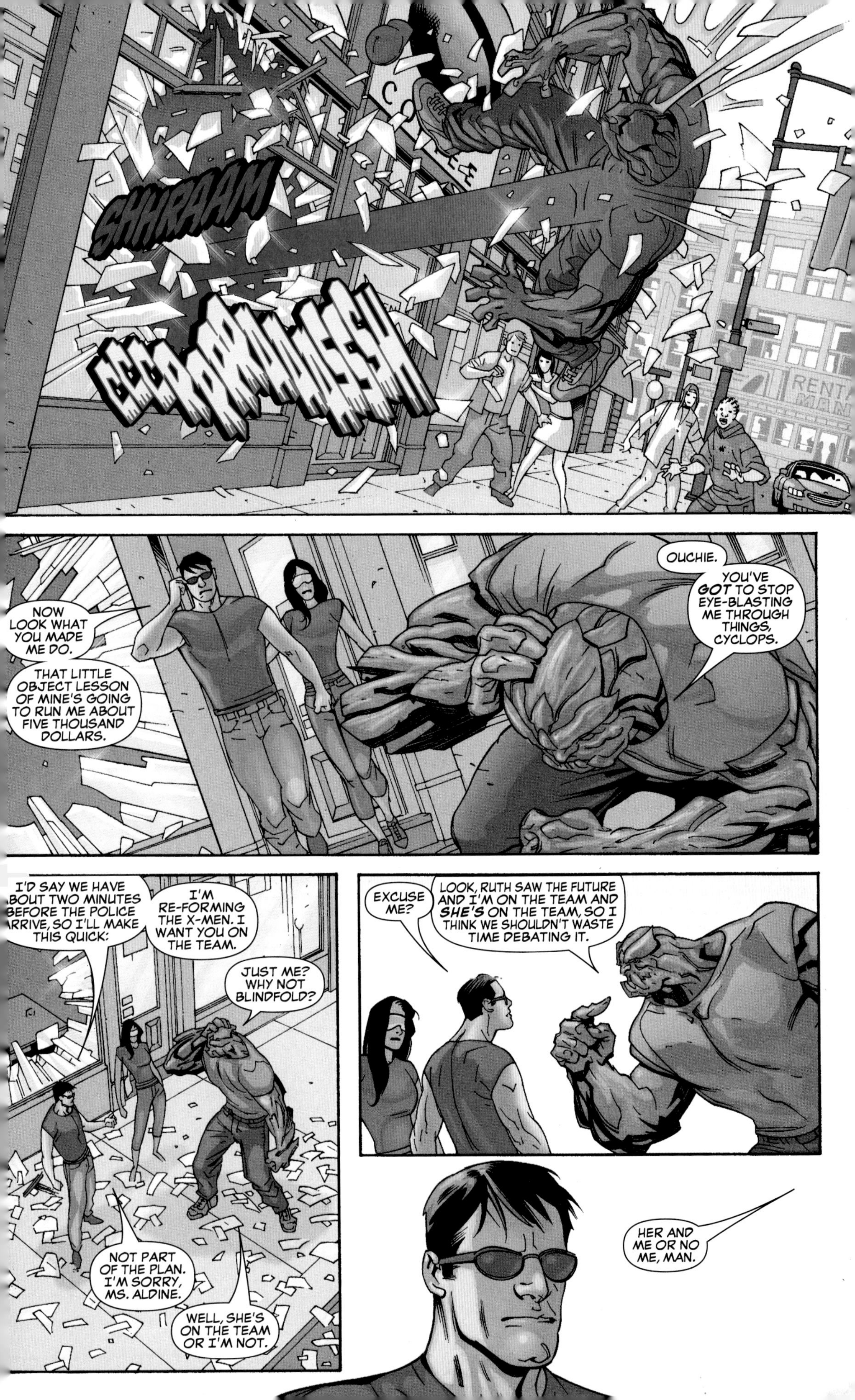
SHHRAAM
CCCRRRRAAASSSH
NOW LOOK WHAT YOU MADE ME DO.
THAT LITTLE OBJECT LESSON OF MINE'S GOING TO RUN ME ABOUT FIVE THOUSAND DOLLARS.
OUCHIE.
YOU'VE GOT TO STOP EYE-BLASTING ME THROUGH THINGS, CYCLOPS.
I'D SAY WE HAVE ABOUT TWO MINUTES BEFORE THE POLICE ARRIVE, SO I'LL MAKE THIS QUICK:
I'M RE-FORMING THE X-MEN. I WANT YOU ON THE TEAM.
JUST ME? WHY NOT BLINDFOLD?
NOT PART OF THE PLAN. I'M SORRY, MS. ALDINE.
WELL, SHE'S ON THE TEAM OR I'M NOT.
EXCUSE ME?
LOOK, RUTH SAW THE FUTURE AND I'M ON THE TEAM AND SHE'S ON THE TEAM, SO I THINK WE SHOULDN'T WASTE TIME DEBATING IT.
HER AND ME OR NO ME, MAN.

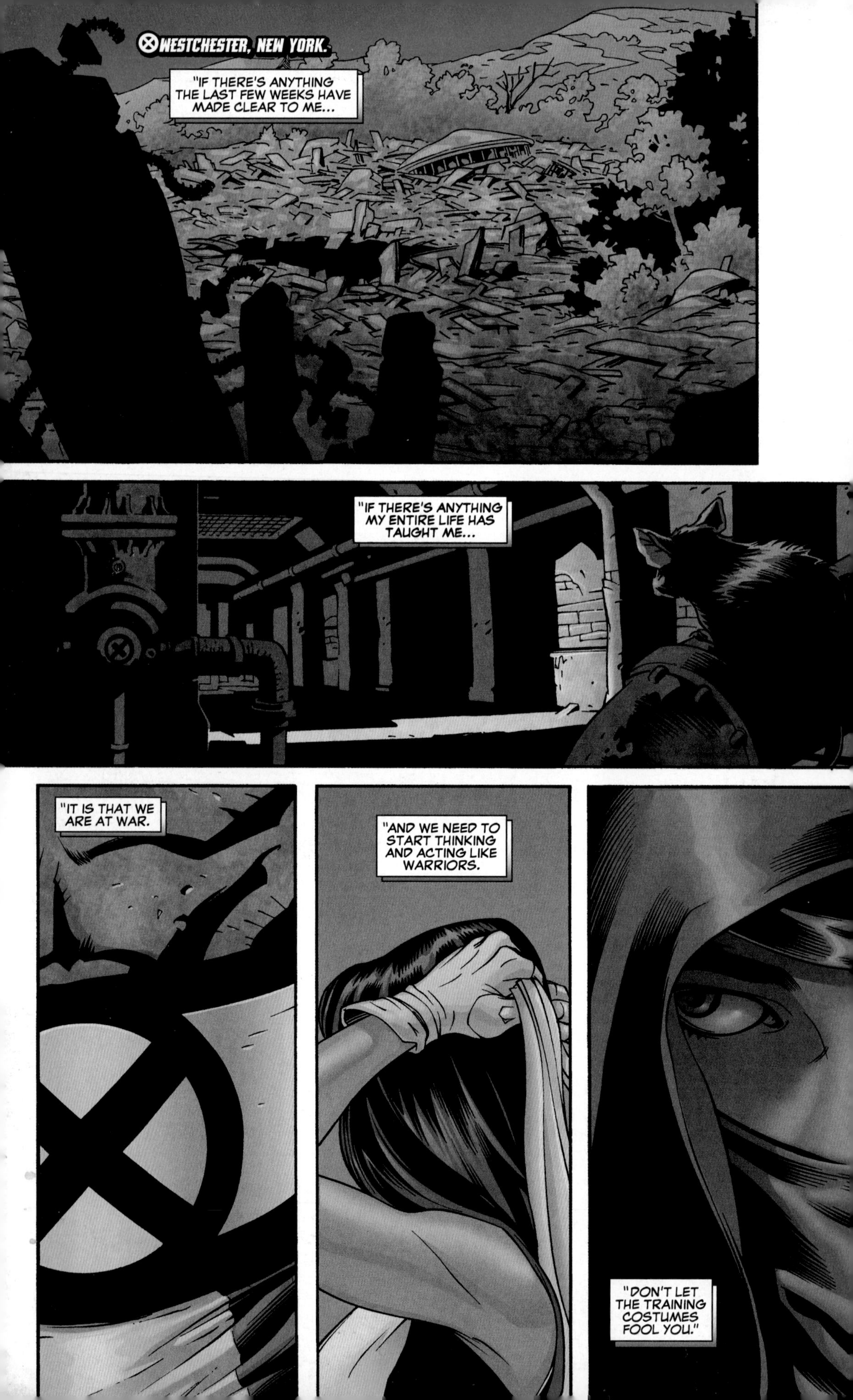
WESTCHESTER, NEW YORK.
"IF THERE'S ANYTHING THE LAST FEW WEEKS HAVE MADE CLEAR TO ME...
"IF THERE'S ANYTHING MY ENTIRE LIFE HAS TAUGHT ME...
"IT IS THAT WE ARE AT WAR.
"AND WE NEED TO START THINKING AND ACTING LIKE WARRIORS.
"DON'T LET THE TRAINING COSTUMES FOOL YOU."

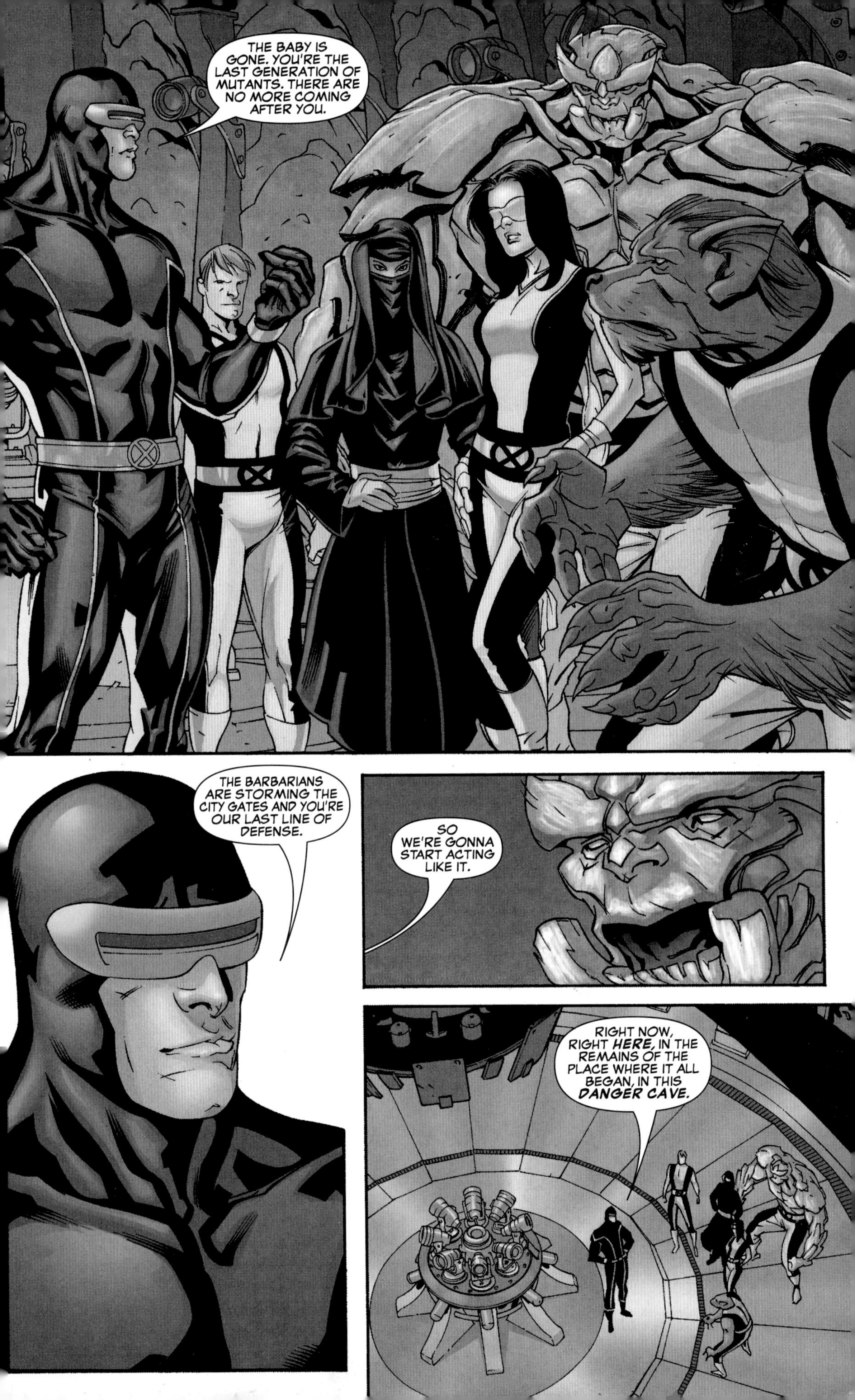
THE BABY IS GONE. YOU'RE THE LAST GENERATION OF MUTANTS. THERE ARE NO MORE COMING AFTER YOU.
THE BARBARIANS ARE STORMING THE CITY GATES AND YOU'RE OUR LAST LINE OF DEFENSE.
SO WE'RE GONNA START ACTING LIKE IT.
RIGHT NOW, RIGHT *HERE*, IN THE REMAINS OF THE PLACE WHERE IT ALL BEGAN, IN THIS ***DANGER CAVE.***

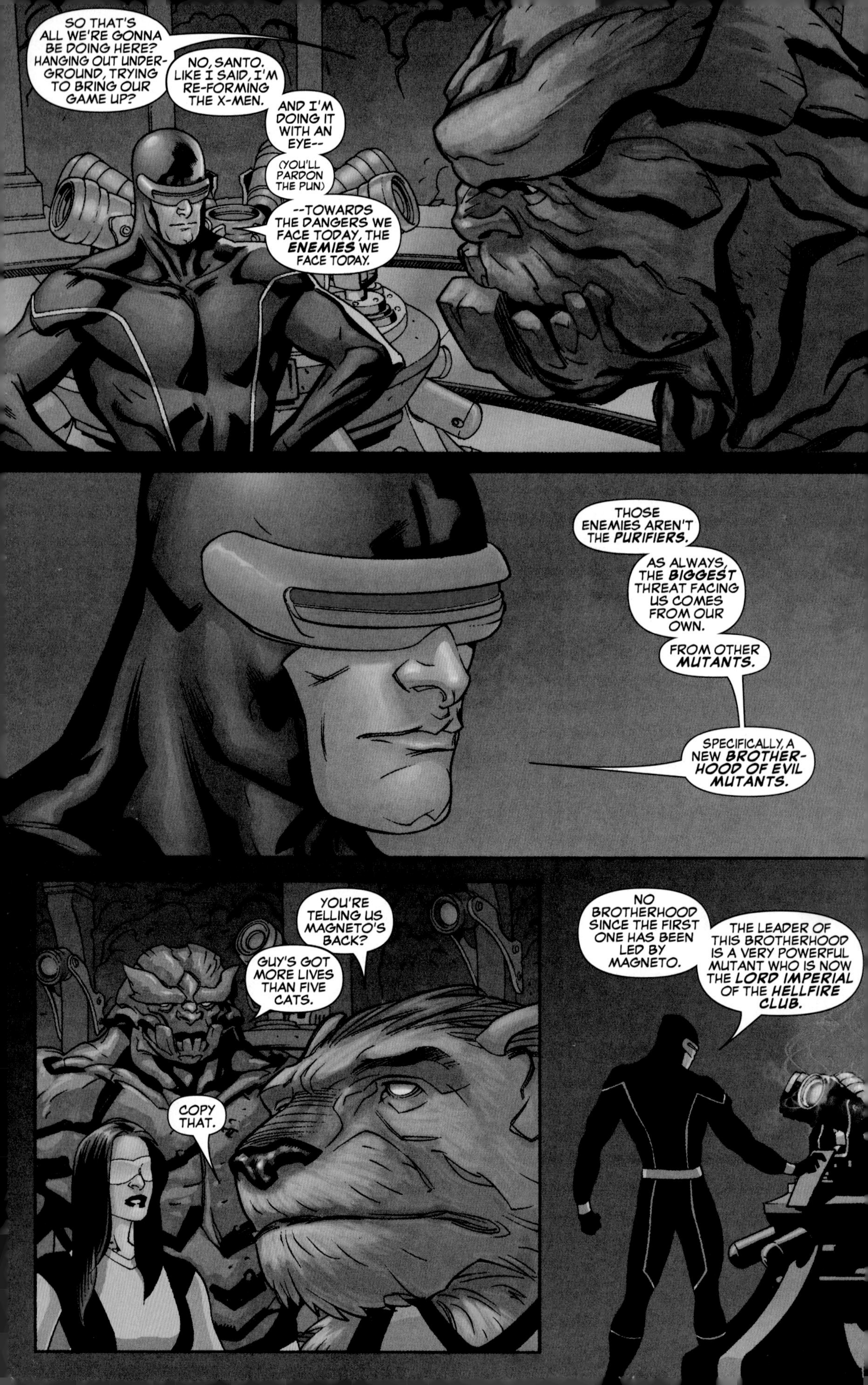
SO THAT'S ALL WE'RE GONNA BE DOING HERE? HANGING OUT UNDER-GROUND, TRYING TO BRING OUR GAME UP?
NO, SANTO. LIKE I SAID, I'M RE-FORMING THE X-MEN.
AND I'M DOING IT WITH AN EYE--
(YOU'LL PARDON THE PUN)
--TOWARDS THE DANGERS WE FACE TODAY, THE ENEMIES WE FACE TODAY.
THOSE ENEMIES AREN'T THE PURIFIERS.
AS ALWAYS, THE BIGGEST THREAT FACING US COMES FROM OUR OWN.
FROM OTHER MUTANTS.
SPECIFICALLY, A NEW BROTHER-HOOD OF EVIL MUTANTS.
YOU'RE TELLING US MAGNETO'S BACK?
GUY'S GOT MORE LIVES THAN FIVE CATS.
COPY THAT.
NO BROTHERHOOD SINCE THE FIRST ONE HAS BEEN LED BY MAGNETO.
THE LEADER OF THIS BROTHERHOOD IS A VERY POWERFUL MUTANT WHO IS NOW THE LORD IMPERIAL OF THE HELLFIRE CLUB.

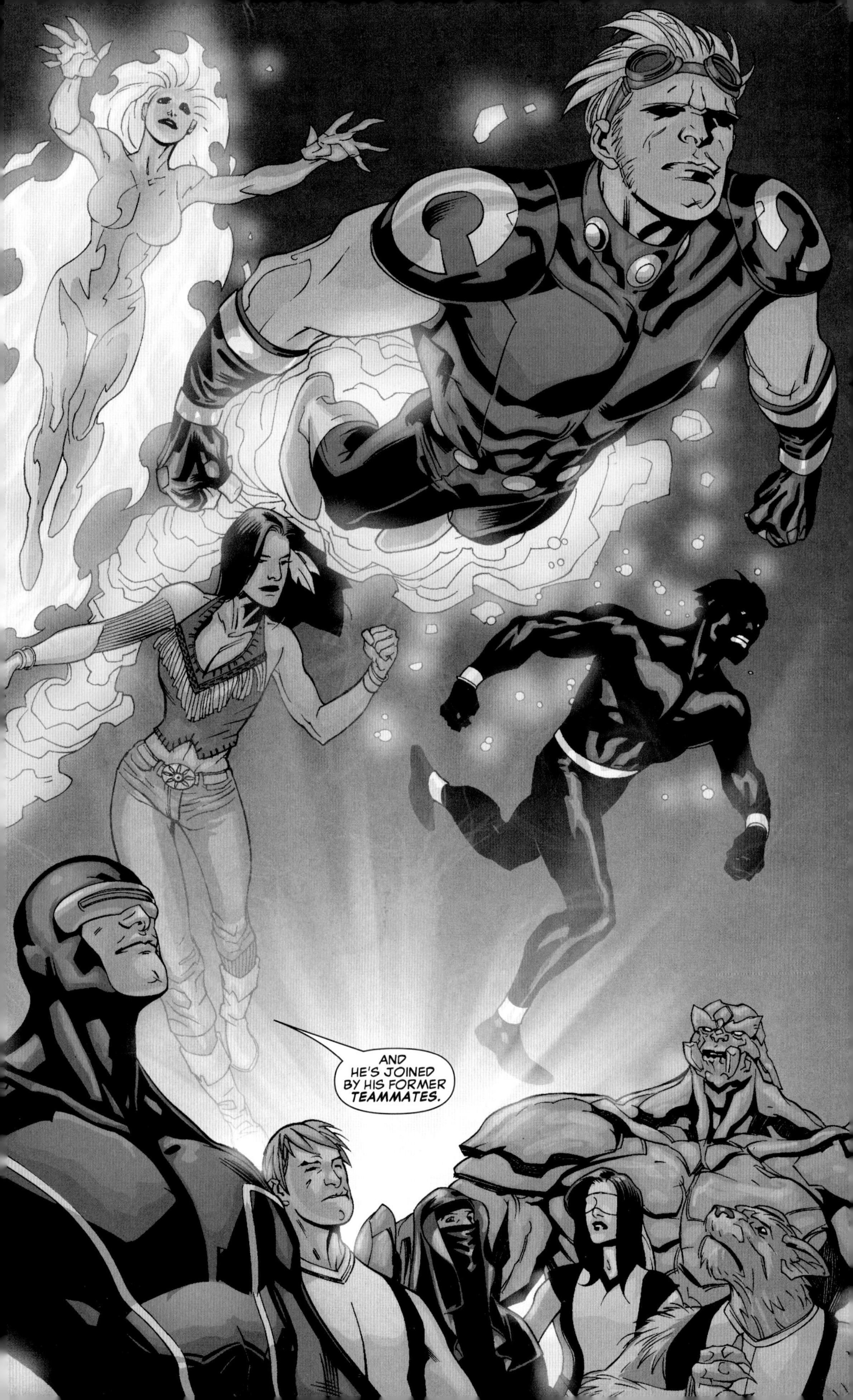
AND HE'S JOINED BY HIS FORMER *TEAMMATES.*

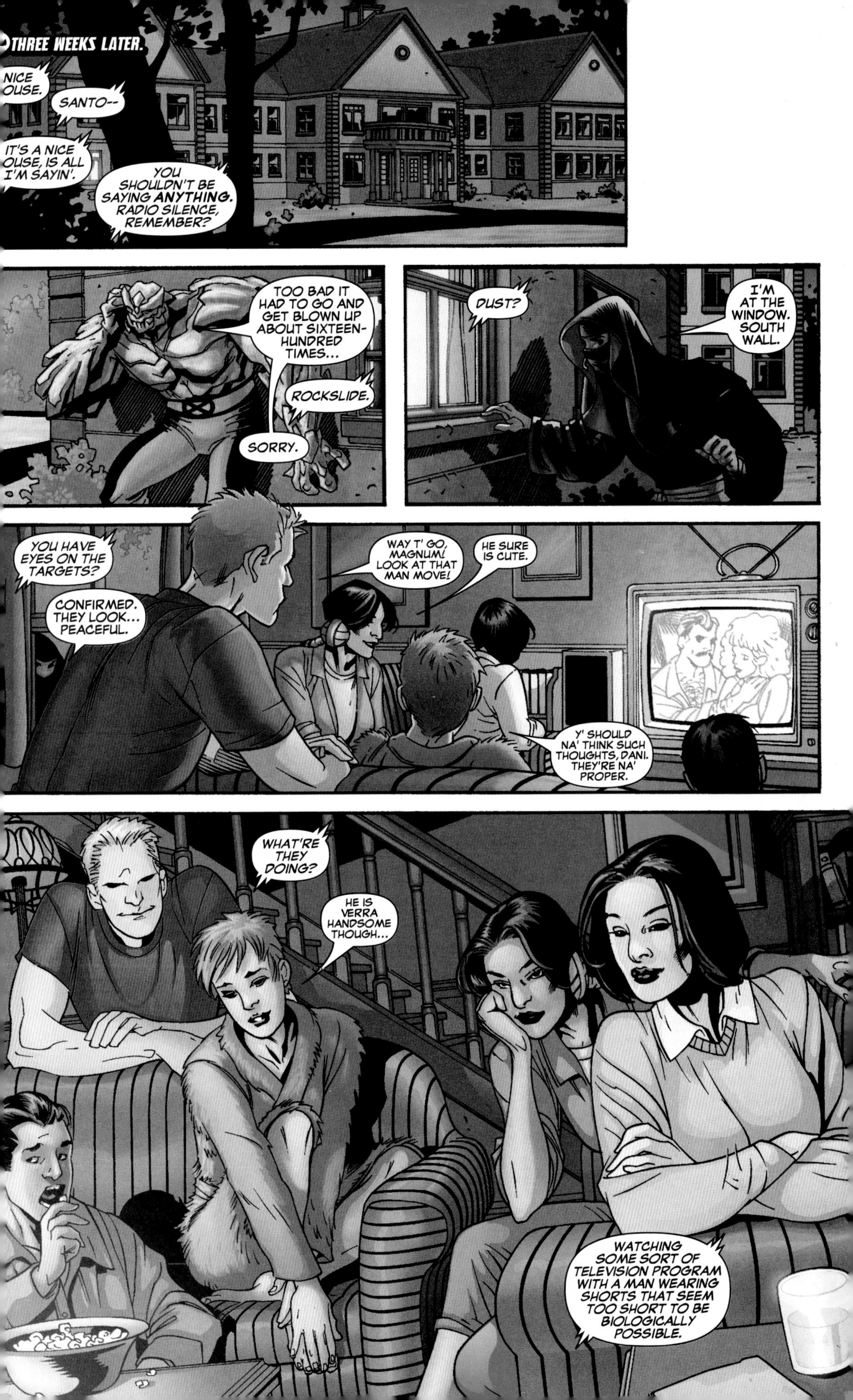
THREE WEEKS LATER.
NICE OUSE.
SANTO--
IT'S A NICE OUSE, IS ALL I'M SAYIN'.
YOU SHOULDN'T BE SAYING ANYTHING. RADIO SILENCE, REMEMBER?
TOO BAD IT HAD TO GO AND GET BLOWN UP ABOUT SIXTEEN-HUNDRED TIMES...
ROCKSLIDE.
SORRY.
DUST?
I'M AT THE WINDOW. SOUTH WALL.
YOU HAVE EYES ON THE TARGETS?
CONFIRMED. THEY LOOK... PEACEFUL.
WAY T' GO, MAGNUM! LOOK AT THAT MAN MOVE!
HE SURE IS CUTE.
Y' SHOULD NA' THINK SUCH THOUGHTS, DANI. THEY'RE NA' PROPER.
WHAT'RE THEY DOING?
HE IS VERRA HANDSOME THOUGH...
WATCHING SOME SORT OF TELEVISION PROGRAM WITH A MAN WEARING SHORTS THAT SEEM TOO SHORT TO BE BIOLOGICALLY POSSIBLE.

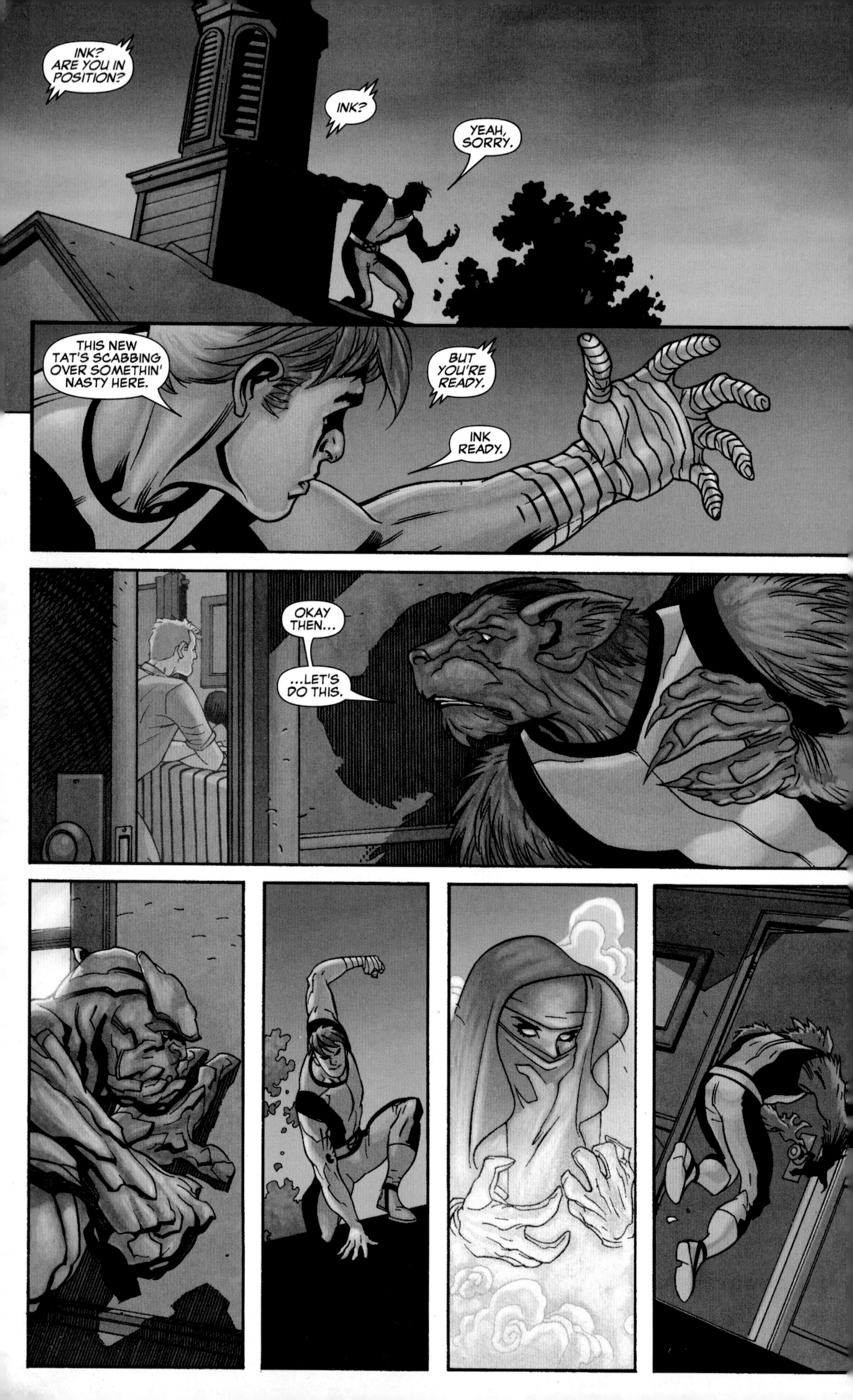
INK? ARE YOU IN POSITION?
INK?
YEAH, SORRY.
THIS NEW TAT'S SCABBING OVER SOMETHIN' NASTY HERE.
BUT YOU'RE READY.
INK READY.
OKAY THEN...
...LET'S DO THIS.

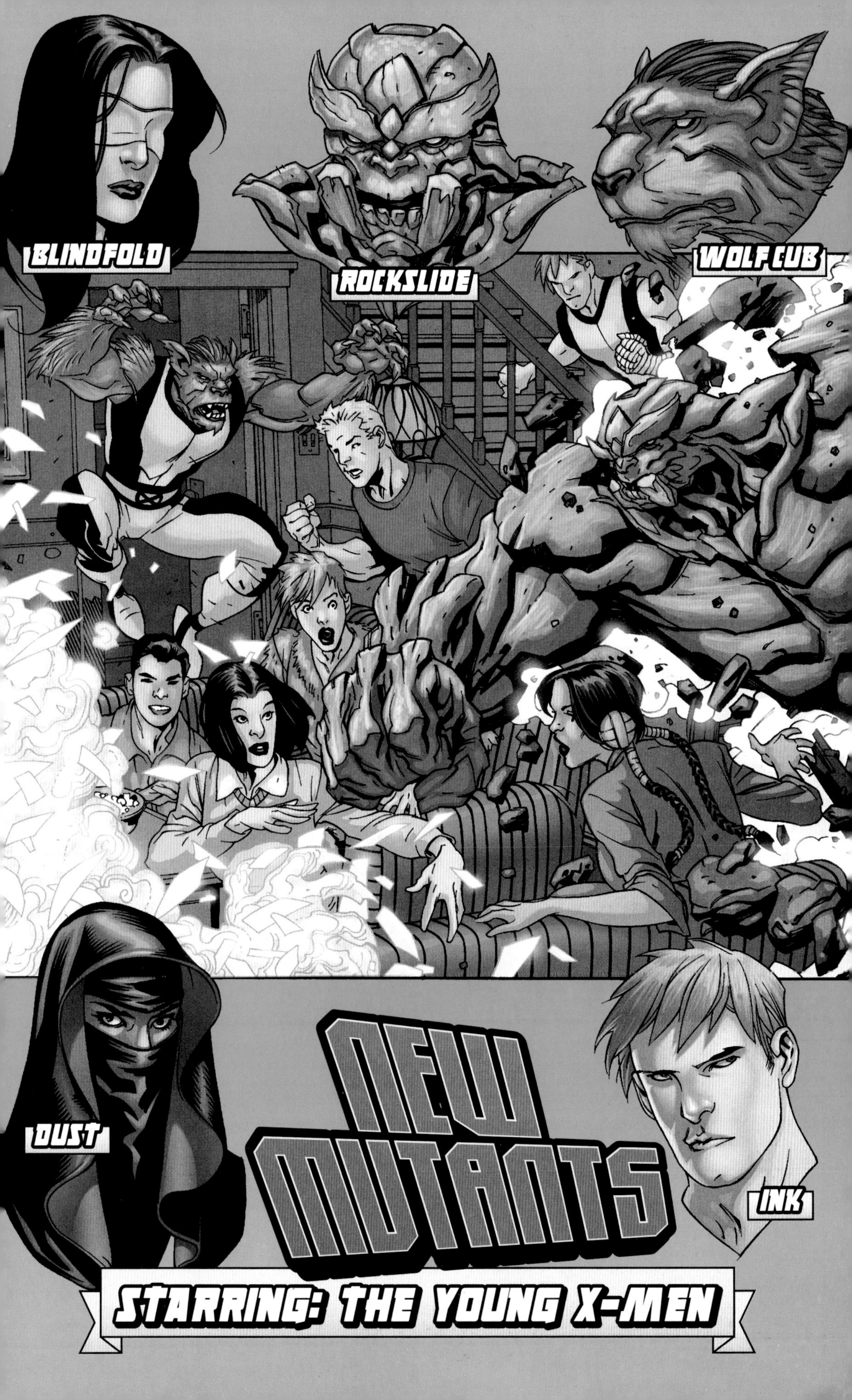
BLINDFOLD
ROCKSLIDE
WOLF CUB
DUST
NEW MUTANTS
INK
STARRING: THE YOUNG X-MEN

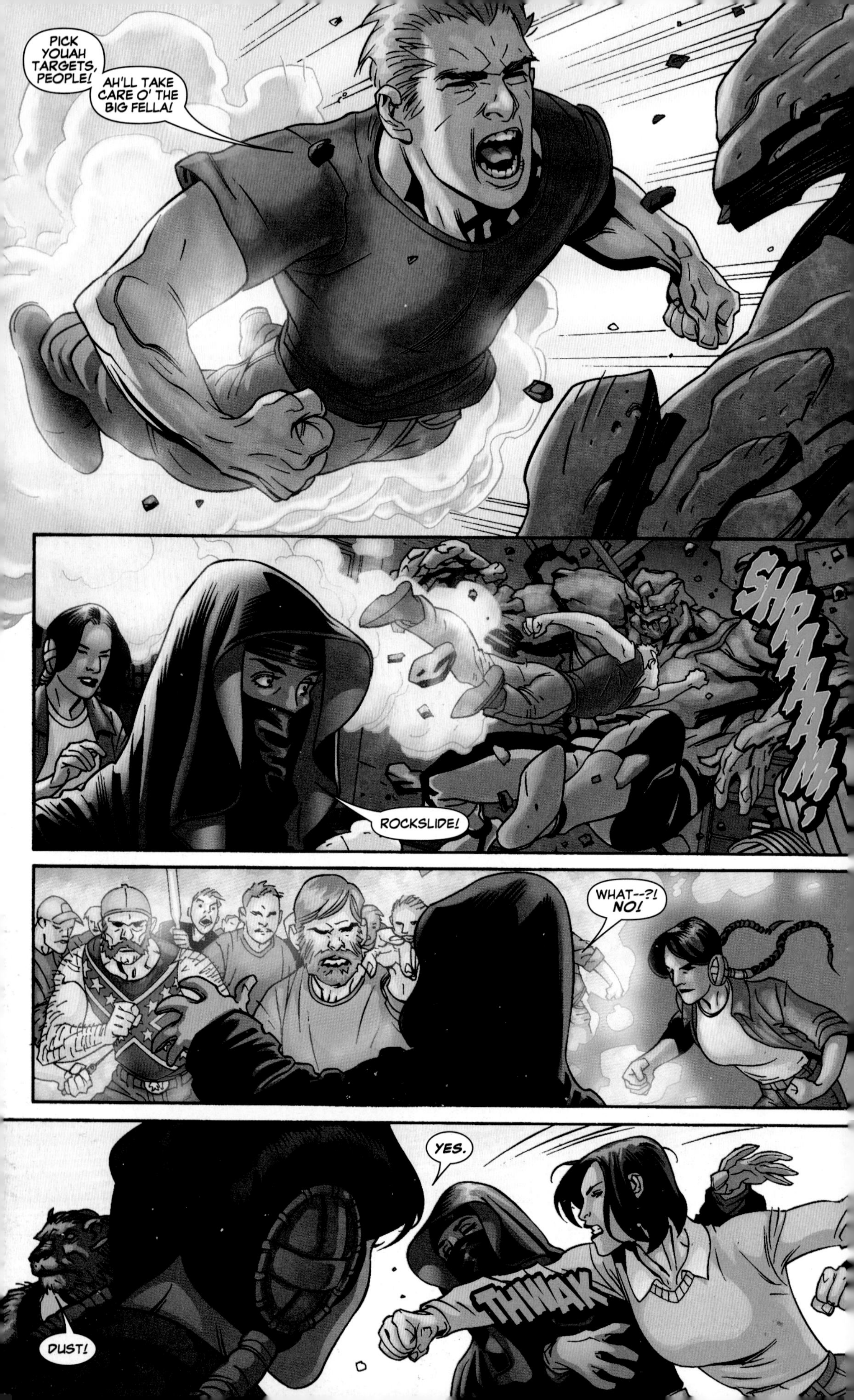
PICK YOUAH TARGETS, PEOPLE!
AH'LL TAKE CARE O' THE BIG FELLA!
SHRAAAAM!
ROCKSLIDE!
WHAT--?! NO!
YES.
THWAK
DUST!

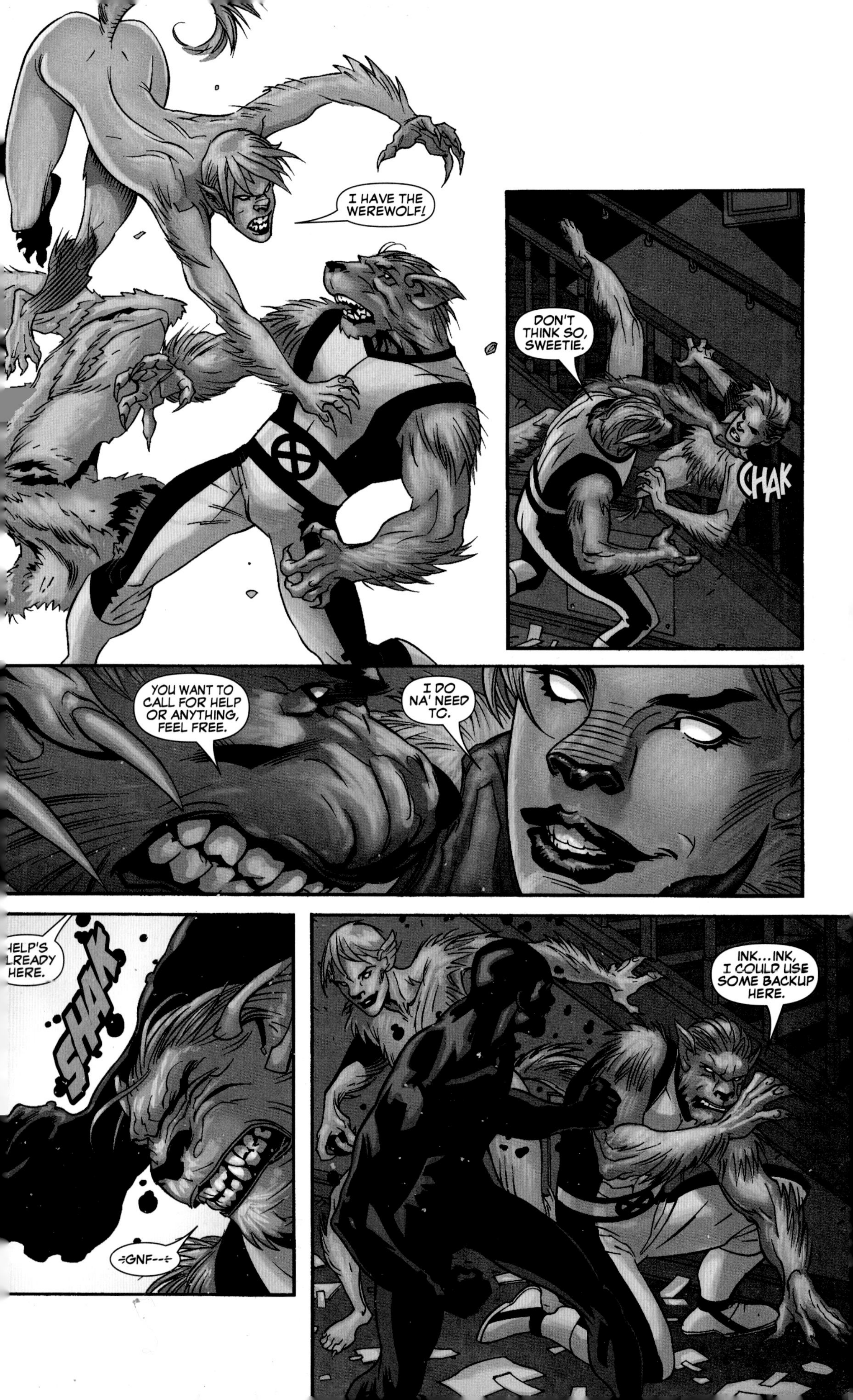
I HAVE THE WEREWOLF!
DON'T THINK SO, SWEETIE.
CHAK
YOU WANT TO CALL FOR HELP OR ANYTHING, FEEL FREE.
I DO NA' NEED TO.
HELP'S ALREADY HERE.
SHAK
GNF--
INK...INK, I COULD USE SOME BACKUP HERE.

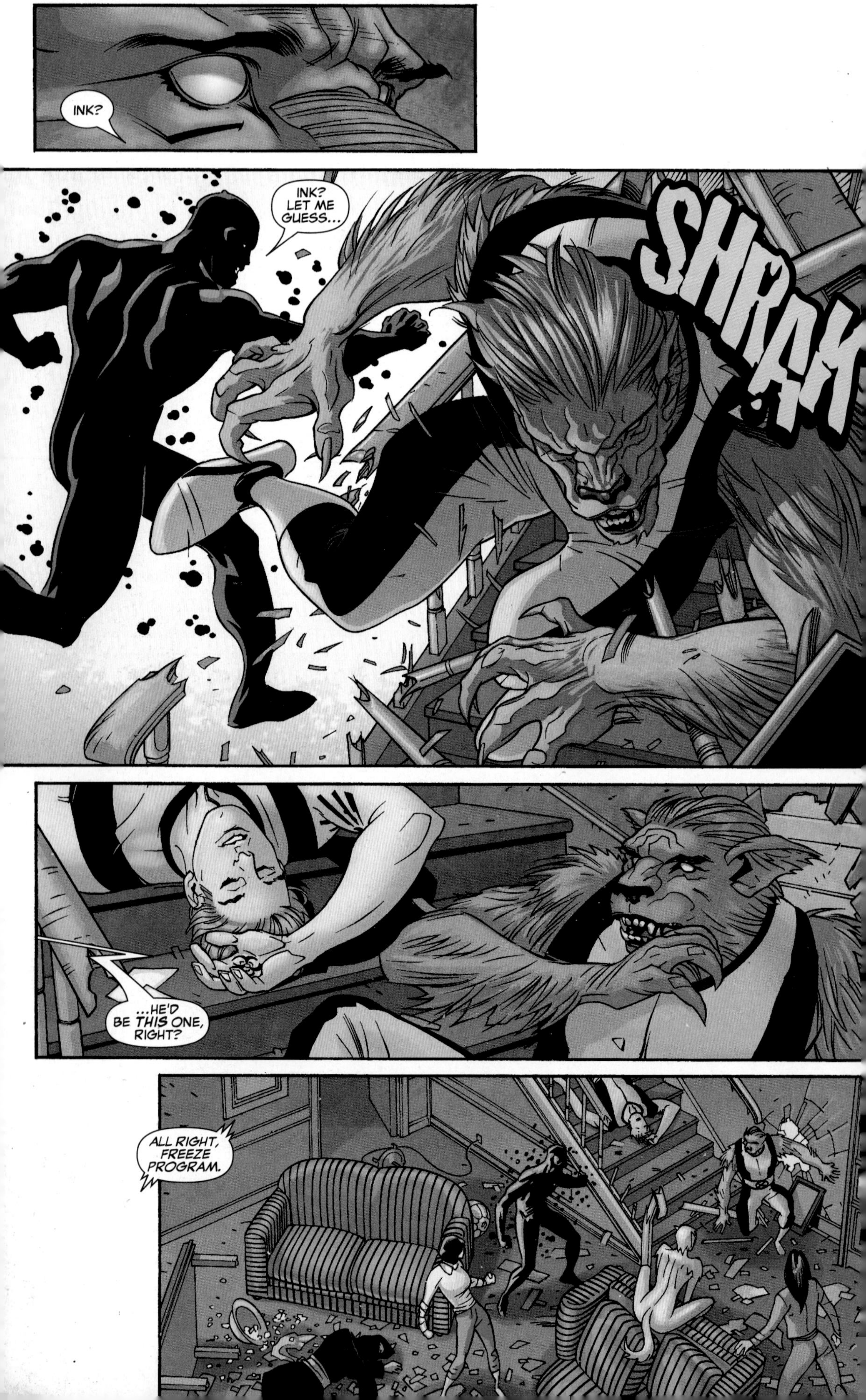
INK?
INK? LET ME GUESS...
SHRAK
...HE'D BE THIS ONE, RIGHT?
ALL RIGHT, FREEZE PROGRAM.

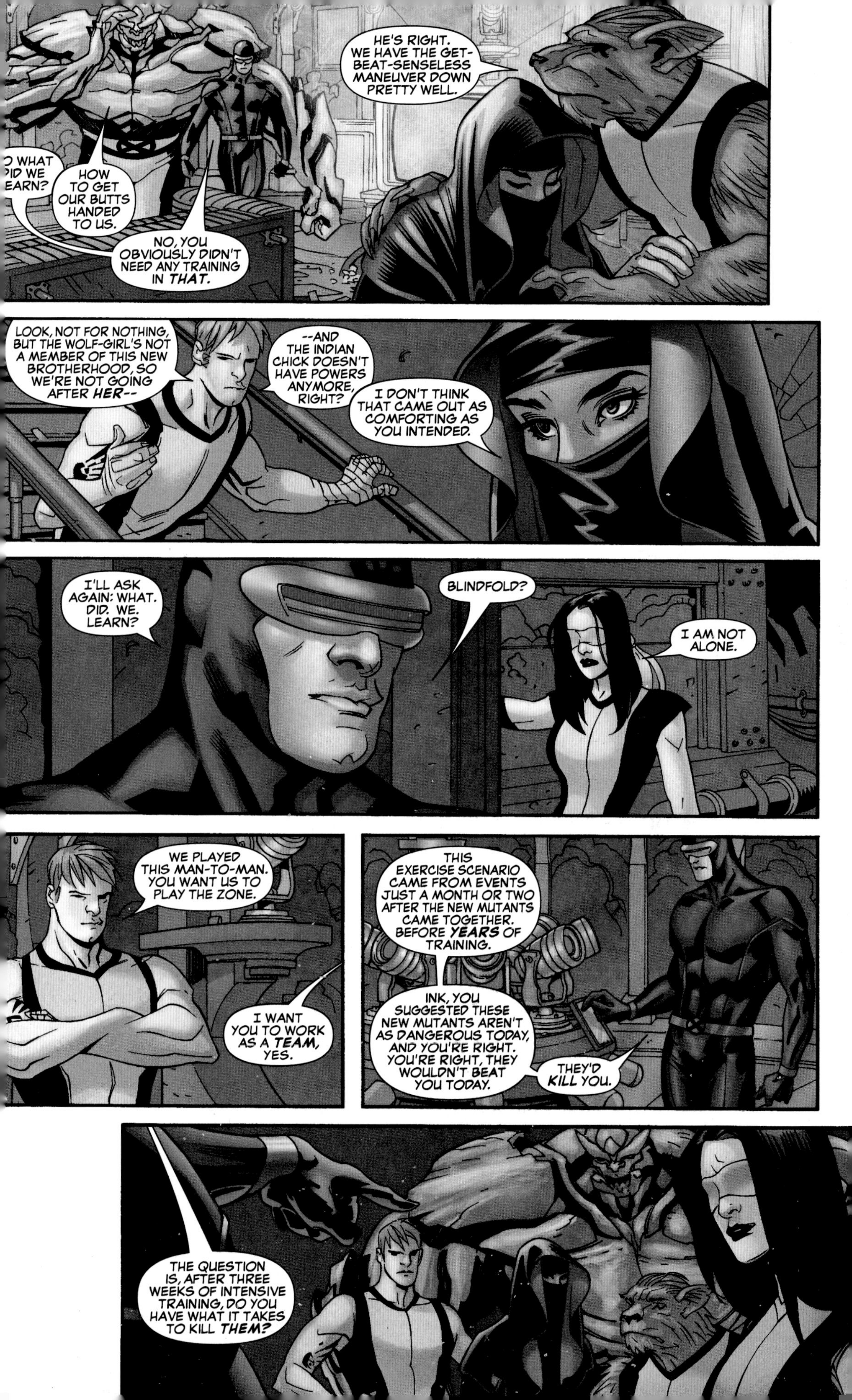
HE'S RIGHT. WE HAVE THE GET-BEAT-SENSELESS MANEUVER DOWN PRETTY WELL.
O WHAT DID WE EARN?
HOW TO GET OUR BUTTS HANDED TO US.
NO, YOU OBVIOUSLY DIDN'T NEED ANY TRAINING IN THAT.
LOOK, NOT FOR NOTHING, BUT THE WOLF-GIRL'S NOT A MEMBER OF THIS NEW BROTHERHOOD, SO WE'RE NOT GOING AFTER HER--
--AND THE INDIAN CHICK DOESN'T HAVE POWERS ANYMORE, RIGHT?
I DON'T THINK THAT CAME OUT AS COMFORTING AS YOU INTENDED.
I'LL ASK AGAIN: WHAT. DID. WE. LEARN?
BLINDFOLD?
I AM NOT ALONE.
WE PLAYED THIS MAN-TO-MAN. YOU WANT US TO PLAY THE ZONE.
I WANT YOU TO WORK AS A TEAM, YES.
THIS EXERCISE SCENARIO CAME FROM EVENTS JUST A MONTH OR TWO AFTER THE NEW MUTANTS CAME TOGETHER. BEFORE YEARS OF TRAINING.
INK, YOU SUGGESTED THESE NEW MUTANTS AREN'T AS DANGEROUS TODAY, AND YOU'RE RIGHT. YOU'RE RIGHT, THEY WOULDN'T BEAT YOU TODAY.
THEY'D KILL YOU.
THE QUESTION IS, AFTER THREE WEEKS OF INTENSIVE TRAINING, DO YOU HAVE WHAT IT TAKES TO KILL THEM?

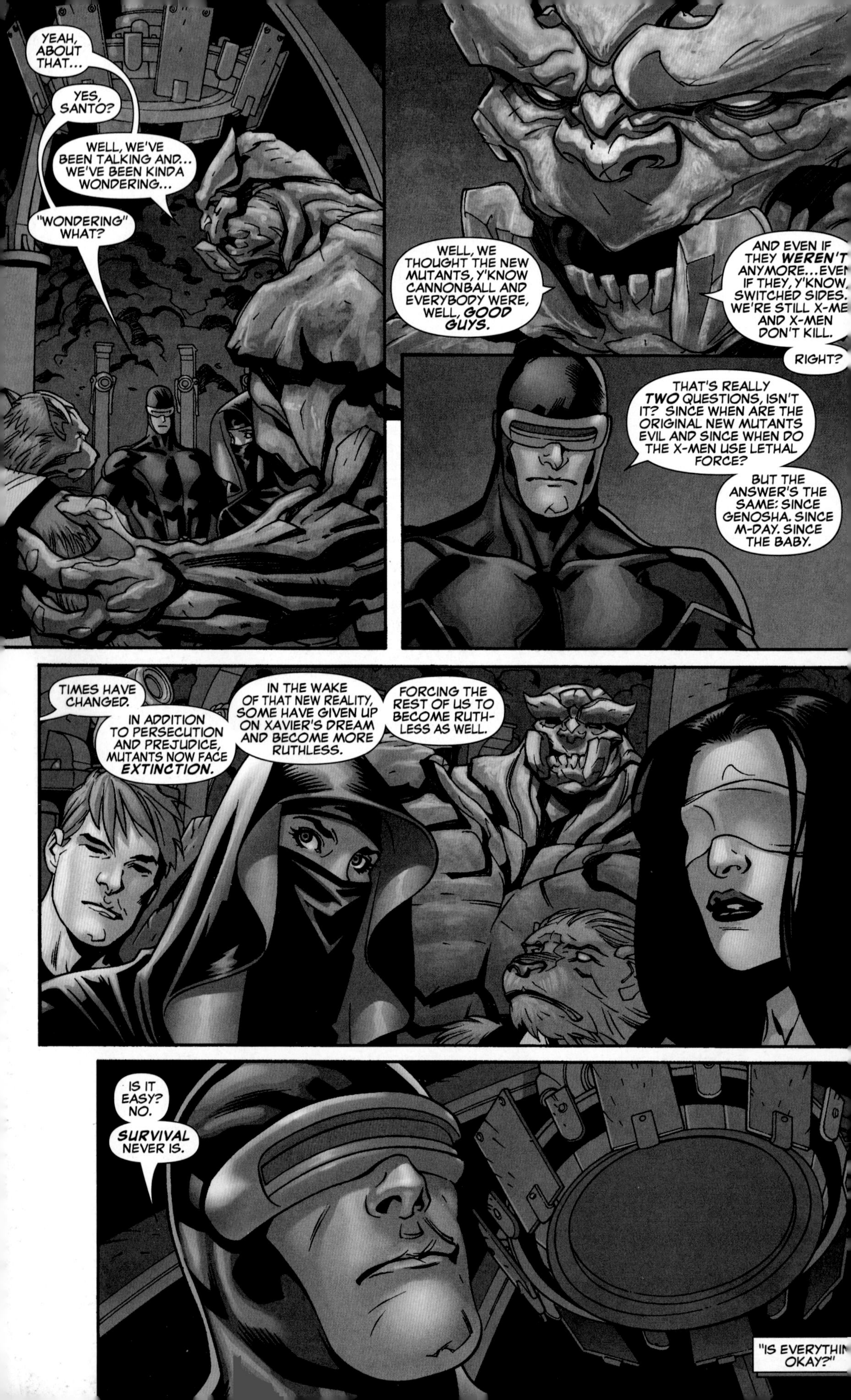

YEAH, ABOUT THAT...
YES, SANTO?
WELL, WE'VE BEEN TALKING AND... WE'VE BEEN KINDA WONDERING...
"WONDERING" WHAT?
WELL, WE THOUGHT THE NEW MUTANTS, Y'KNOW CANNONBALL AND EVERYBODY WERE, WELL, GOOD GUYS.
AND EVEN IF THEY WEREN'T ANYMORE...EVEN IF THEY, Y'KNOW, SWITCHED SIDES. WE'RE STILL X-MEN AND X-MEN DON'T KILL.
RIGHT?
THAT'S REALLY TWO QUESTIONS, ISN'T IT? SINCE WHEN ARE THE ORIGINAL NEW MUTANTS EVIL AND SINCE WHEN DO THE X-MEN USE LETHAL FORCE?
BUT THE ANSWER'S THE SAME: SINCE GENOSHA. SINCE M-DAY. SINCE THE BABY.
TIMES HAVE CHANGED.
IN ADDITION TO PERSECUTION AND PREJUDICE, MUTANTS NOW FACE EXTINCTION.
IN THE WAKE OF THAT NEW REALITY, SOME HAVE GIVEN UP ON XAVIER'S DREAM AND BECOME MORE RUTHLESS.
FORCING THE REST OF US TO BECOME RUTHLESS AS WELL.
IS IT EASY? NO.
SURVIVAL NEVER IS.
"IS EVERYTHIN OKAY?"

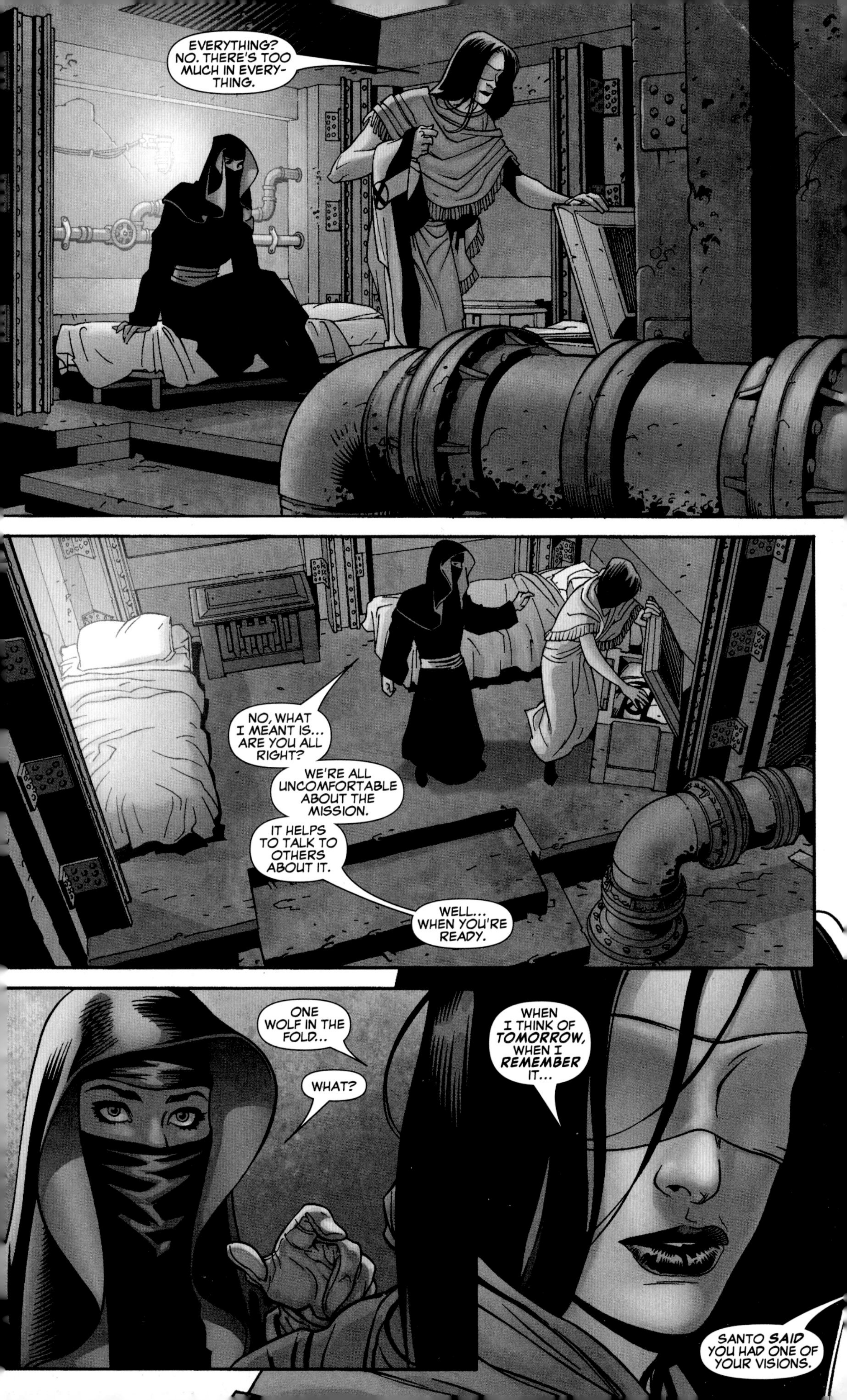
EVERYTHING? NO. THERE'S TOO MUCH IN EVERY-THING.
NO, WHAT I MEANT IS... ARE YOU ALL RIGHT?
WE'RE ALL UNCOMFORTABLE ABOUT THE MISSION.
IT HELPS TO TALK TO OTHERS ABOUT IT.
WELL... WHEN YOU'RE READY.
ONE WOLF IN THE FOLD...
WHAT?
WHEN I THINK OF *TOMORROW*, WHEN I *REMEMBER* IT...
SANTO **SAID** YOU HAD ONE OF YOUR VISIONS.

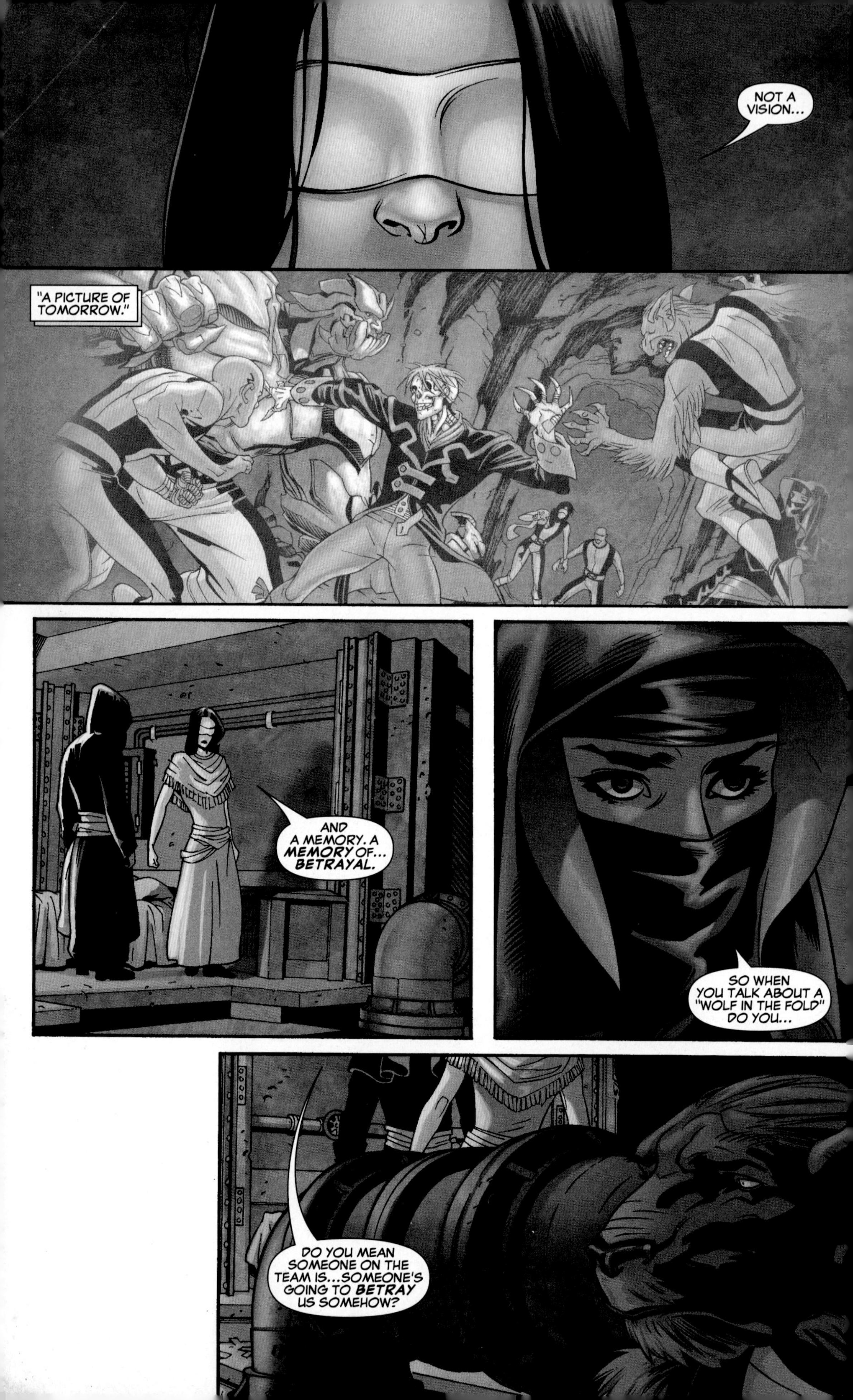
NOT A VISION...
"A PICTURE OF TOMORROW."
AND A MEMORY. A MEMORY OF... BETRAYAL.
SO WHEN YOU TALK ABOUT A "WOLF IN THE FOLD" DO YOU...
DO YOU MEAN SOMEONE ON THE TEAM IS...SOMEONE'S GOING TO BETRAY US SOMEHOW?

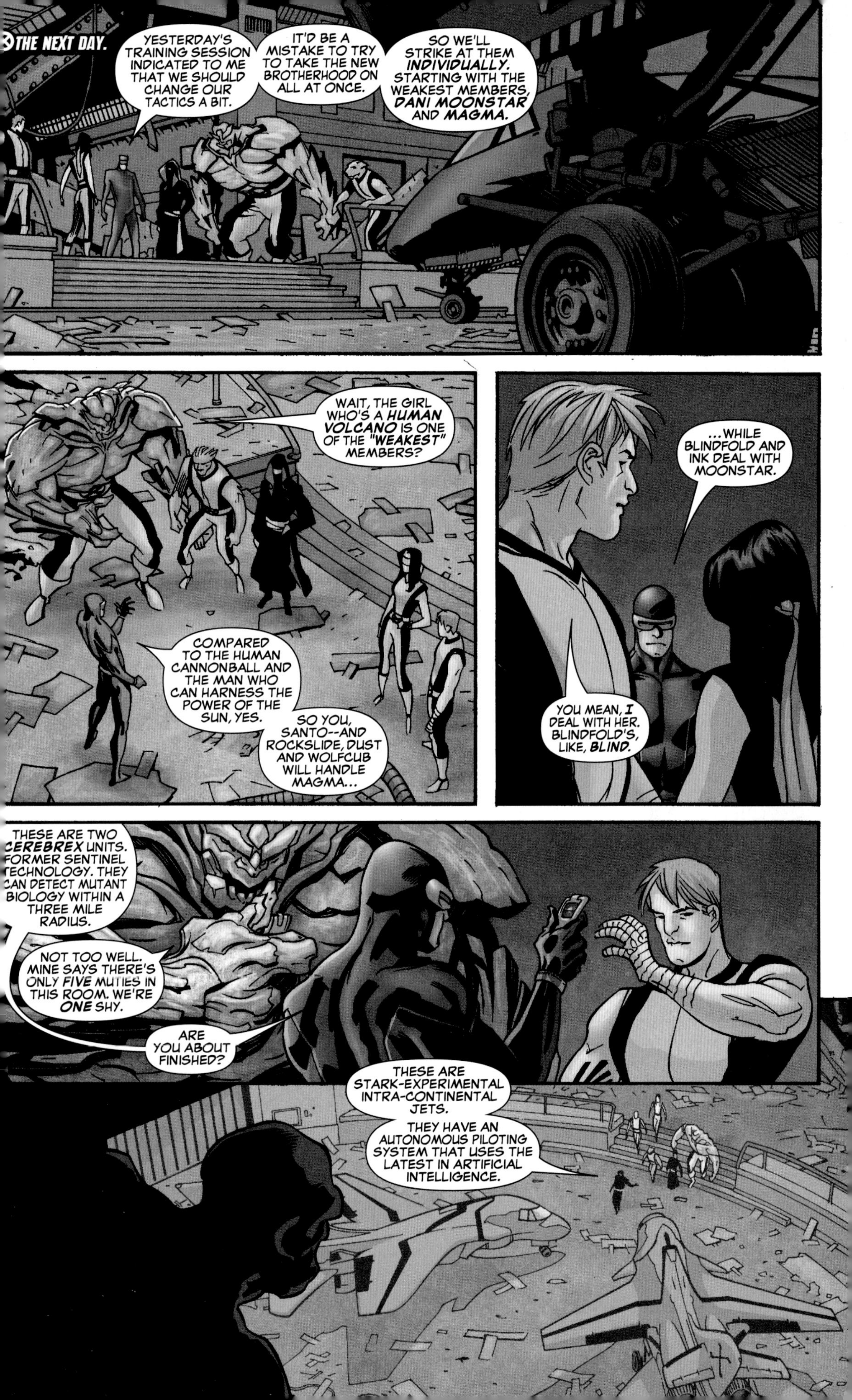
THE NEXT DAY.
YESTERDAY'S TRAINING SESSION INDICATED TO ME THAT WE SHOULD CHANGE OUR TACTICS A BIT.
IT'D BE A MISTAKE TO TRY TO TAKE THE NEW BROTHERHOOD ON ALL AT ONCE.
SO WE'LL STRIKE AT THEM INDIVIDUALLY. STARTING WITH THE WEAKEST MEMBERS, DANI MOONSTAR AND MAGMA.
WAIT, THE GIRL WHO'S A HUMAN VOLCANO IS ONE OF THE "WEAKEST" MEMBERS?
COMPARED TO THE HUMAN CANNONBALL AND THE MAN WHO CAN HARNESS THE POWER OF THE SUN, YES.
SO YOU, SANTO--AND ROCKSLIDE, DUST AND WOLFCUB WILL HANDLE MAGMA...
...WHILE BLINDFOLD AND INK DEAL WITH MOONSTAR.
YOU MEAN, I DEAL WITH HER. BLINDFOLD'S, LIKE, BLIND.
THESE ARE TWO CEREBREX UNITS. FORMER SENTINEL TECHNOLOGY. THEY CAN DETECT MUTANT BIOLOGY WITHIN A THREE MILE RADIUS.
NOT TOO WELL. MINE SAYS THERE'S ONLY FIVE MUTIES IN THIS ROOM. WE'RE ONE SHY.
ARE YOU ABOUT FINISHED?
THESE ARE STARK-EXPERIMENTAL INTRA-CONTINENTAL JETS.
THEY HAVE AN AUTONOMOUS PILOTING SYSTEM THAT USES THE LATEST IN ARTIFICIAL INTELLIGENCE.

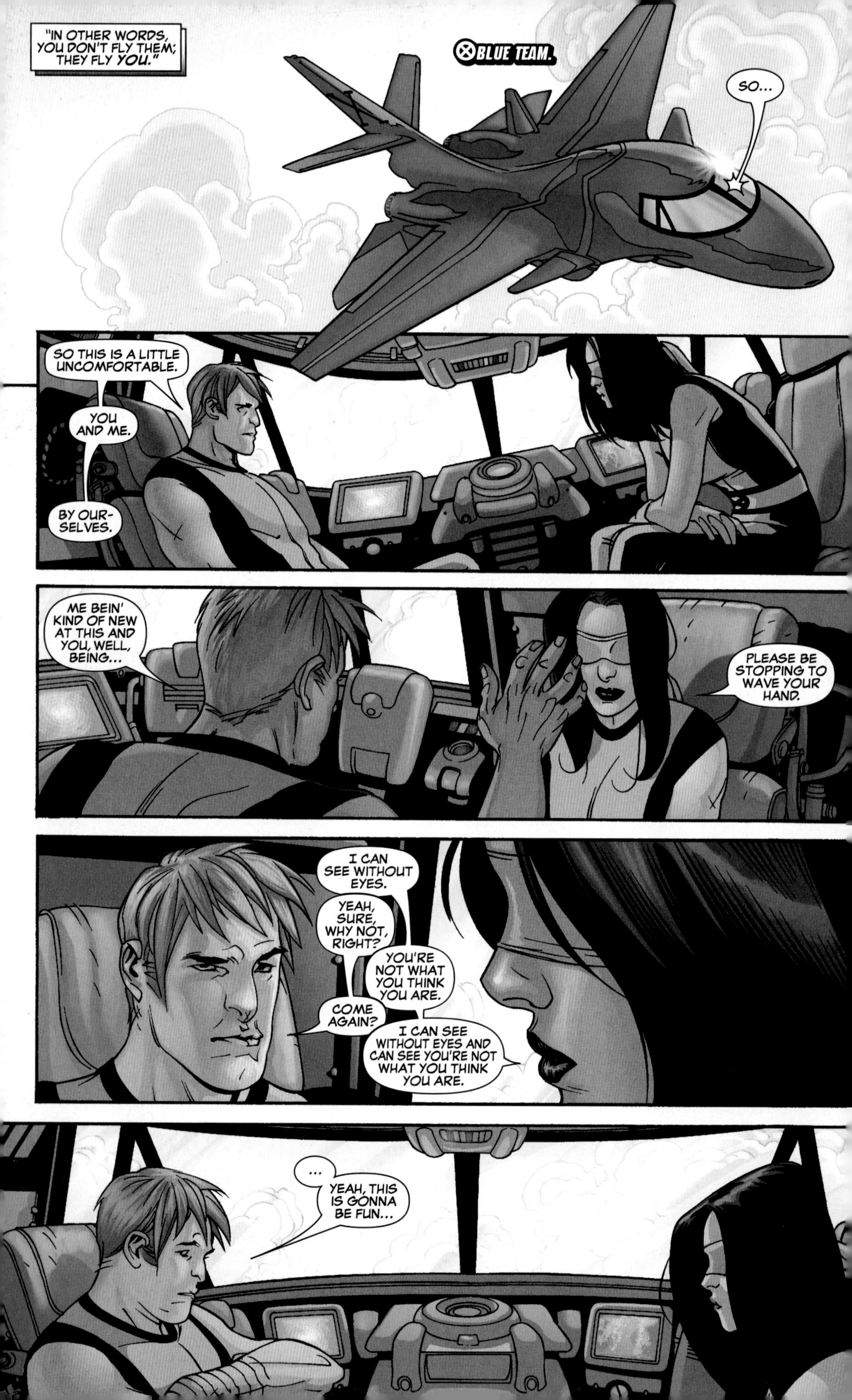
"IN OTHER WORDS, YOU DON'T FLY THEM; THEY FLY YOU."
BLUE TEAM.
SO...
SO THIS IS A LITTLE UNCOMFORTABLE.
YOU AND ME.
BY OURSELVES.
ME BEIN' KIND OF NEW AT THIS AND YOU, WELL, BEING...
PLEASE BE STOPPING TO WAVE YOUR HAND.
I CAN SEE WITHOUT EYES.
YEAH, SURE, WHY NOT, RIGHT?
YOU'RE NOT WHAT YOU THINK YOU ARE.
COME AGAIN?
I CAN SEE WITHOUT EYES AND CAN SEE YOU'RE NOT WHAT YOU THINK YOU ARE.
...
YEAH, THIS IS GONNA BE FUN...

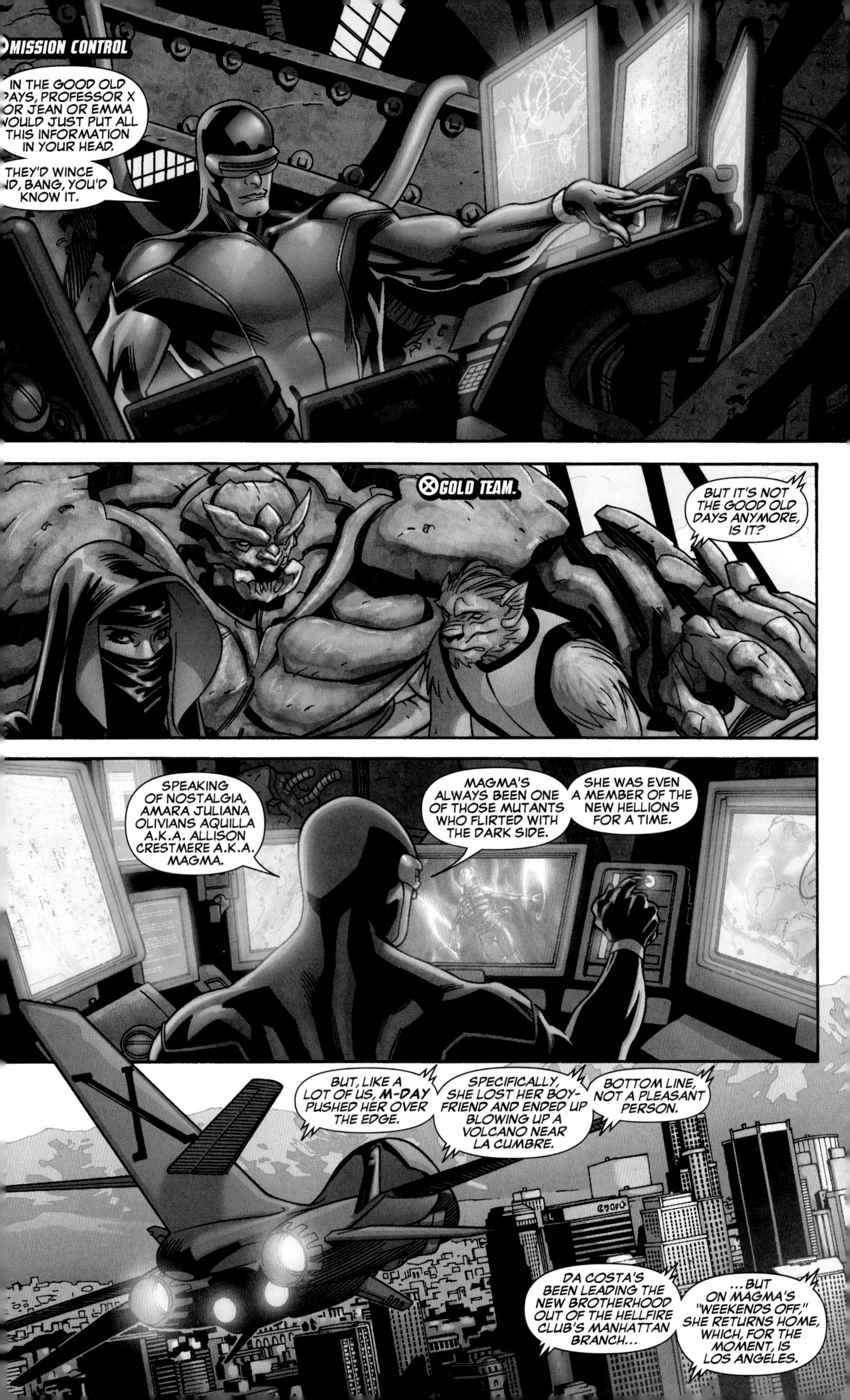
MISSION CONTROL
IN THE GOOD OLD DAYS, PROFESSOR X OR JEAN OR EMMA WOULD JUST PUT ALL THIS INFORMATION IN YOUR HEAD.
THEY'D WINCE AND, BANG, YOU'D KNOW IT.
GOLD TEAM.
BUT IT'S NOT THE GOOD OLD DAYS ANYMORE, IS IT?
SPEAKING OF NOSTALGIA, AMARA JULIANA OLIVIANS AQUILLA A.K.A. ALLISON CRESTMERE A.K.A. MAGMA.
MAGMA'S ALWAYS BEEN ONE OF THOSE MUTANTS WHO FLIRTED WITH THE DARK SIDE.
SHE WAS EVEN A MEMBER OF THE NEW HELLIONS FOR A TIME.
BUT, LIKE A LOT OF US, M-DAY PUSHED HER OVER THE EDGE.
SPECIFICALLY, SHE LOST HER BOY-FRIEND AND ENDED UP BLOWING UP A VOLCANO NEAR LA CUMBRE.
BOTTOM LINE, NOT A PLEASANT PERSON.
DA COSTA'S BEEN LEADING THE NEW BROTHERHOOD OUT OF THE HELLFIRE CLUB'S MANHATTAN BRANCH...
...BUT ON MAGMA'S "WEEKENDS OFF," SHE RETURNS HOME, WHICH, FOR THE MOMENT, IS LOS ANGELES.

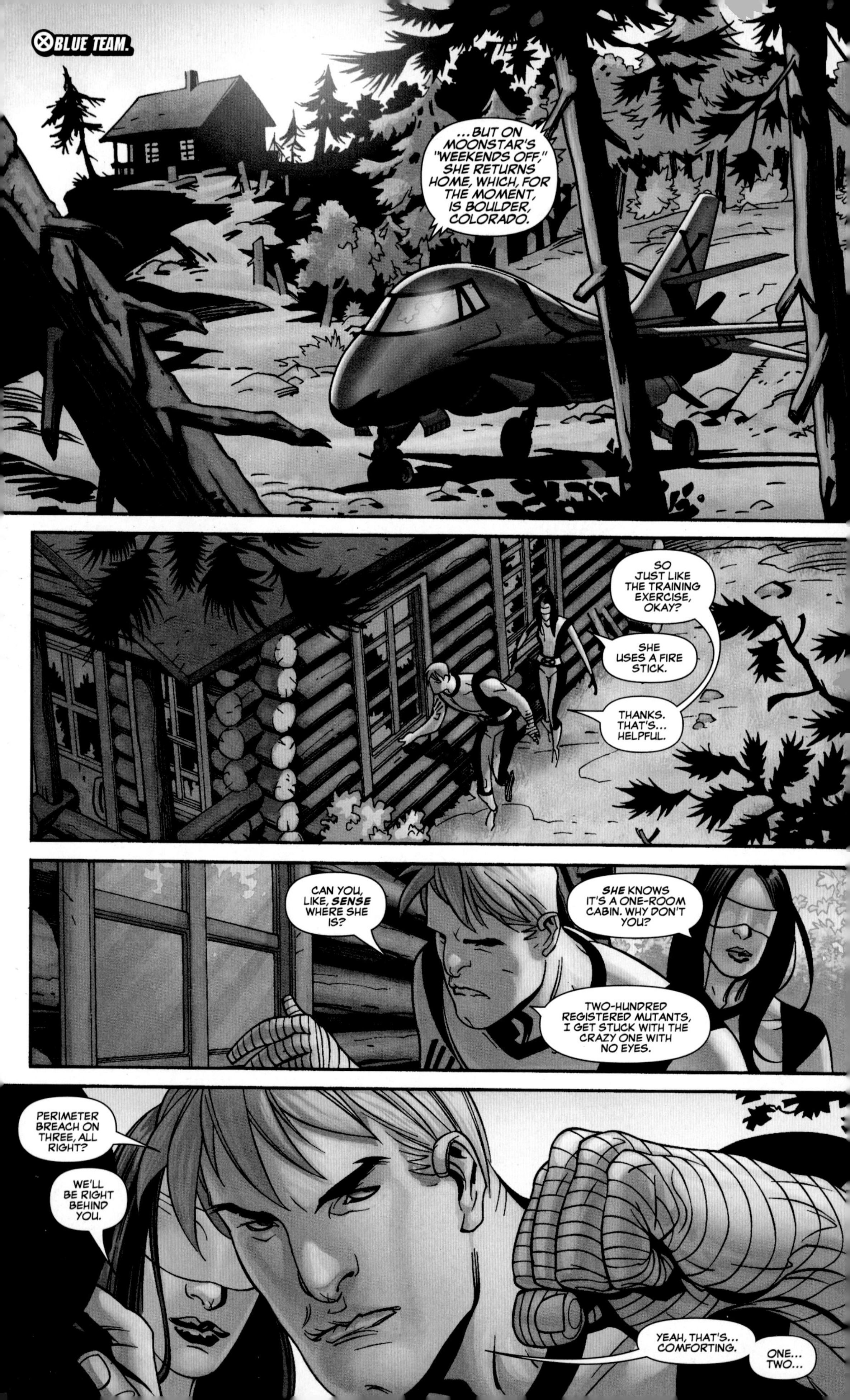
BLUE TEAM.
...BUT ON MOONSTAR'S "WEEKENDS OFF," SHE RETURNS HOME, WHICH, FOR THE MOMENT, IS BOULDER, COLORADO.
SO JUST LIKE THE TRAINING EXERCISE, OKAY?
SHE USES A FIRE STICK.
THANKS. THAT'S... HELPFUL.
CAN YOU, LIKE, SENSE WHERE SHE IS?
SHE KNOWS IT'S A ONE-ROOM CABIN. WHY DON'T YOU?
TWO-HUNDRED REGISTERED MUTANTS, I GET STUCK WITH THE CRAZY ONE WITH NO EYES.
PERIMETER BREACH ON THREE, ALL RIGHT?
WE'LL BE RIGHT BEHIND YOU.
YEAH, THAT'S... COMFORTING.
ONE... TWO...

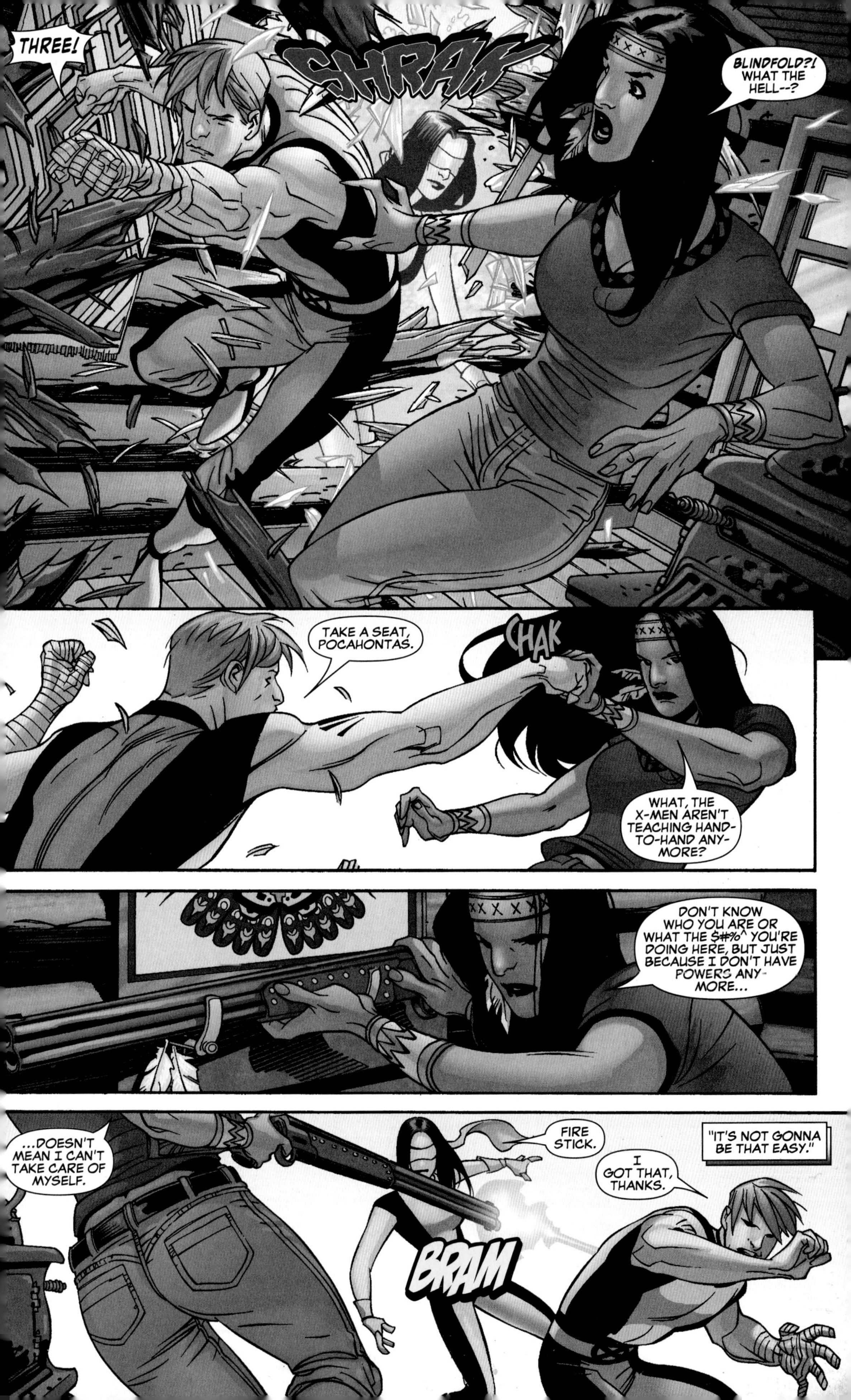
THREE!
SHRAK
BLINDFOLD?! WHAT THE HELL--?
TAKE A SEAT, POCAHONTAS.
CHAK
WHAT, THE X-MEN AREN'T TEACHING HAND-TO-HAND ANY-MORE?
DON'T KNOW WHO YOU ARE OR WHAT THE $#%^ YOU'RE DOING HERE, BUT JUST BECAUSE I DON'T HAVE POWERS ANY-MORE...
...DOESN'T MEAN I CAN'T TAKE CARE OF MYSELF.
FIRE STICK.
I GOT THAT, THANKS.
"IT'S NOT GONNA BE THAT EASY."
BRAM

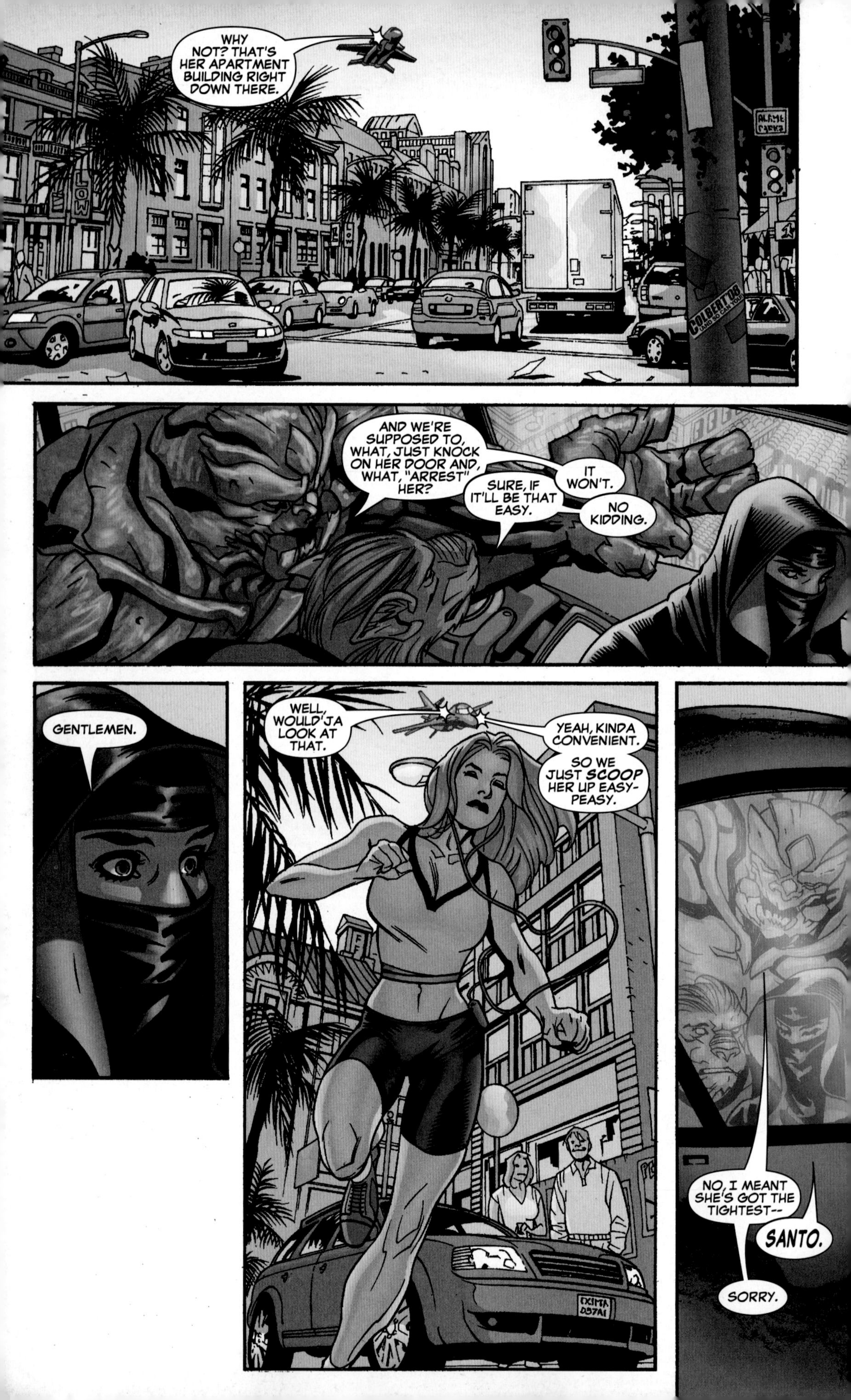

WHY NOT? THAT'S HER APARTMENT BUILDING RIGHT DOWN THERE.
COLBERT'08 AND SO CAN YOU!
AND WE'RE SUPPOSED TO, WHAT, JUST KNOCK ON HER DOOR AND, WHAT, "ARREST" HER?
SURE, IF IT'LL BE THAT EASY.
IT WON'T.
NO KIDDING.
GENTLEMEN.
WELL, WOULD'JA LOOK AT THAT.
YEAH, KINDA CONVENIENT.
SO WE JUST SCOOP HER UP EASY-PEASY.
NO, I MEANT SHE'S GOT THE TIGHTEST--
SANTO.
SORRY.

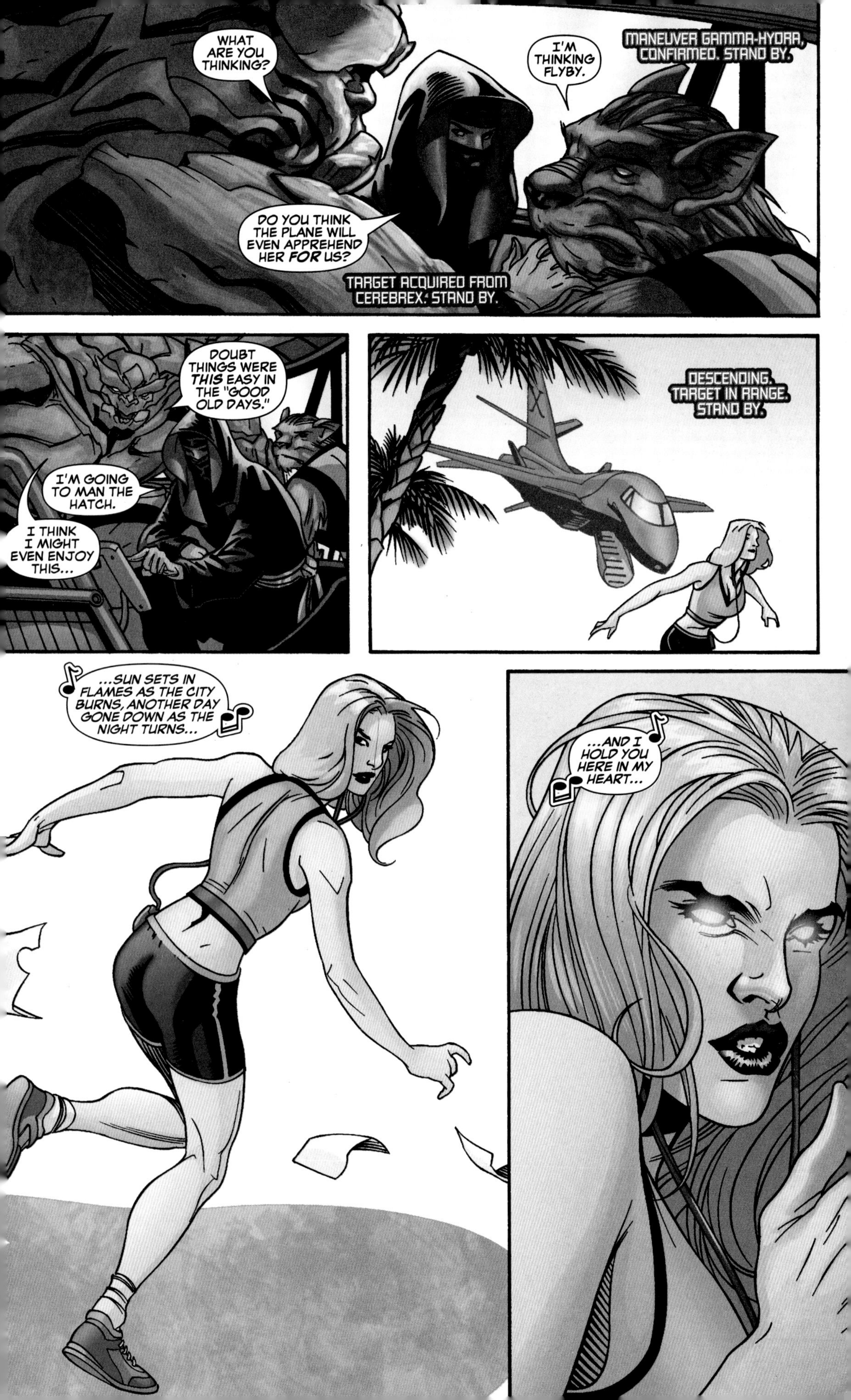
WHAT ARE YOU THINKING?
I'M THINKING FLYBY.
MANEUVER GAMMA-HYDRA, CONFIRMED. STAND BY.
DO YOU THINK THE PLANE WILL EVEN APPREHEND HER FOR US?
TARGET ACQUIRED FROM CEREBREX. STAND BY.
DOUBT THINGS WERE THIS EASY IN THE "GOOD OLD DAYS."
I'M GOING TO MAN THE HATCH.
I THINK I MIGHT EVEN ENJOY THIS...
DESCENDING. TARGET IN RANGE. STAND BY.
...SUN SETS IN FLAMES AS THE CITY BURNS, ANOTHER DAY GONE DOWN AS THE NIGHT TURNS...
...AND I HOLD YOU HERE IN MY HEART...

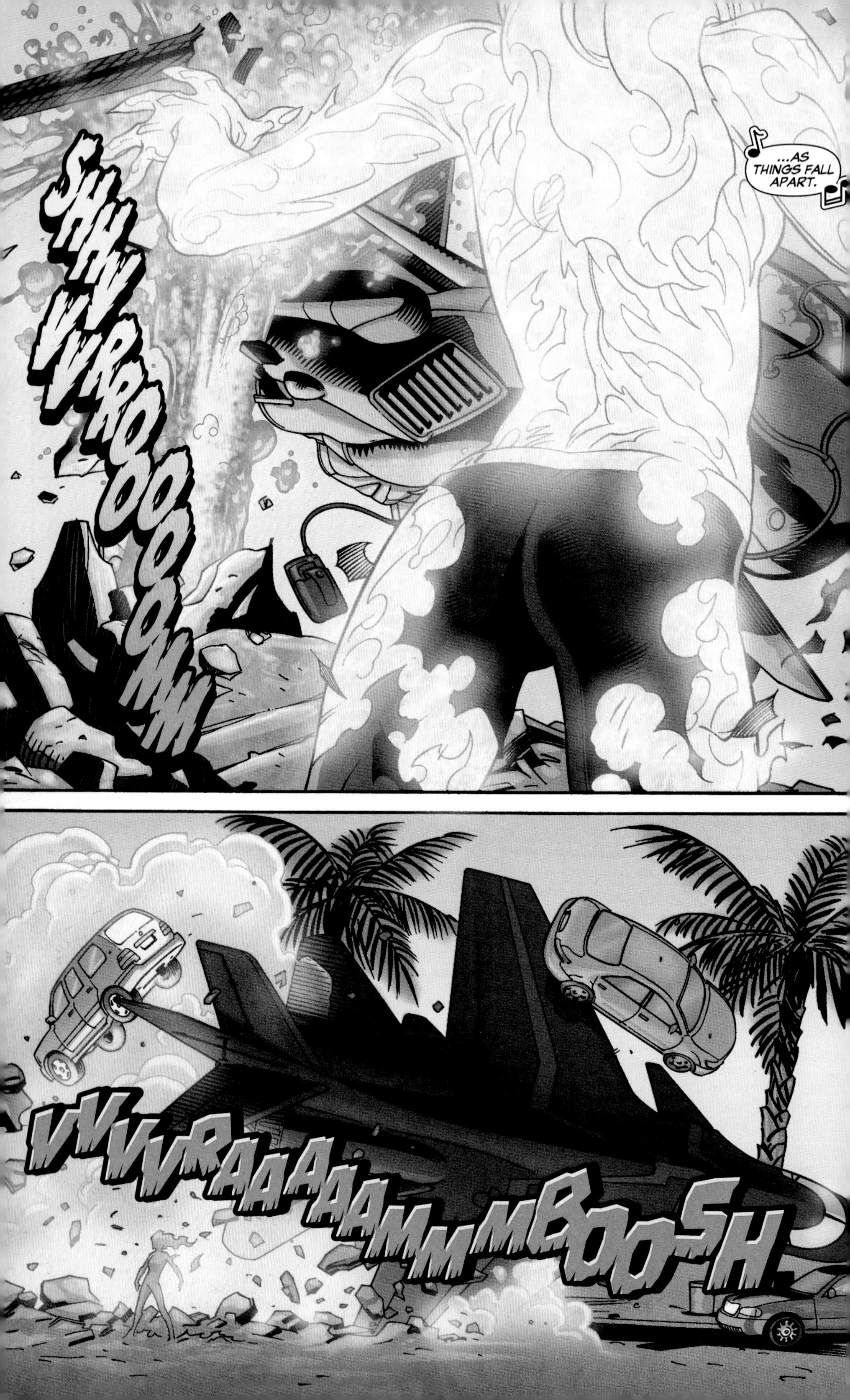
...AS THINGS FALL APART.
SHHVVROOOOOOMM
VVVVRAAAAAMMMMBOO-SH

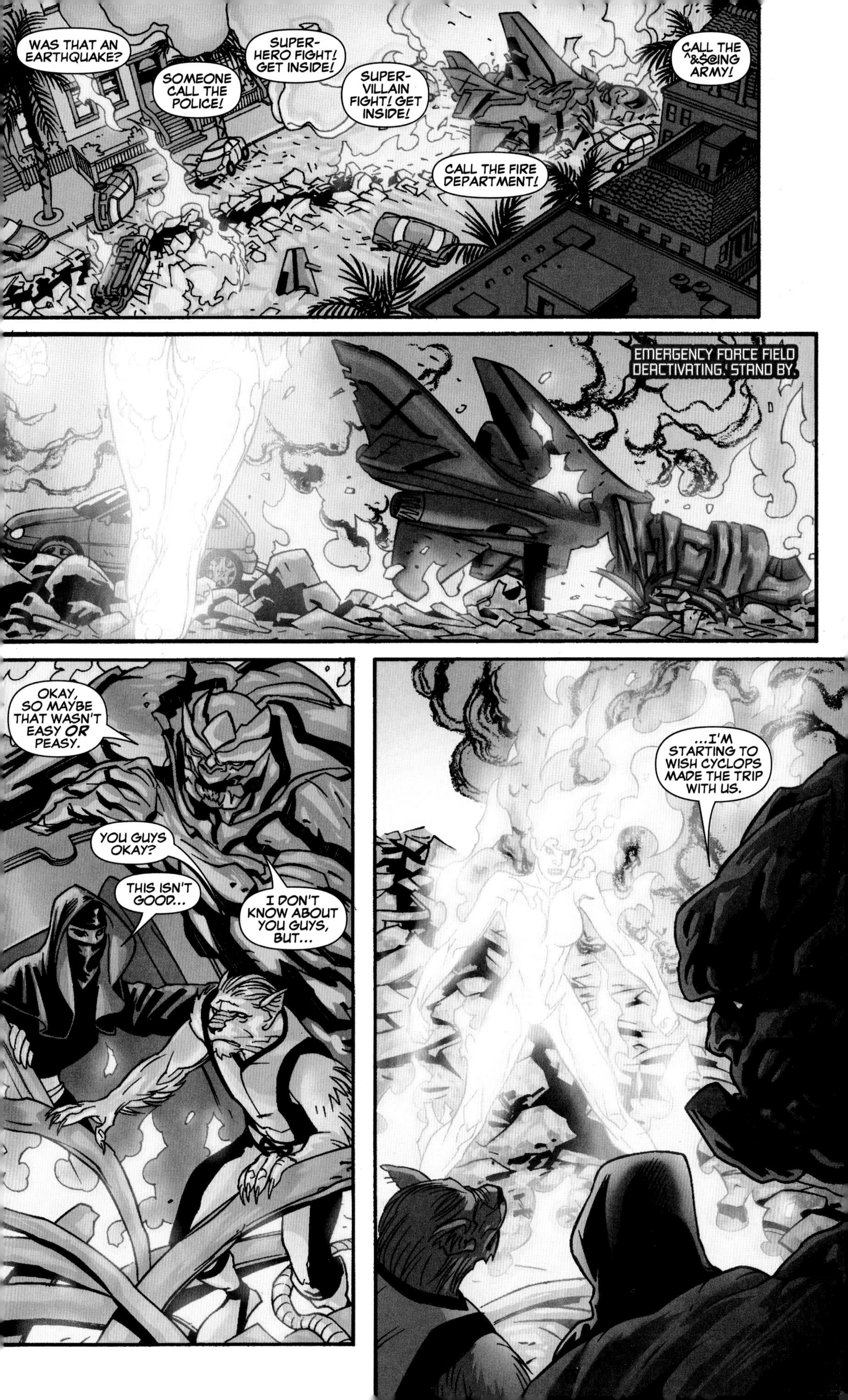
WAS THAT AN EARTHQUAKE?
SOMEONE CALL THE POLICE!
SUPER-HERO FIGHT! GET INSIDE!
SUPER-VILLAIN FIGHT! GET INSIDE!
CALL THE ^&$@ING ARMY!
CALL THE FIRE DEPARTMENT!
EMERGENCY FORCE FIELD DEACTIVATING. STAND BY.
OKAY, SO MAYBE THAT WASN'T EASY OR PEASY.
YOU GUYS OKAY?
THIS ISN'T GOOD...
I DON'T KNOW ABOUT YOU GUYS, BUT...
...I'M STARTING TO WISH CYCLOPS MADE THE TRIP WITH US.

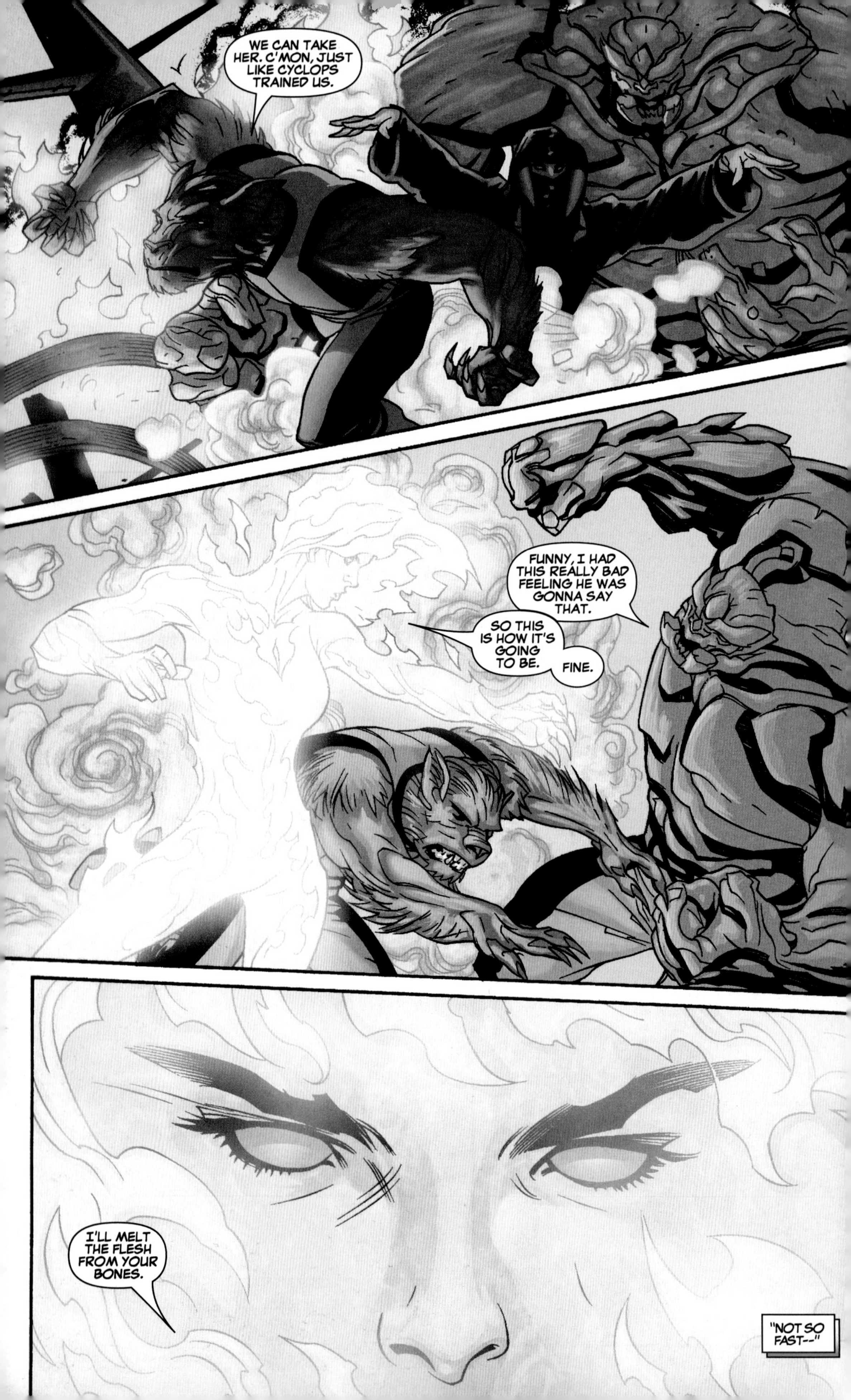
WE CAN TAKE HER. C'MON, JUST LIKE CYCLOPS TRAINED US.
FUNNY, I HAD THIS REALLY BAD FEELING HE WAS GONNA SAY THAT.
SO THIS IS HOW IT'S GOING TO BE.
FINE.
I'LL MELT THE FLESH FROM YOUR BONES.
"NOT SO FAST--"

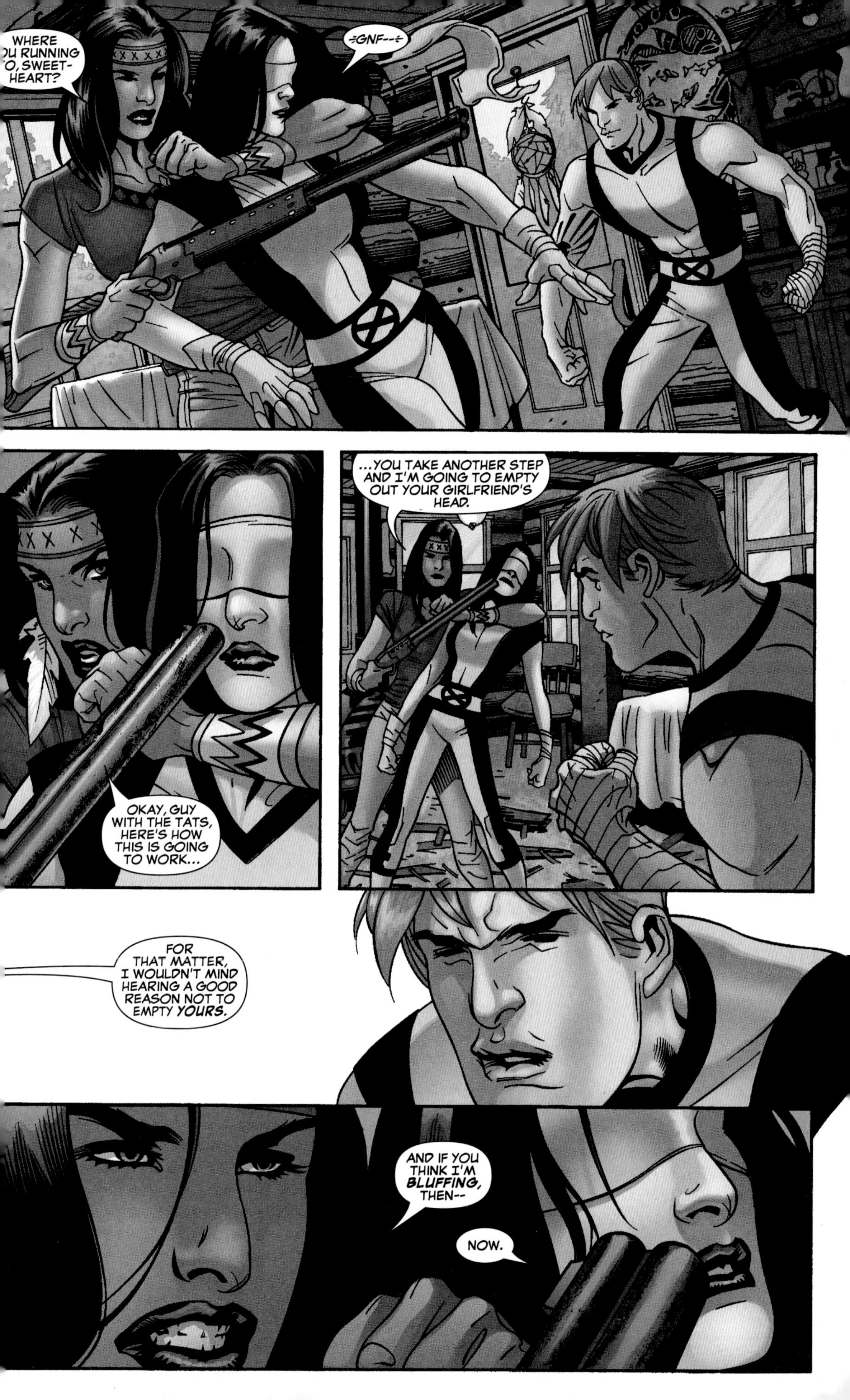

WHERE YOU RUNNING TO, SWEET-HEART?
GNF--
OKAY, GUY WITH THE TATS, HERE'S HOW THIS IS GOING TO WORK...
...YOU TAKE ANOTHER STEP AND I'M GOING TO EMPTY OUT YOUR GIRLFRIEND'S HEAD.
FOR THAT MATTER, I WOULDN'T MIND HEARING A GOOD REASON NOT TO EMPTY YOURS.
AND IF YOU THINK I'M BLUFFING, THEN--
NOW.

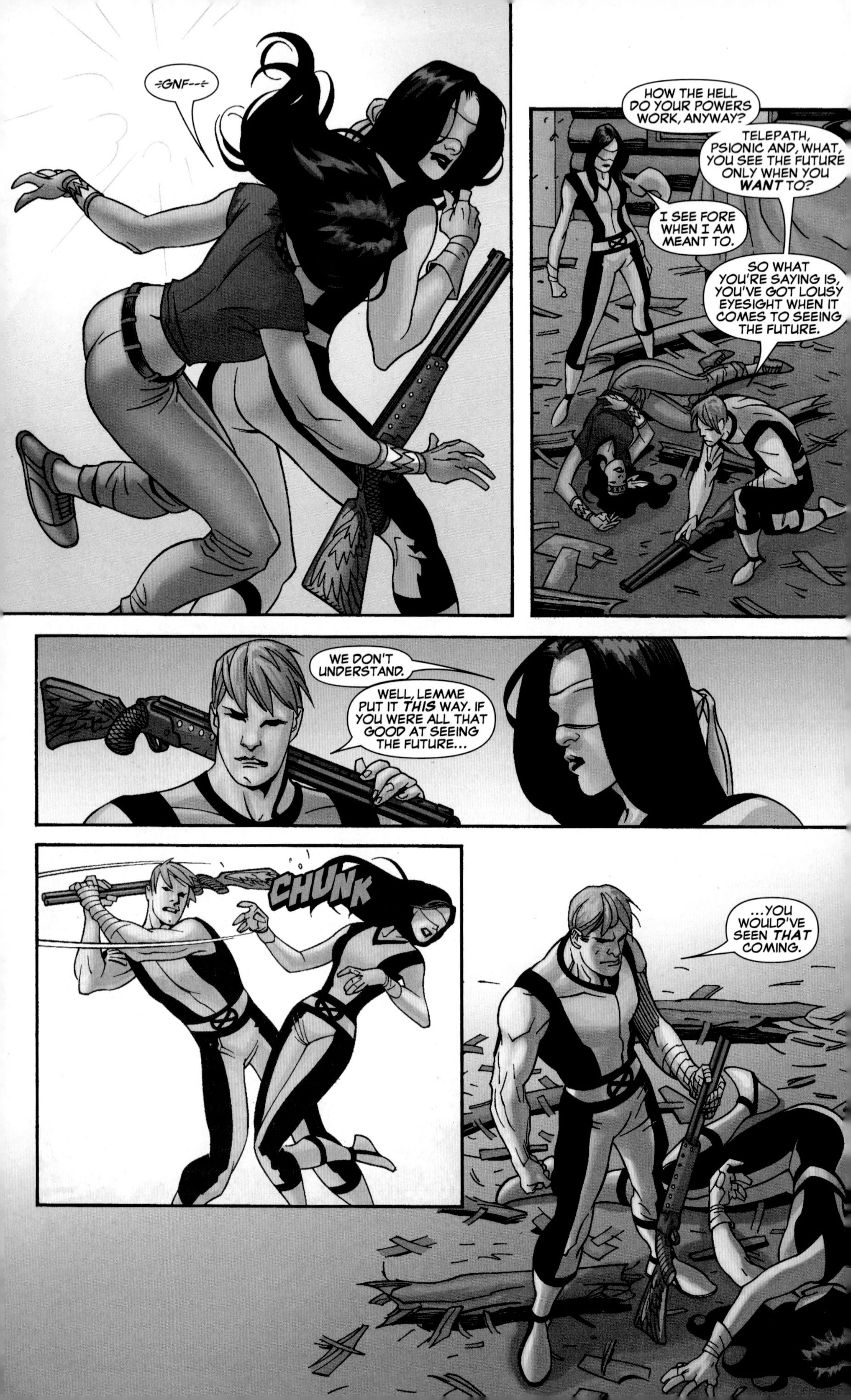

GNF--
HOW THE HELL DO YOUR POWERS WORK, ANYWAY?
TELEPATH, PSIONIC AND, WHAT, YOU SEE THE FUTURE ONLY WHEN YOU WANT TO?
I SEE FORE WHEN I AM MEANT TO.
SO WHAT YOU'RE SAYING IS, YOU'VE GOT LOUSY EYESIGHT WHEN IT COMES TO SEEING THE FUTURE.
WE DON'T UNDERSTAND.
WELL, LEMME PUT IT THIS WAY. IF YOU WERE ALL THAT GOOD AT SEEING THE FUTURE...
CHUNK
...YOU WOULD'VE SEEN THAT COMING.

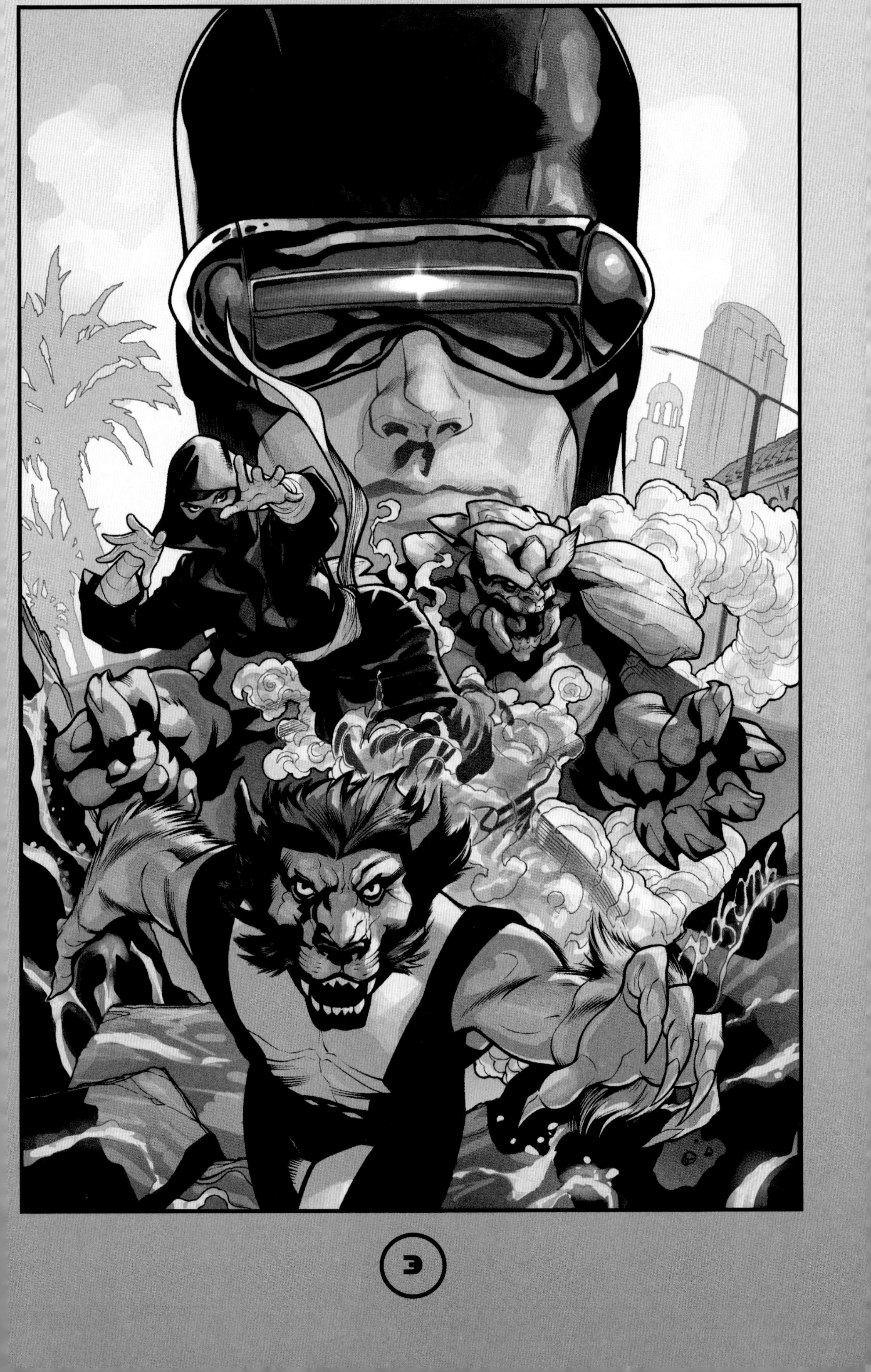

3

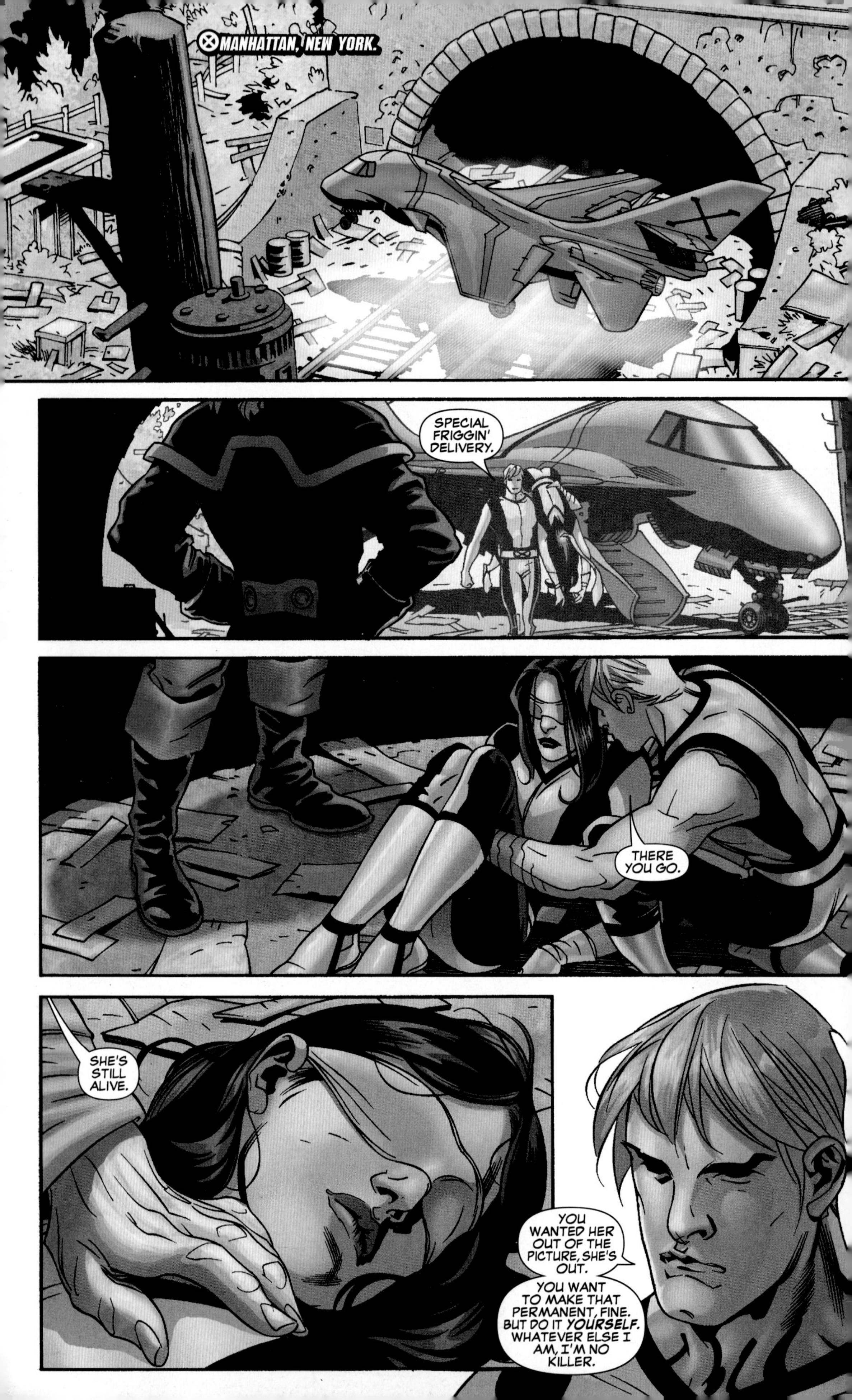
MANHATTAN, NEW YORK.
SPECIAL FRIGGIN' DELIVERY.
THERE YOU GO.
SHE'S STILL ALIVE.
YOU WANTED HER OUT OF THE PICTURE, SHE'S OUT.
YOU WANT TO MAKE THAT PERMANENT, FINE. BUT DO IT YOURSELF. WHATEVER ELSE I AM, I'M NO KILLER.

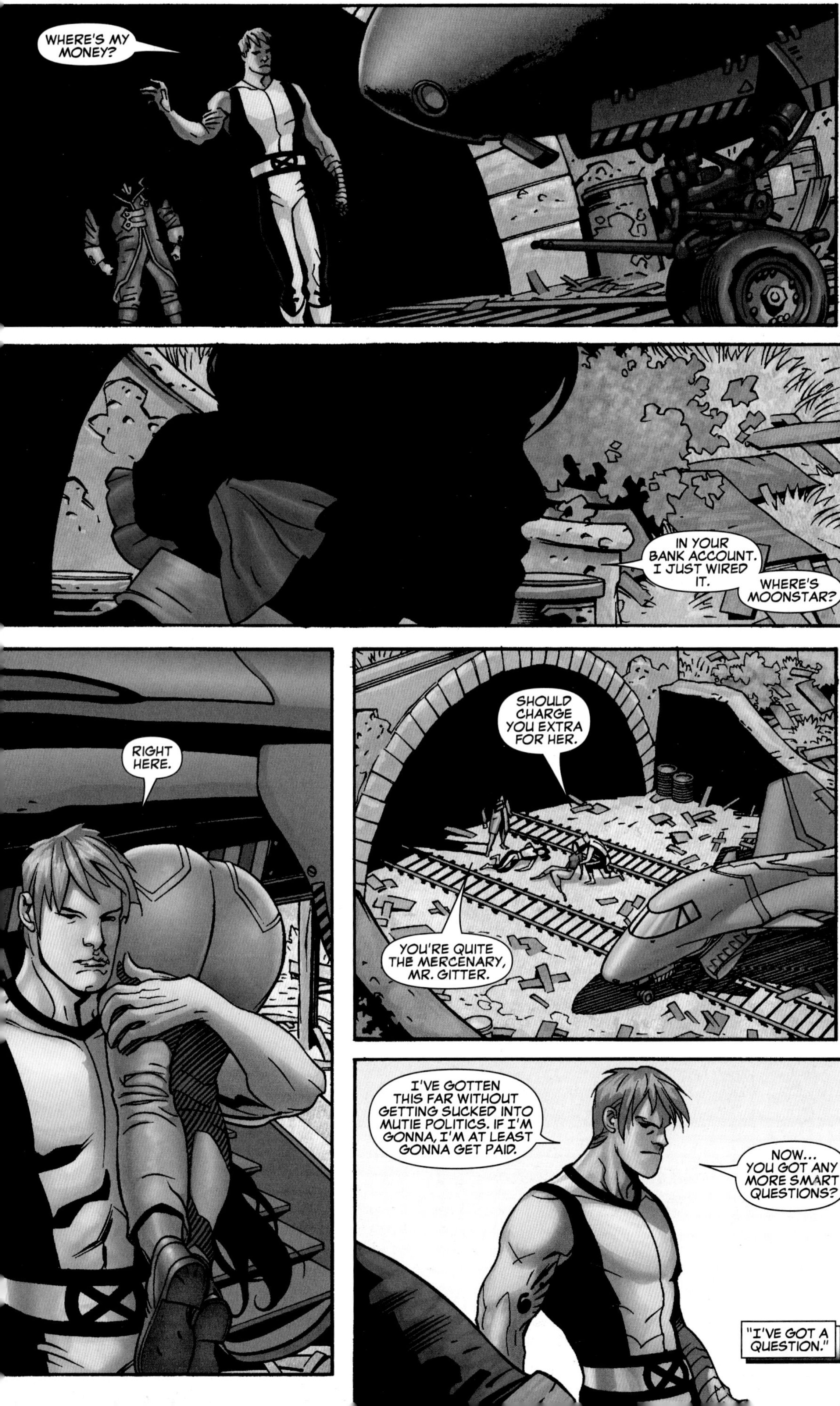

WHERE'S MY MONEY?
IN YOUR BANK ACCOUNT. I JUST WIRED IT.
WHERE'S MOONSTAR?
RIGHT HERE.
SHOULD CHARGE YOU EXTRA FOR HER.
YOU'RE QUITE THE MERCENARY, MR. GITTER.
I'VE GOTTEN THIS FAR WITHOUT GETTING SUCKED INTO MUTIE POLITICS. IF I'M GONNA, I'M AT LEAST GONNA GET PAID.
NOW... YOU GOT ANY MORE SMART QUESTIONS?
"I'VE GOT A QUESTION."

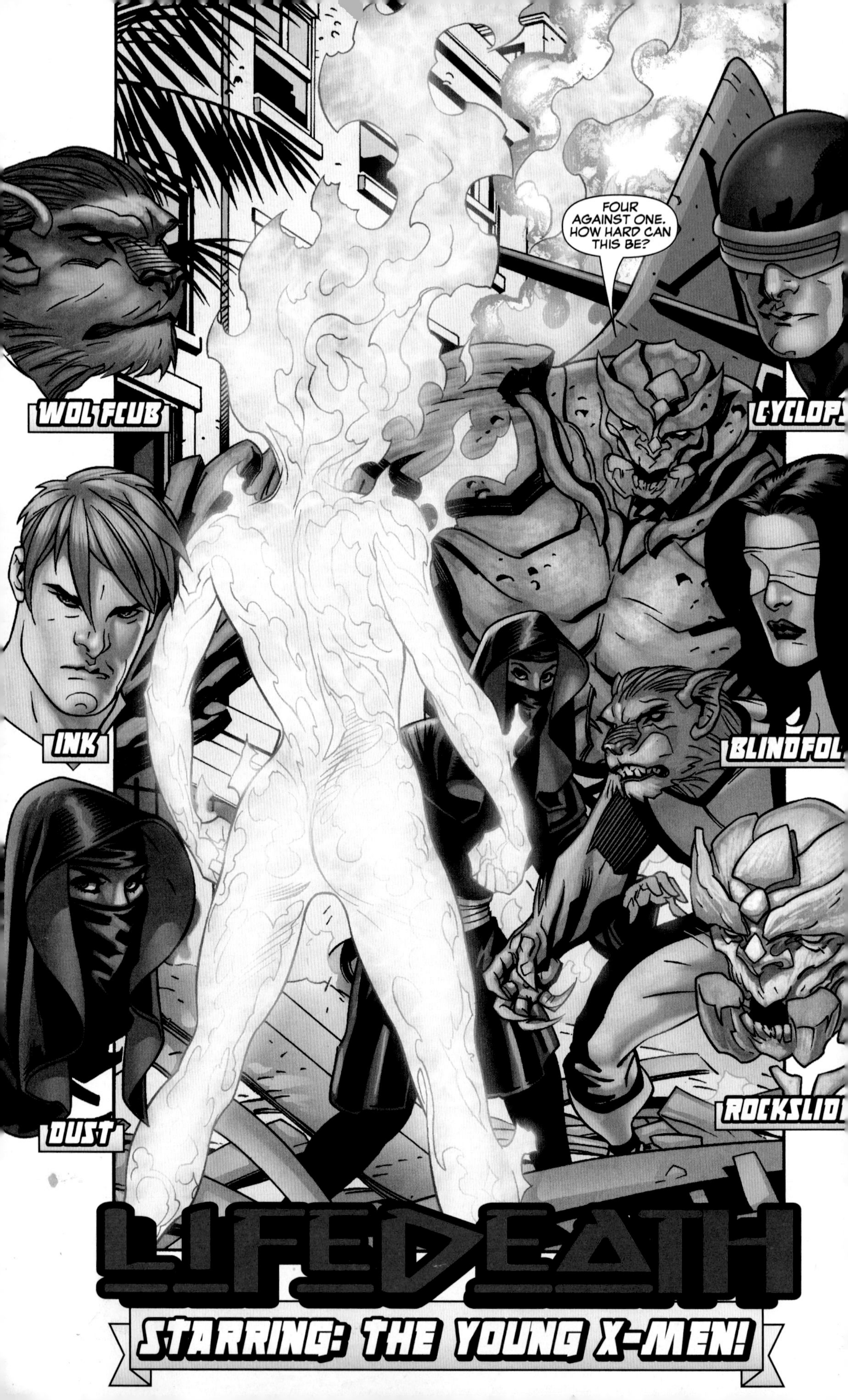
FOUR AGAINST ONE. HOW HARD CAN THIS BE?
WOLFCUB
CYCLOP
INK
BLINDFOL
DUST
ROCKSLID
LIFEDEATH
STARRING: THE YOUNG X-MEN!

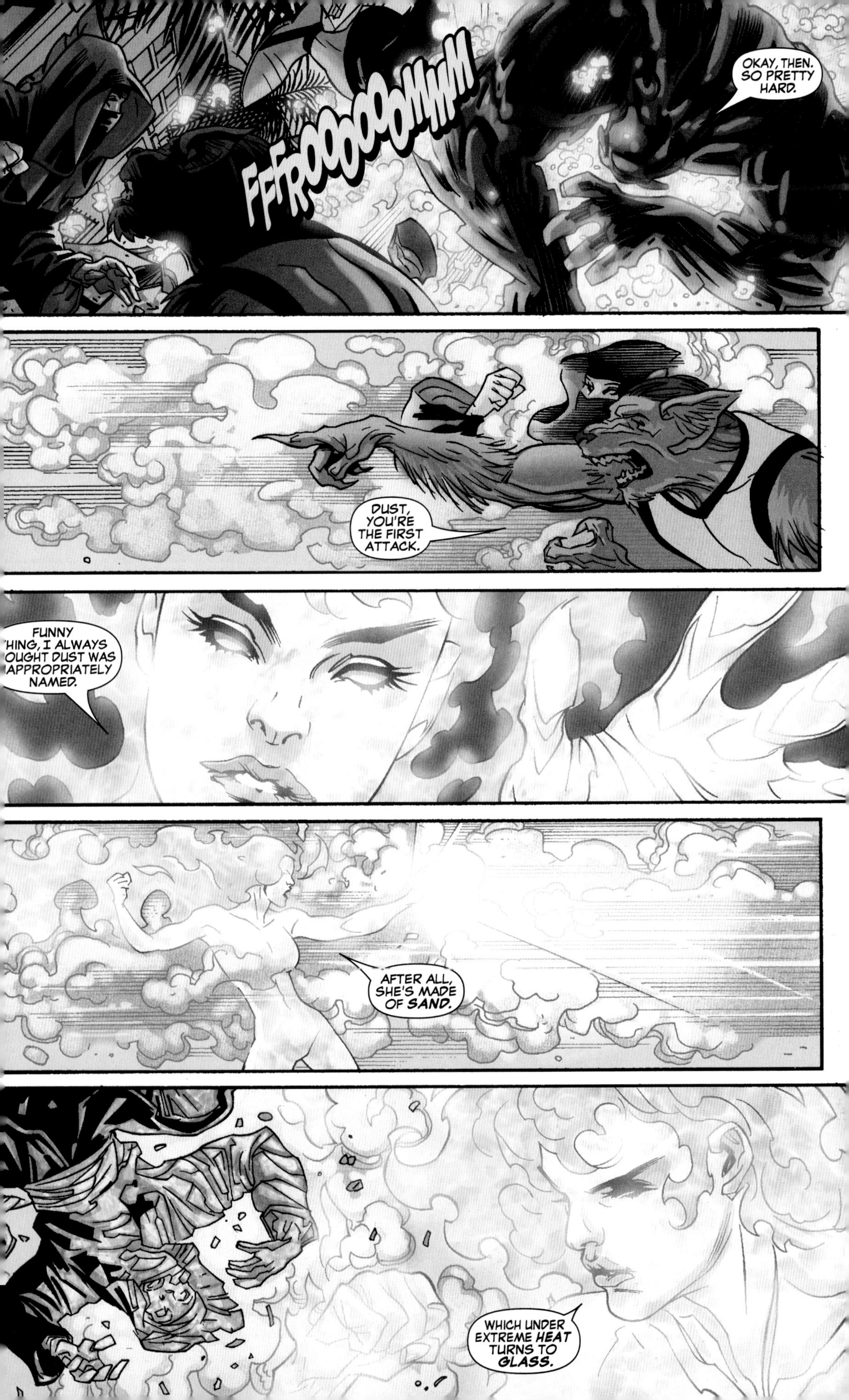
FFFROOOOOOMMMM
OKAY, THEN. SO PRETTY HARD.
DUST, YOU'RE THE FIRST ATTACK.
FUNNY THING, I ALWAYS THOUGHT DUST WAS APPROPRIATELY NAMED.
AFTER ALL, SHE'S MADE OF SAND.
WHICH UNDER EXTREME HEAT TURNS TO GLASS.

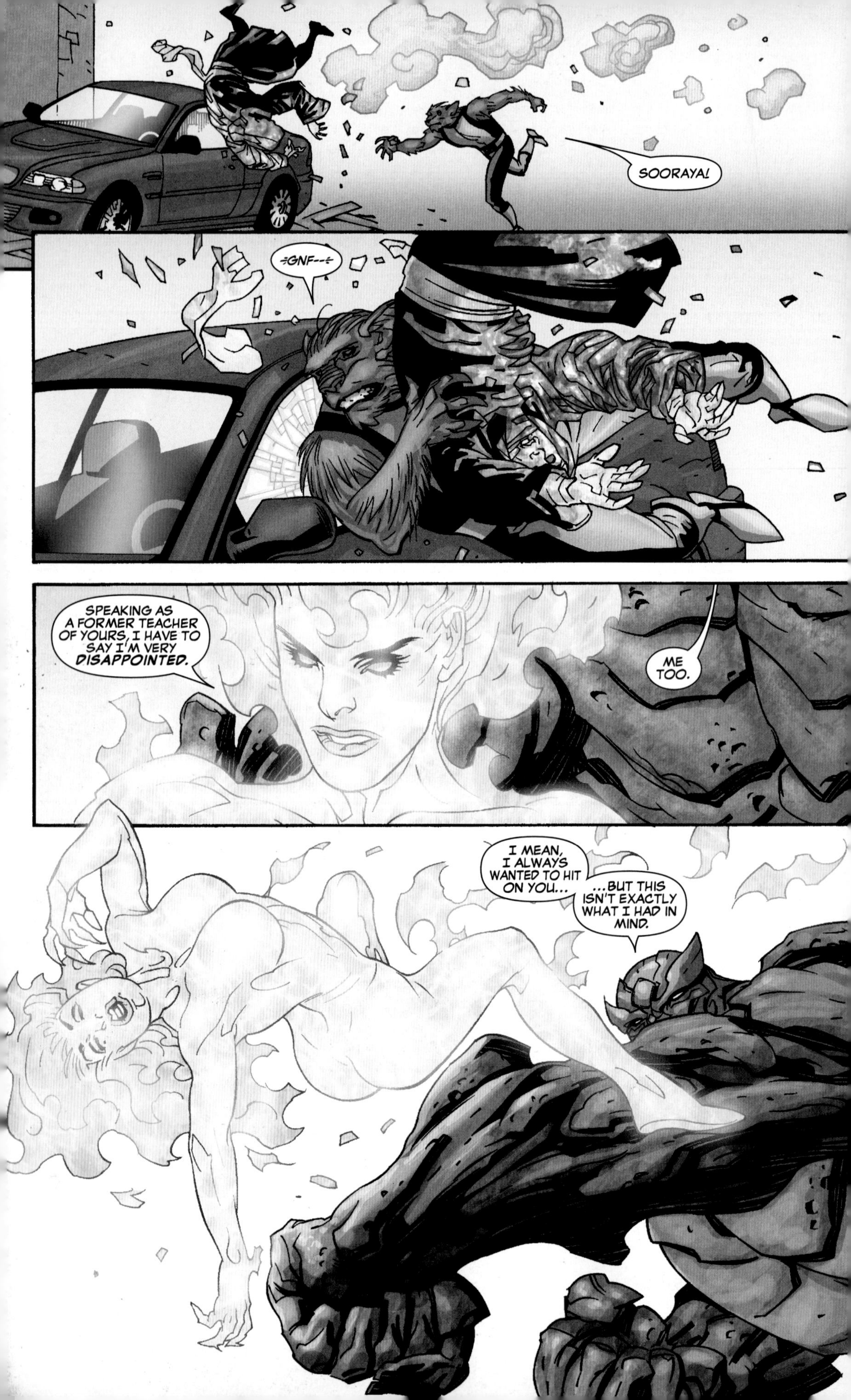
SOORAYA!
=GNF--=
SPEAKING AS A FORMER TEACHER OF YOURS, I HAVE TO SAY I'M VERY DISAPPOINTED.
ME TOO.
I MEAN, I ALWAYS WANTED TO HIT ON YOU...
...BUT THIS ISN'T EXACTLY WHAT I HAD IN MIND.

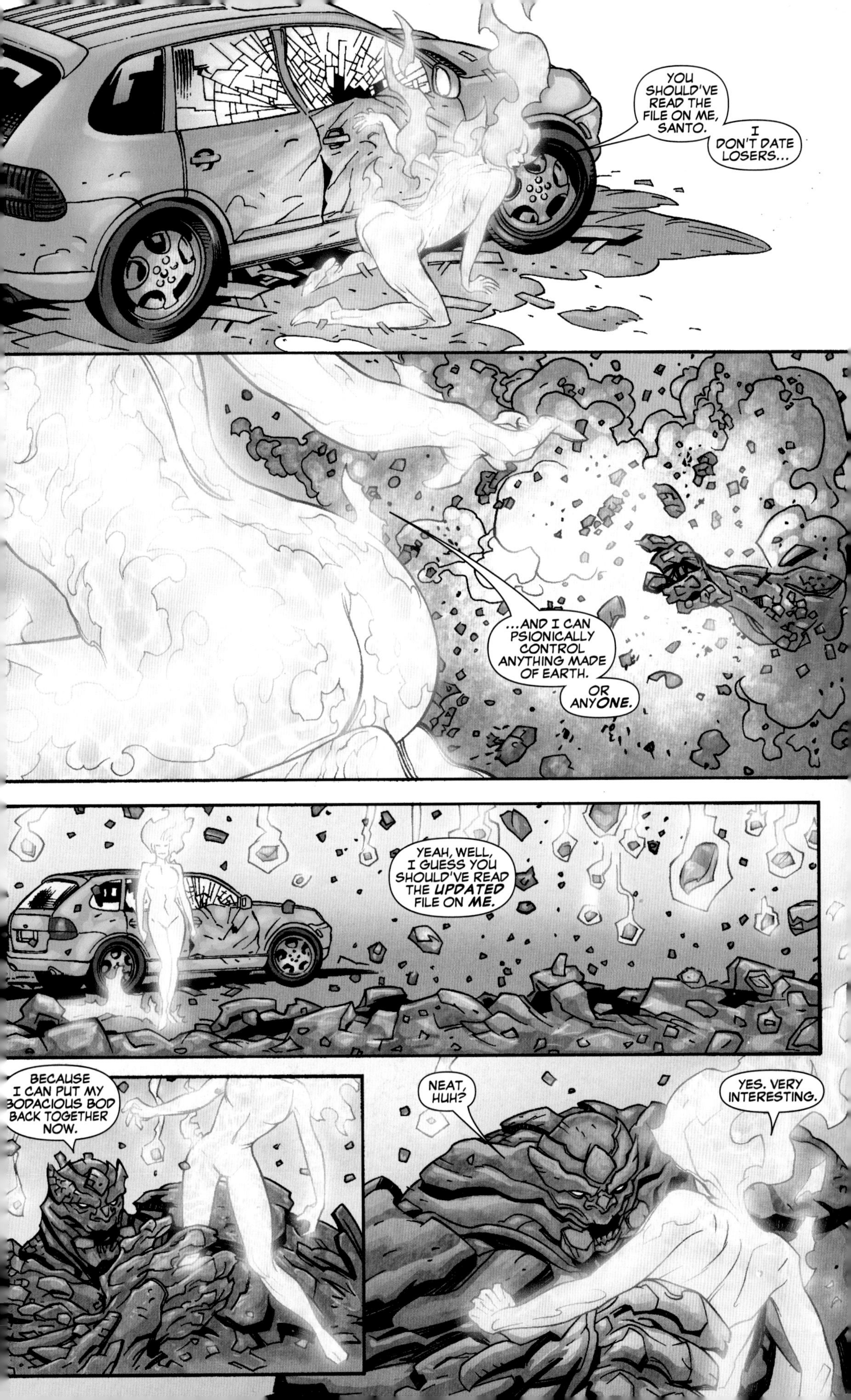

YOU SHOULD'VE READ THE FILE ON ME, SANTO.
I DON'T DATE LOSERS...
...AND I CAN PSIONICALLY CONTROL ANYTHING MADE OF EARTH.
OR ANYONE.
YEAH, WELL, I GUESS YOU SHOULD'VE READ THE UPDATED FILE ON ME.
BECAUSE I CAN PUT MY BODACIOUS BOD BACK TOGETHER NOW.
NEAT, HUH?
YES. VERY INTERESTING.

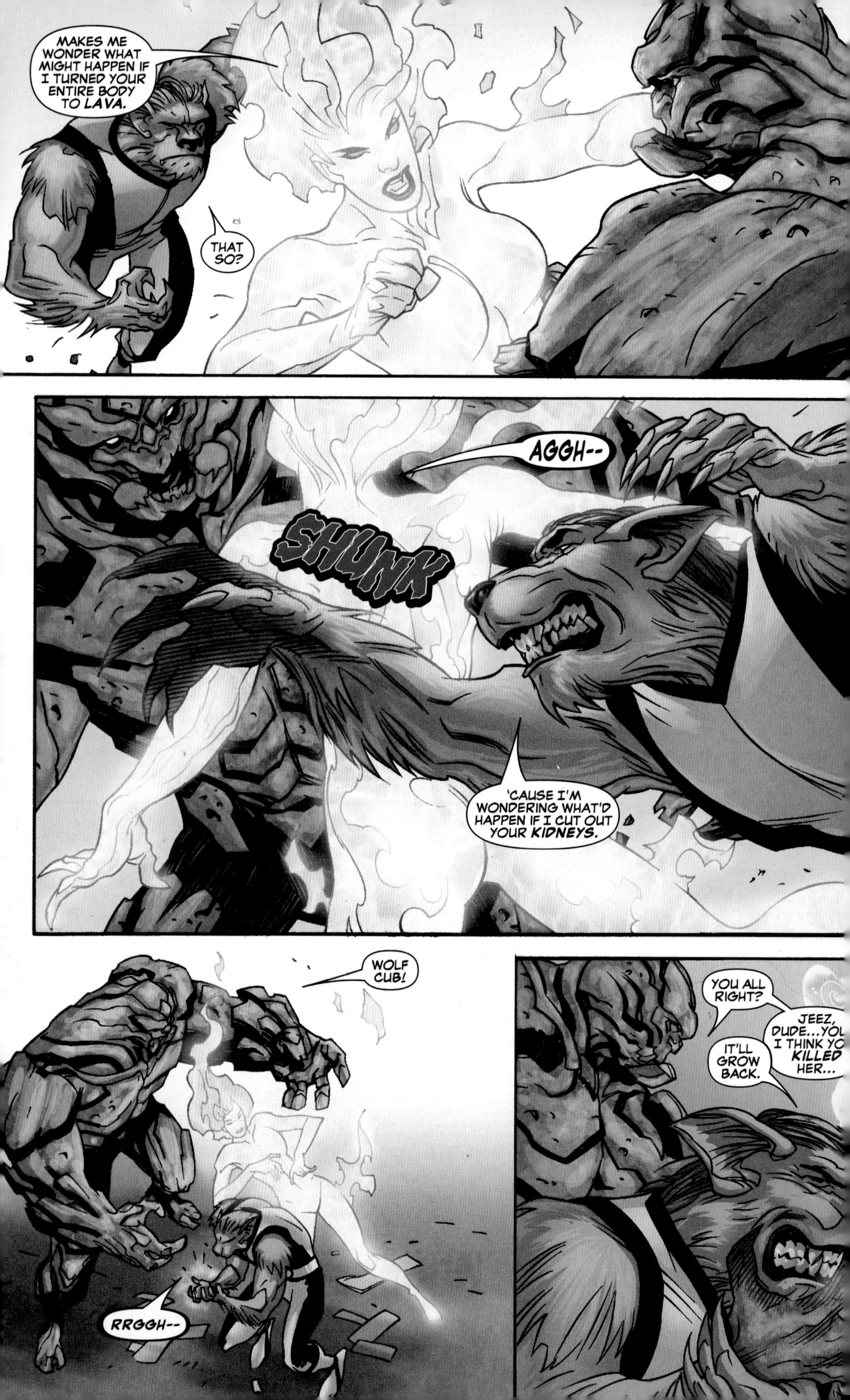
MAKES ME WONDER WHAT MIGHT HAPPEN IF I TURNED YOUR ENTIRE BODY TO LAVA.
THAT SO?
AGGH--
SHUNK
'CAUSE I'M WONDERING WHAT'D HAPPEN IF I CUT OUT YOUR KIDNEYS.
WOLF CUB!
RRGGH--
YOU ALL RIGHT?
JEEZ, DUDE...YO I THINK YO KILLED HER...
IT'LL GROW BACK.

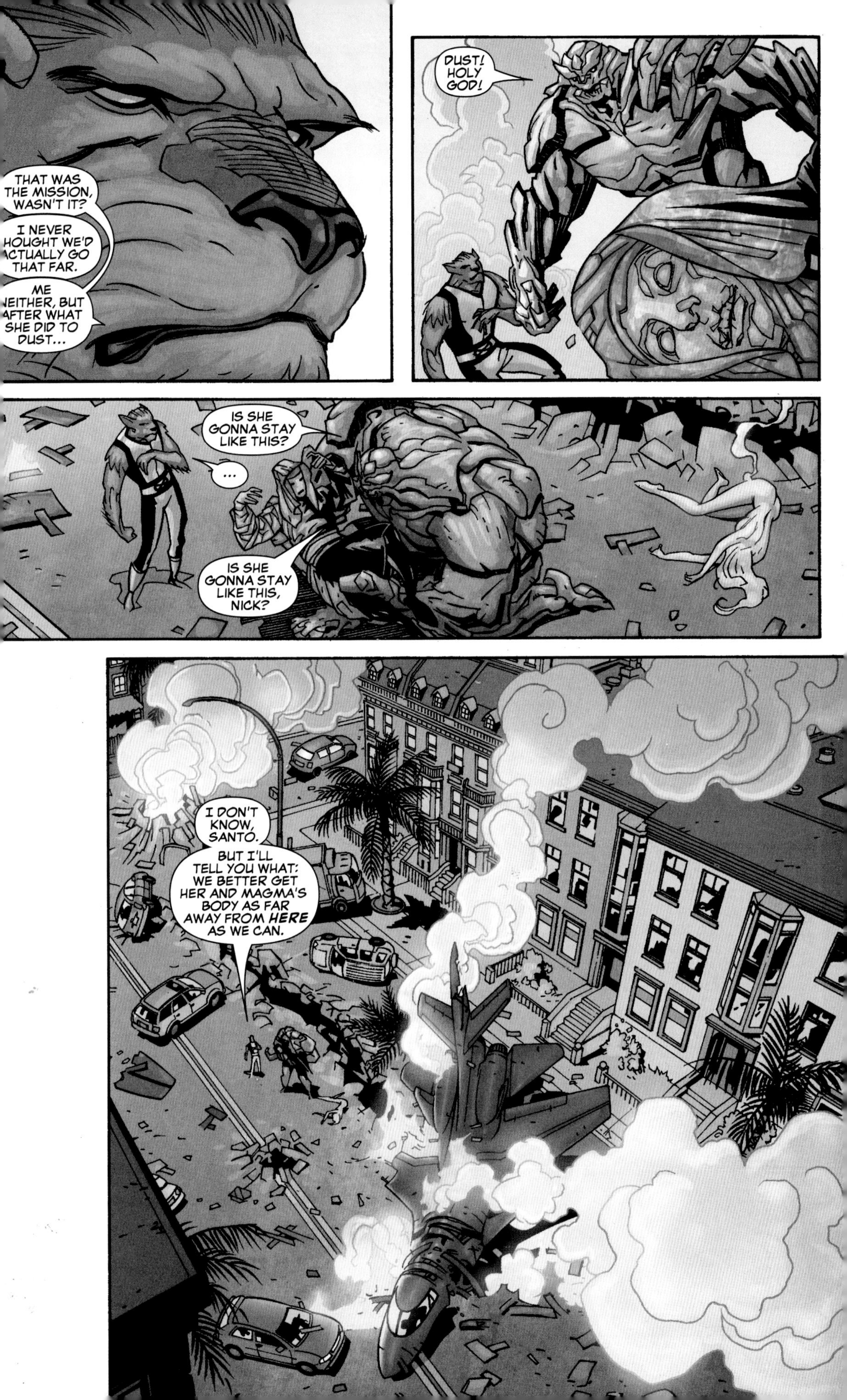
THAT WAS THE MISSION, WASN'T IT?
I NEVER THOUGHT WE'D ACTUALLY GO THAT FAR.
ME NEITHER, BUT AFTER WHAT SHE DID TO DUST...
DUST! HOLY GOD!
IS SHE GONNA STAY LIKE THIS?
...
IS SHE GONNA STAY LIKE THIS, NICK?
I DON'T KNOW, SANTO.
BUT I'LL TELL YOU WHAT: WE BETTER GET HER AND MAGMA'S BODY AS FAR AWAY FROM HERE AS WE CAN.

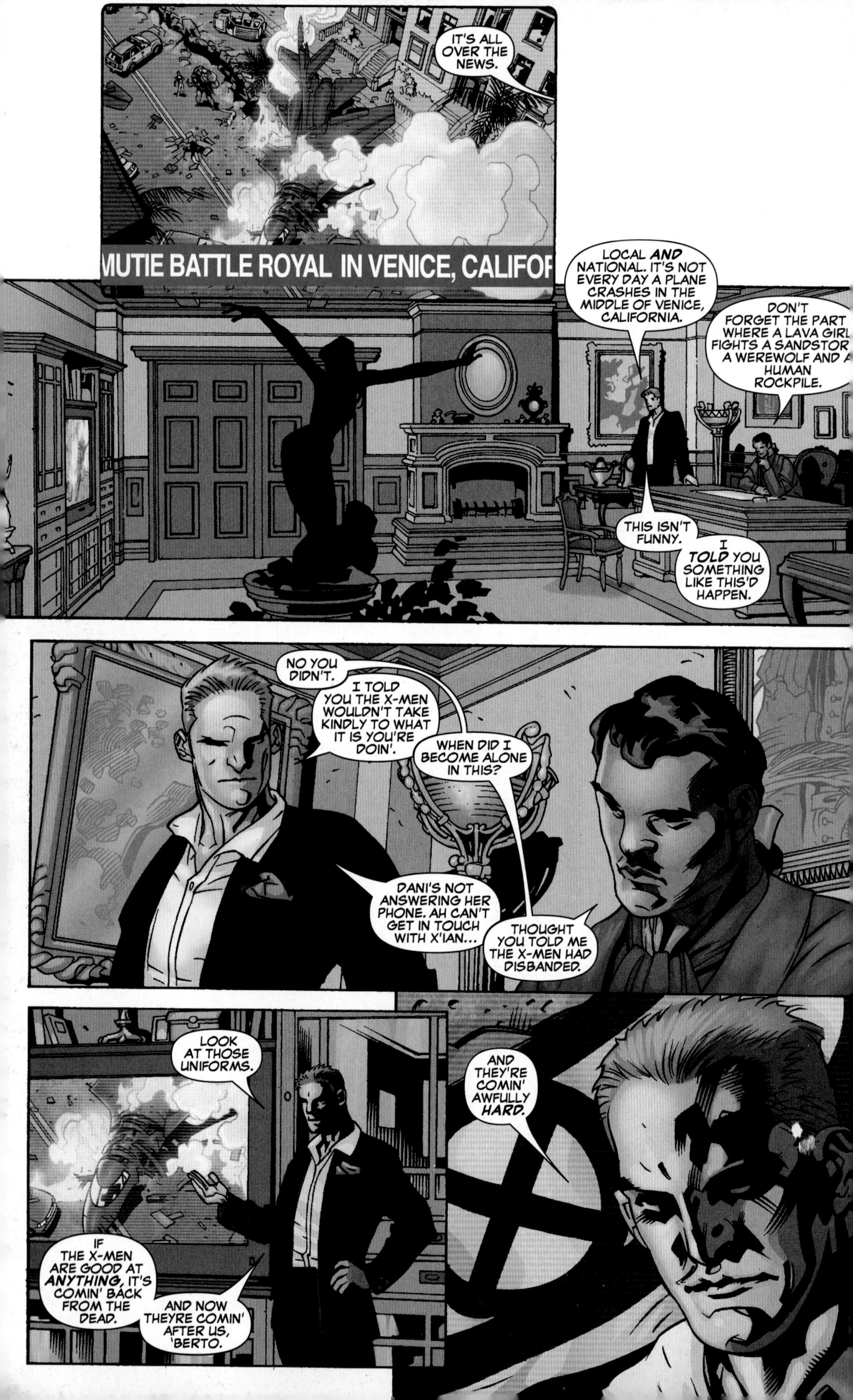
IT'S ALL OVER THE NEWS.
MUTIE BATTLE ROYAL IN VENICE, CALIFOR
LOCAL AND NATIONAL. IT'S NOT EVERY DAY A PLANE CRASHES IN THE MIDDLE OF VENICE, CALIFORNIA.
DON'T FORGET THE PART WHERE A LAVA GIRL FIGHTS A SANDSTOR A WEREWOLF AND A HUMAN ROCKPILE.
THIS ISN'T FUNNY.
I TOLD YOU SOMETHING LIKE THIS'D HAPPEN.
NO YOU DIDN'T.
I TOLD YOU THE X-MEN WOULDN'T TAKE KINDLY TO WHAT IT IS YOU'RE DOIN'.
WHEN DID I BECOME ALONE IN THIS?
DANI'S NOT ANSWERING HER PHONE. AH CAN'T GET IN TOUCH WITH X'IAN...
THOUGHT YOU TOLD ME THE X-MEN HAD DISBANDED.
LOOK AT THOSE UNIFORMS.
AND THEY'RE COMIN' AWFULLY HARD.
IF THE X-MEN ARE GOOD AT ANYTHING, IT'S COMIN' BACK FROM THE DEAD.
AND NOW THEYRE COMIN' AFTER US, 'BERTO.

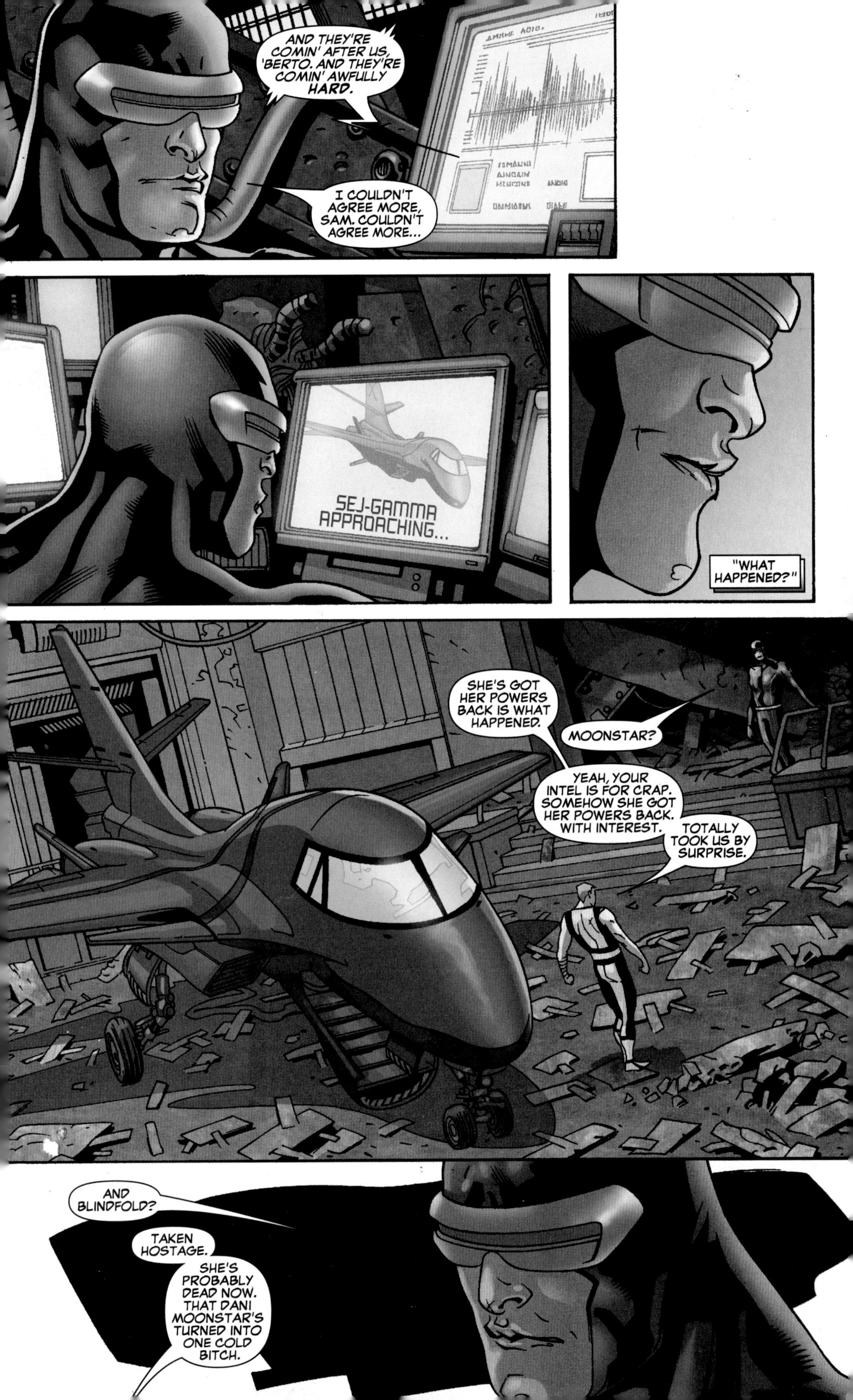
AND THEY'RE COMIN' AFTER US, 'BERTO. AND THEY'RE COMIN' AWFULLY HARD.
I COULDN'T AGREE MORE, SAM. COULDN'T AGREE MORE...
SEJ-GAMMA APPROACHING...
"WHAT HAPPENED?"
SHE'S GOT HER POWERS BACK IS WHAT HAPPENED.
MOONSTAR?
YEAH, YOUR INTEL IS FOR CRAP. SOMEHOW SHE GOT HER POWERS BACK. WITH INTEREST.
TOTALLY TOOK US BY SURPRISE.
AND BLINDFOLD?
TAKEN HOSTAGE.
SHE'S PROBABLY DEAD NOW. THAT DANI MOONSTAR'S TURNED INTO ONE COLD BITCH.

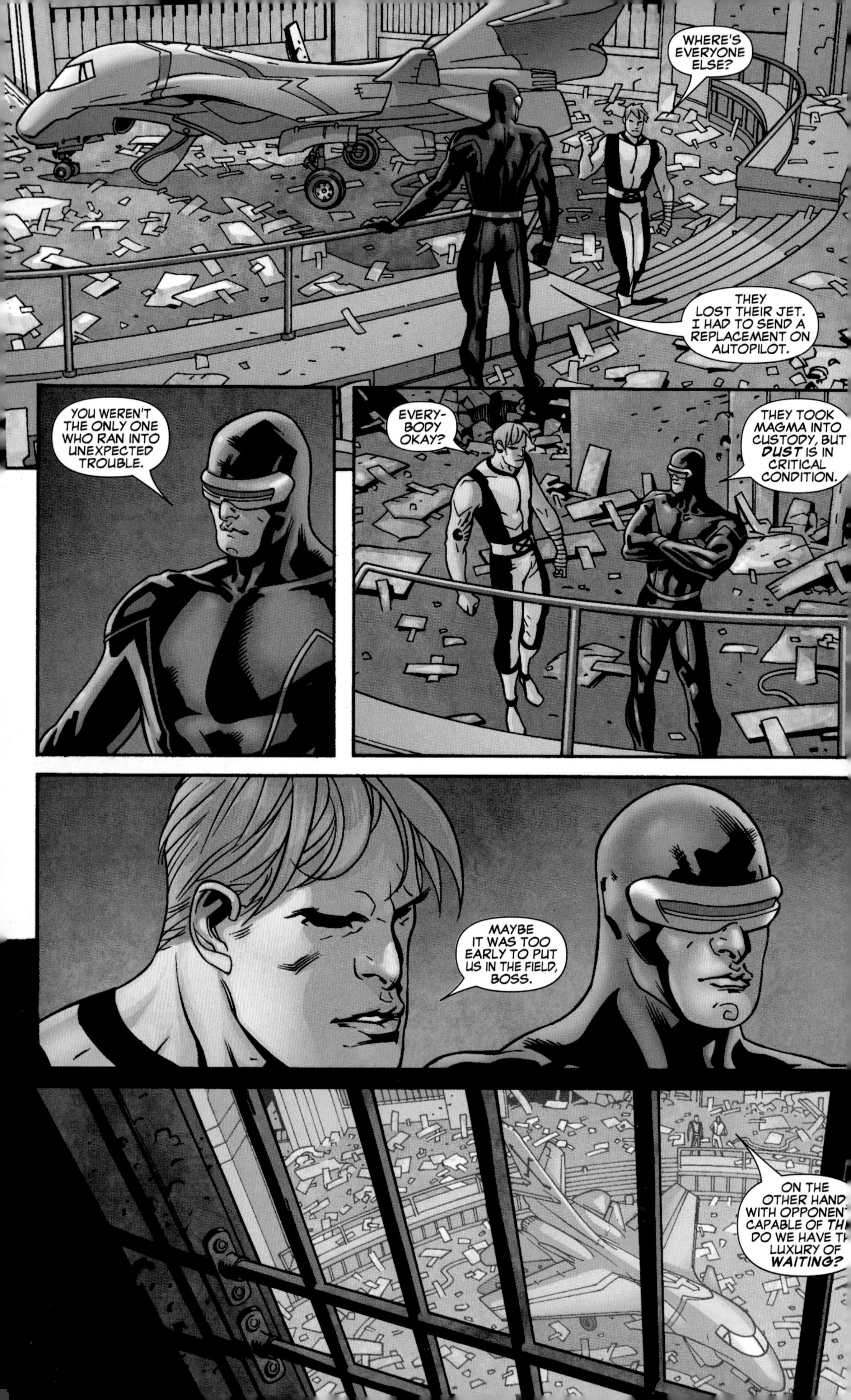
WHERE'S EVERYONE ELSE?
THEY LOST THEIR JET. I HAD TO SEND A REPLACEMENT ON AUTOPILOT.
YOU WEREN'T THE ONLY ONE WHO RAN INTO UNEXPECTED TROUBLE.
EVERY-BODY OKAY?
THEY TOOK MAGMA INTO CUSTODY, BUT DUST IS IN CRITICAL CONDITION.
MAYBE IT WAS TOO EARLY TO PUT US IN THE FIELD, BOSS.
ON THE OTHER HAND WITH OPPONENT CAPABLE OF TH DO WE HAVE T LUXURY OF WAITING?

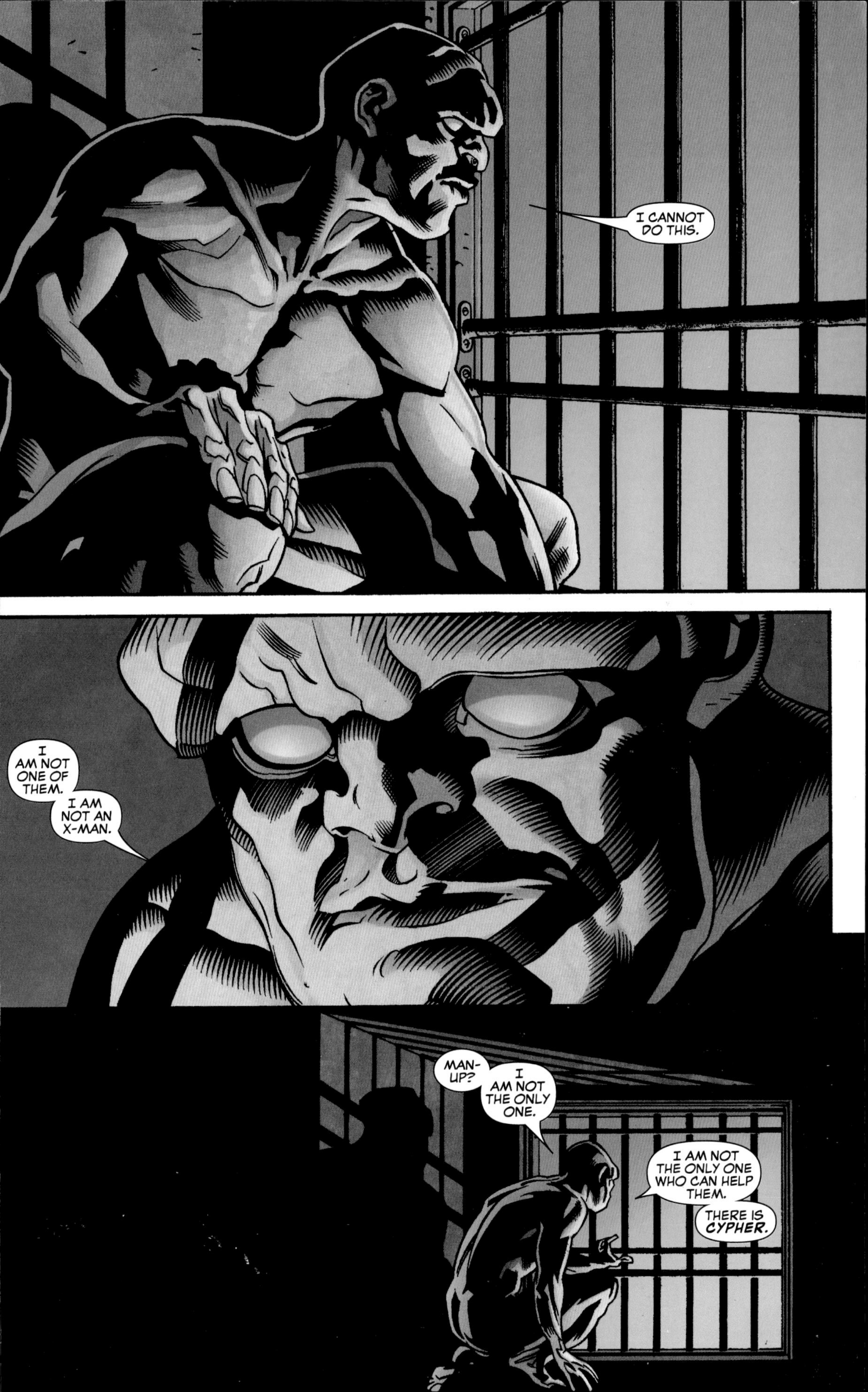
I CANNOT DO THIS.
I AM NOT ONE OF THEM.
I AM NOT AN X-MAN.
MAN-UP?
I AM NOT THE ONLY ONE.
I AM NOT THE ONLY ONE WHO CAN HELP THEM.
THERE IS CYPHER.

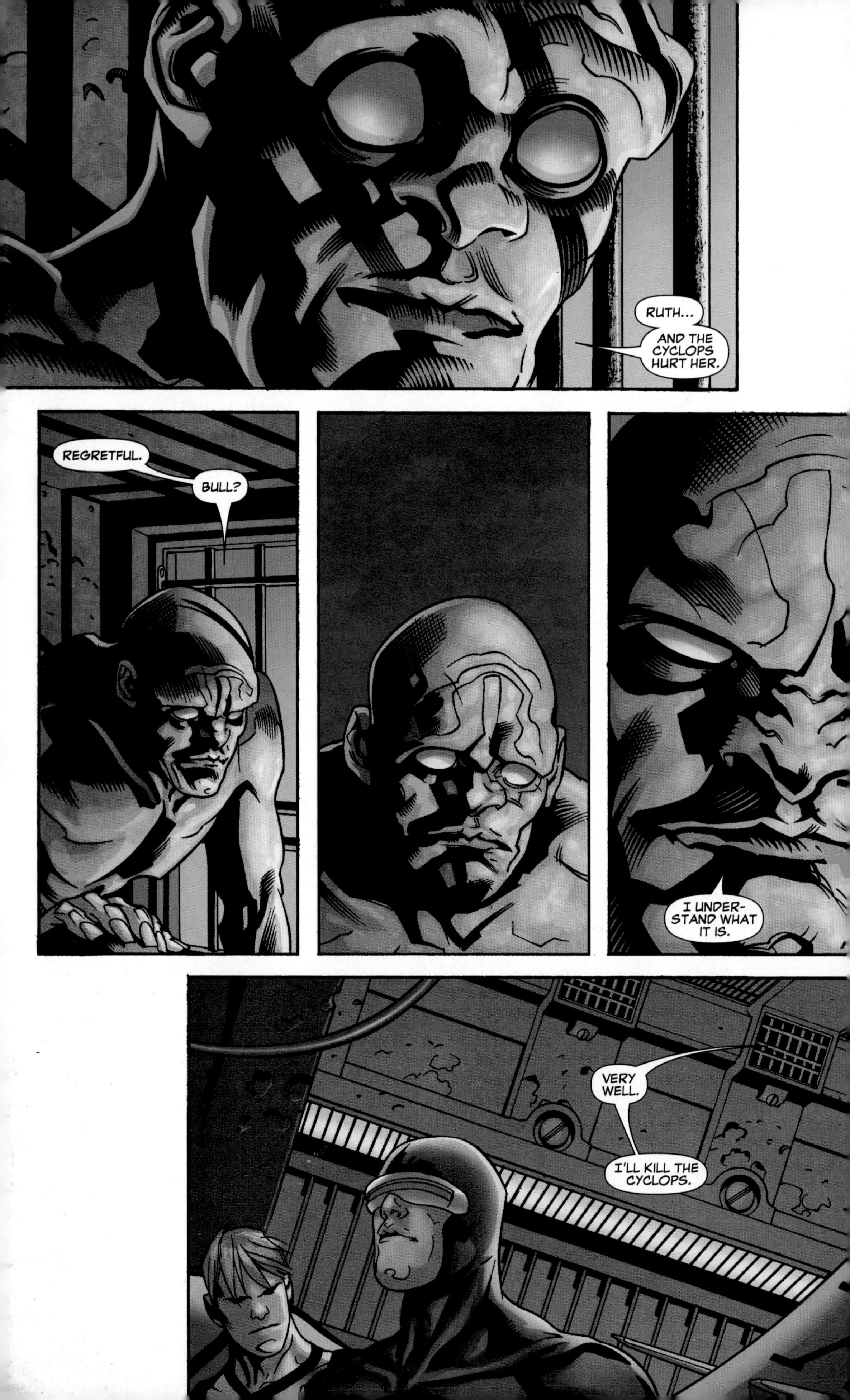
RUTH...
AND THE CYCLOPS HURT HER.
REGRETFUL.
BULL?
I UNDER-STAND WHAT IT IS.
VERY WELL.
I'LL KILL THE CYCLOPS.

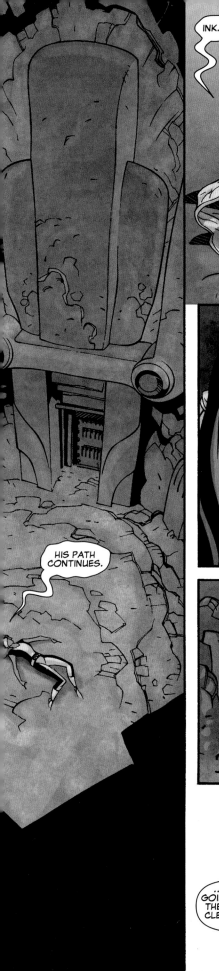

HIS PATH
CONTINUES.

INK...

BLINDFOLD...

...YOU'VE
GOT A LOT OF
EXPLAINING
TO DO...

I'VE
GOT SOME
QUESTIONS,
BITCH...

...AND I'M
GOING TO BEAT
THE ANSWERS
CLEAN OUT OF
YOU.

"BLINDFOLD'S
NOT DEAD."

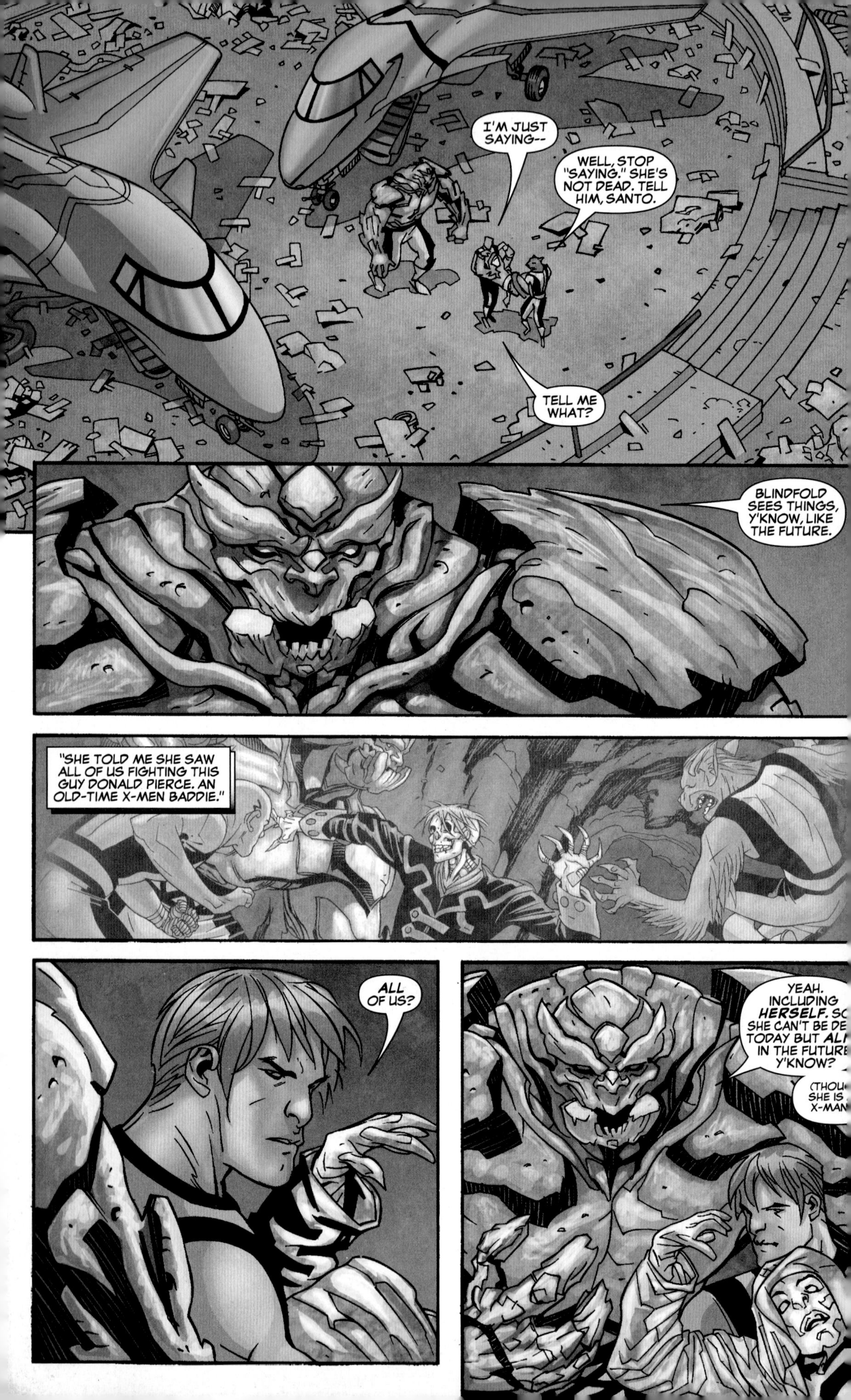
I'M JUST SAYING--
WELL, STOP "SAYING." SHE'S NOT DEAD. TELL HIM, SANTO.
TELL ME WHAT?
BLINDFOLD SEES THINGS, Y'KNOW, LIKE THE FUTURE.
"SHE TOLD ME SHE SAW ALL OF US FIGHTING THIS GUY DONALD PIERCE. AN OLD-TIME X-MEN BADDIE."
ALL OF US?
YEAH. INCLUDING HERSELF. SO SHE CAN'T BE DE TODAY BUT ALI IN THE FUTURE Y'KNOW?
(THOU SHE IS X-MAN

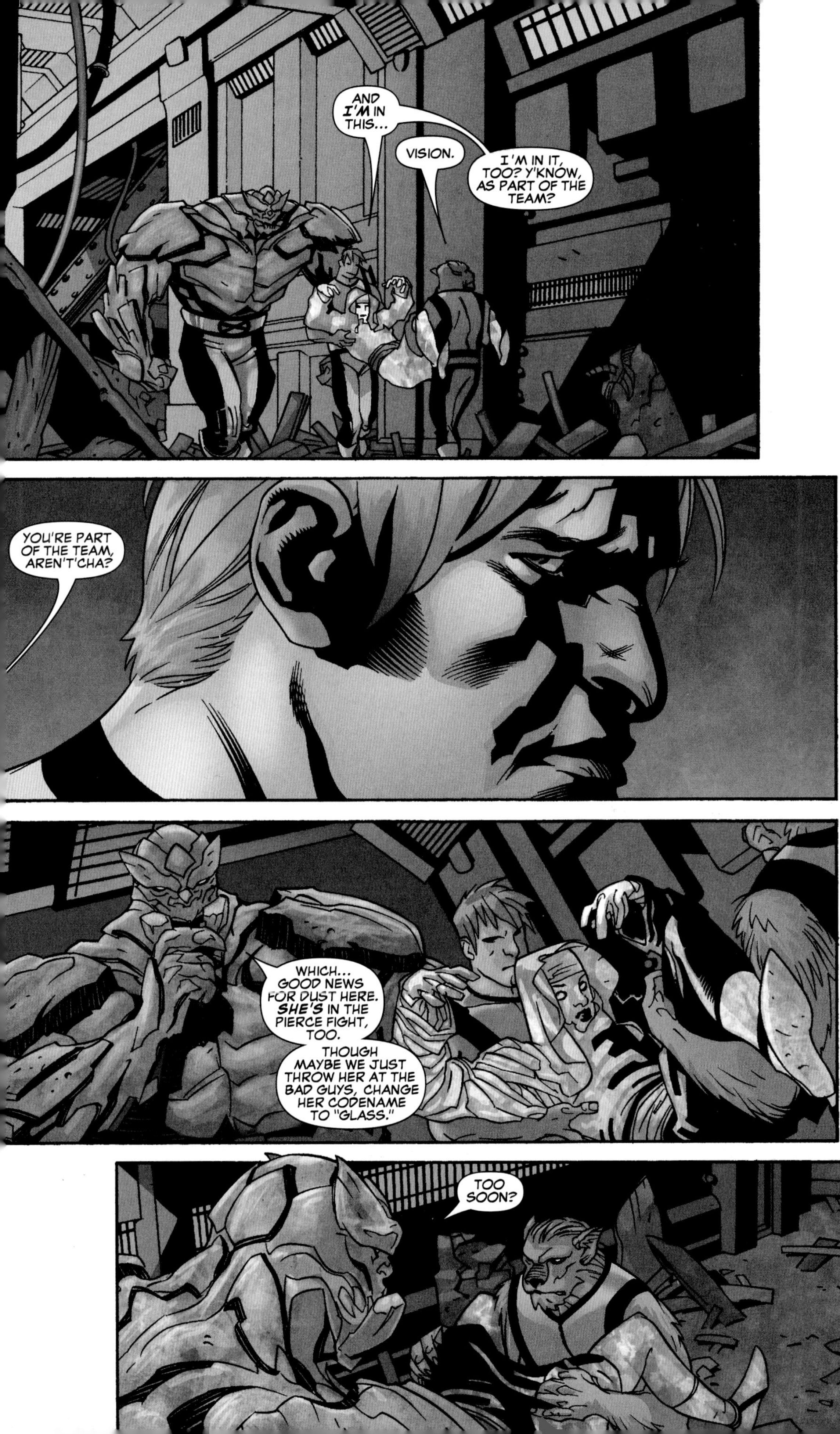
AND I'M IN THIS...
VISION.
I'M IN IT, TOO? Y'KNOW, AS PART OF THE TEAM?
YOU'RE PART OF THE TEAM, AREN'T'CHA?
WHICH... GOOD NEWS FOR DUST HERE. SHE'S IN THE PIERCE FIGHT, TOO.
THOUGH MAYBE WE JUST THROW HER AT THE BAD GUYS, CHANGE HER CODENAME TO "GLASS."
TOO SOON?

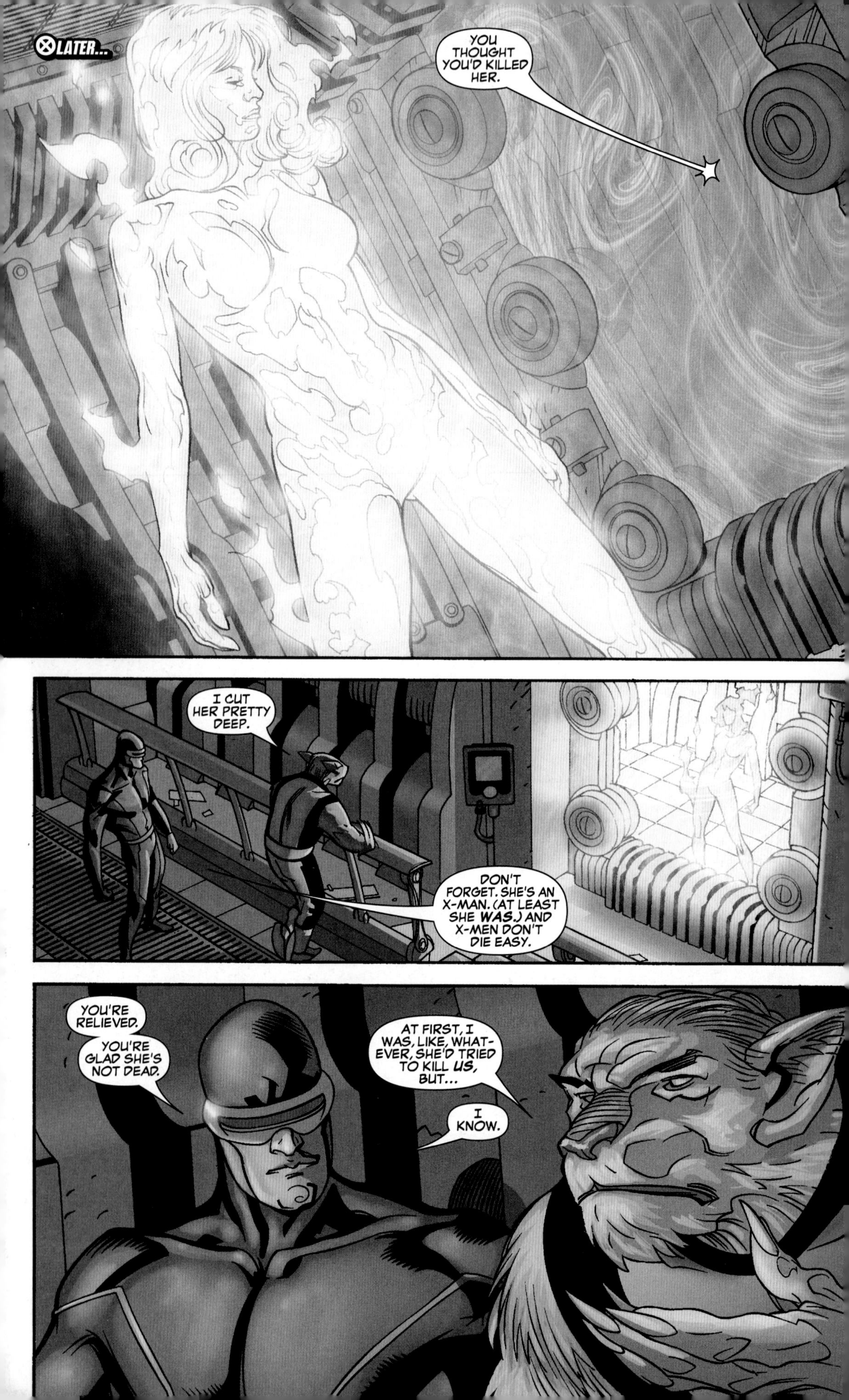
LATER...
YOU THOUGHT YOU'D KILLED HER.
I CUT HER PRETTY DEEP.
DON'T FORGET. SHE'S AN X-MAN. (AT LEAST SHE WAS.) AND X-MEN DON'T DIE EASY.
YOU'RE RELIEVED.
YOU'RE GLAD SHE'S NOT DEAD.
AT FIRST, I WAS, LIKE, WHAT-EVER, SHE'D TRIED TO KILL US, BUT...
I KNOW.

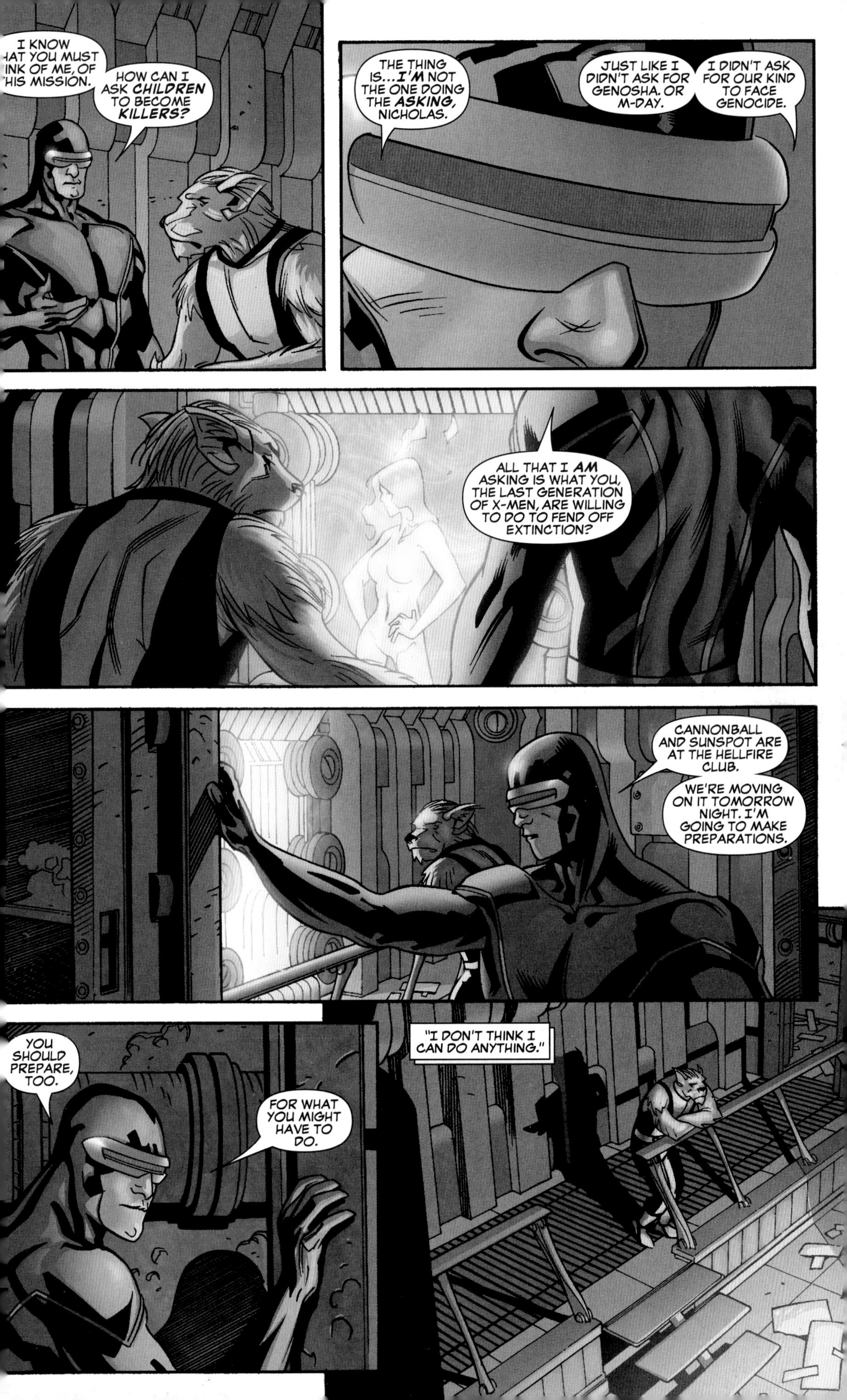
I KNOW HAT YOU MUST INK OF ME, OF THIS MISSION.
HOW CAN I ASK CHILDREN TO BECOME KILLERS?
THE THING IS...I'M NOT THE ONE DOING THE ASKING, NICHOLAS.
JUST LIKE I DIDN'T ASK FOR GENOSHA. OR M-DAY.
I DIDN'T ASK FOR OUR KIND TO FACE GENOCIDE.
ALL THAT I AM ASKING IS WHAT YOU, THE LAST GENERATION OF X-MEN, ARE WILLING TO DO TO FEND OFF EXTINCTION?
CANNONBALL AND SUNSPOT ARE AT THE HELLFIRE CLUB.
WE'RE MOVING ON IT TOMORROW NIGHT. I'M GOING TO MAKE PREPARATIONS.
YOU SHOULD PREPARE, TOO.
FOR WHAT YOU MIGHT HAVE TO DO.
"I DON'T THINK I CAN DO ANYTHING."

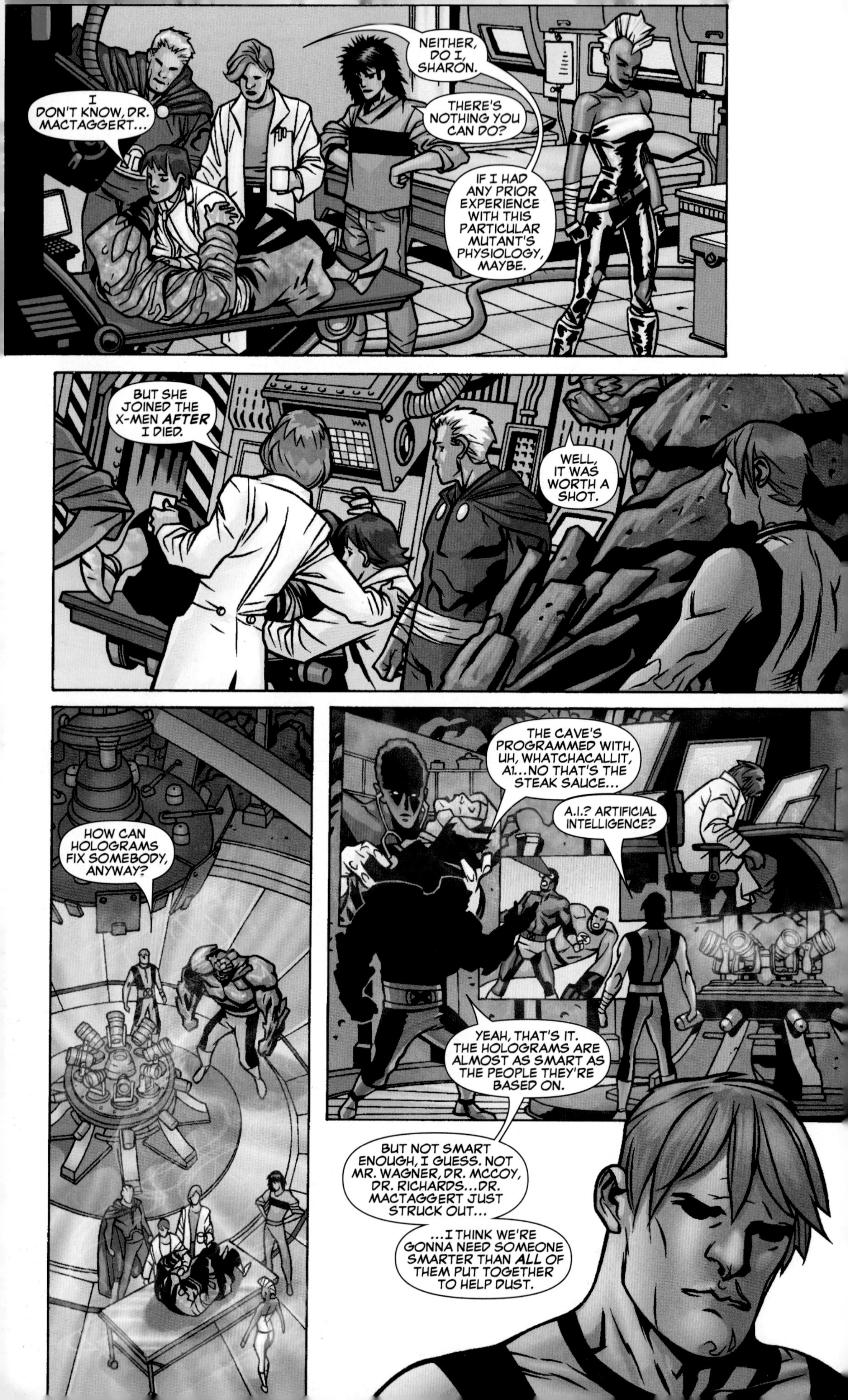
I DON'T KNOW, DR. MACTAGGERT...
NEITHER, DO I, SHARON.
THERE'S NOTHING YOU CAN DO?
IF I HAD ANY PRIOR EXPERIENCE WITH THIS PARTICULAR MUTANT'S PHYSIOLOGY, MAYBE.
BUT SHE JOINED THE X-MEN AFTER I DIED.
WELL, IT WAS WORTH A SHOT.
HOW CAN HOLOGRAMS FIX SOMEBODY, ANYWAY?
THE CAVE'S PROGRAMMED WITH, UH, WHATCHACALLIT, A1...NO THAT'S THE STEAK SAUCE...
A.I.? ARTIFICIAL INTELLIGENCE?
YEAH, THAT'S IT. THE HOLOGRAMS ARE ALMOST AS SMART AS THE PEOPLE THEY'RE BASED ON.
BUT NOT SMART ENOUGH, I GUESS. NOT MR. WAGNER, DR. MCCOY, DR. RICHARDS...DR. MACTAGGERT JUST STRUCK OUT...
...I THINK WE'RE GONNA NEED SOMEONE SMARTER THAN ALL OF THEM PUT TOGETHER TO HELP DUST.

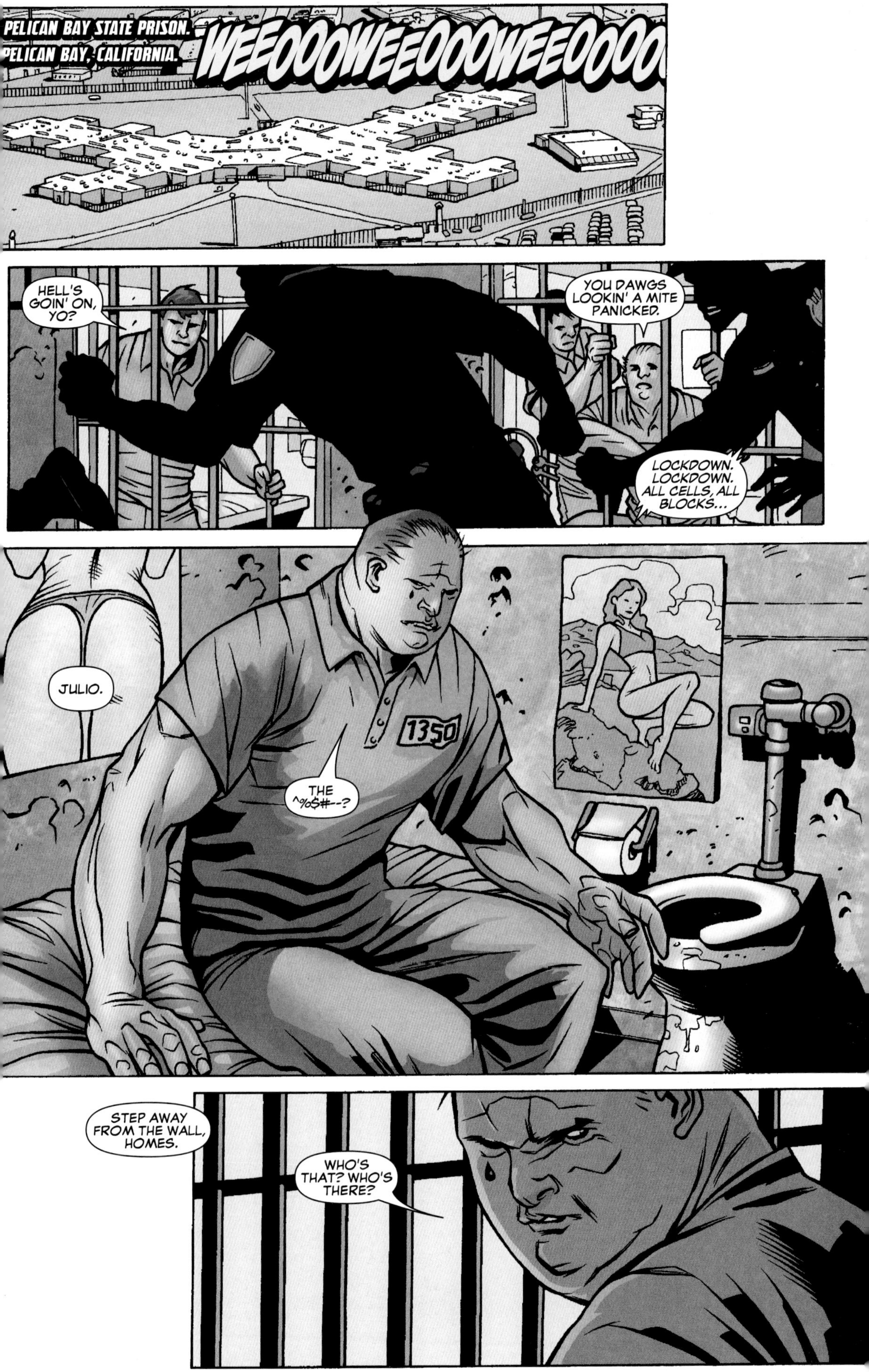
PELICAN BAY STATE PRISON.
PELICAN BAY, CALIFORNIA.
WEEOOOWEEOOOWEEOOOO
HELL'S GOIN' ON, YO?
YOU DAWGS LOOKIN' A MITE PANICKED.
LOCKDOWN. LOCKDOWN. ALL CELLS, ALL BLOCKS...
JULIO.
1350
THE ^%$#--?
STEP AWAY FROM THE WALL, HOMES.
WHO'S THAT? WHO'S THERE?

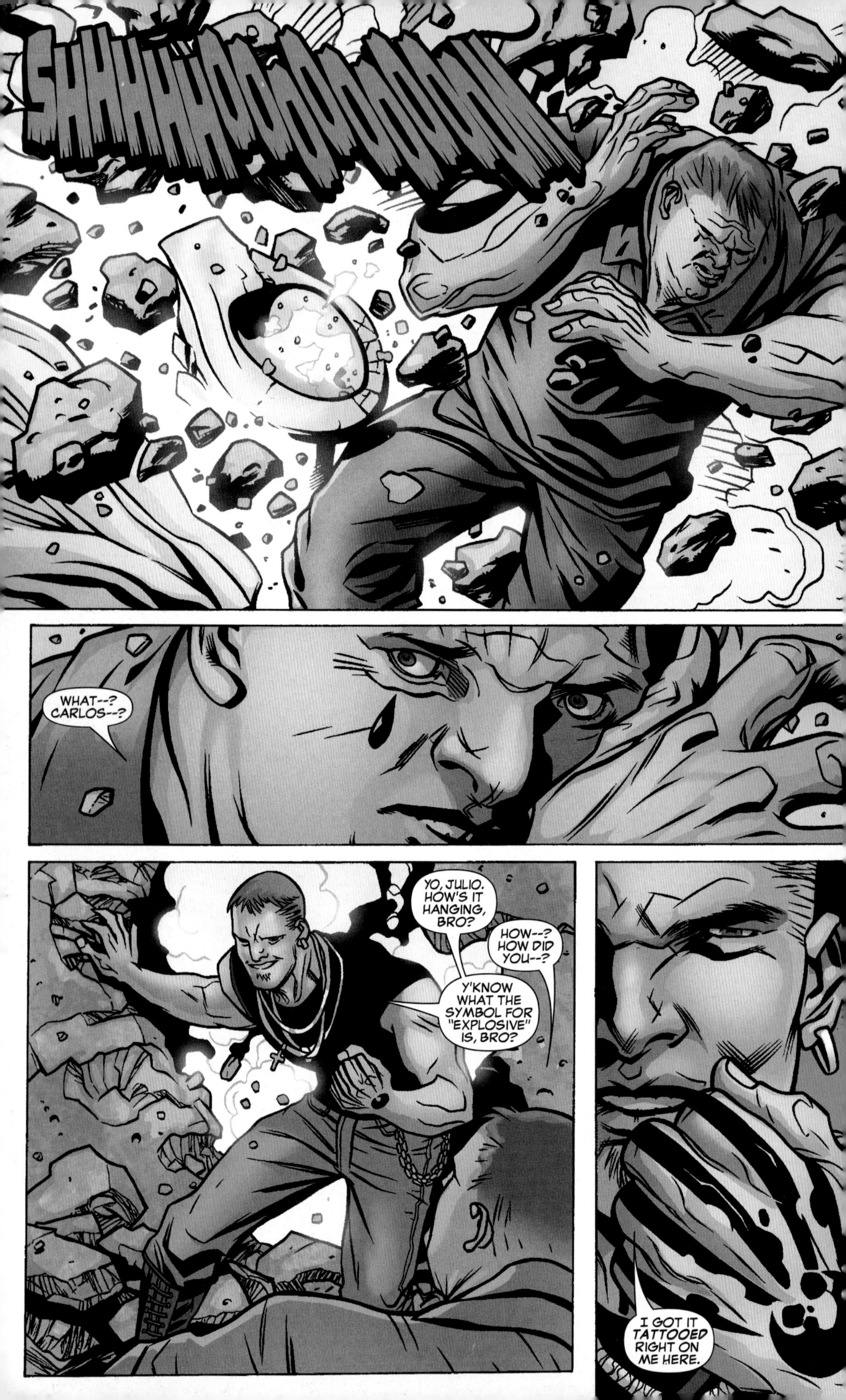
SHHHHOOOOOOOOOM
WHAT--? CARLOS--?
YO, JULIO. HOW'S IT HANGING, BRO?
HOW--? HOW DID YOU--?
Y'KNOW WHAT THE SYMBOL FOR "EXPLOSIVE" IS, BRO?
I GOT IT TATTOOED RIGHT ON ME HERE.

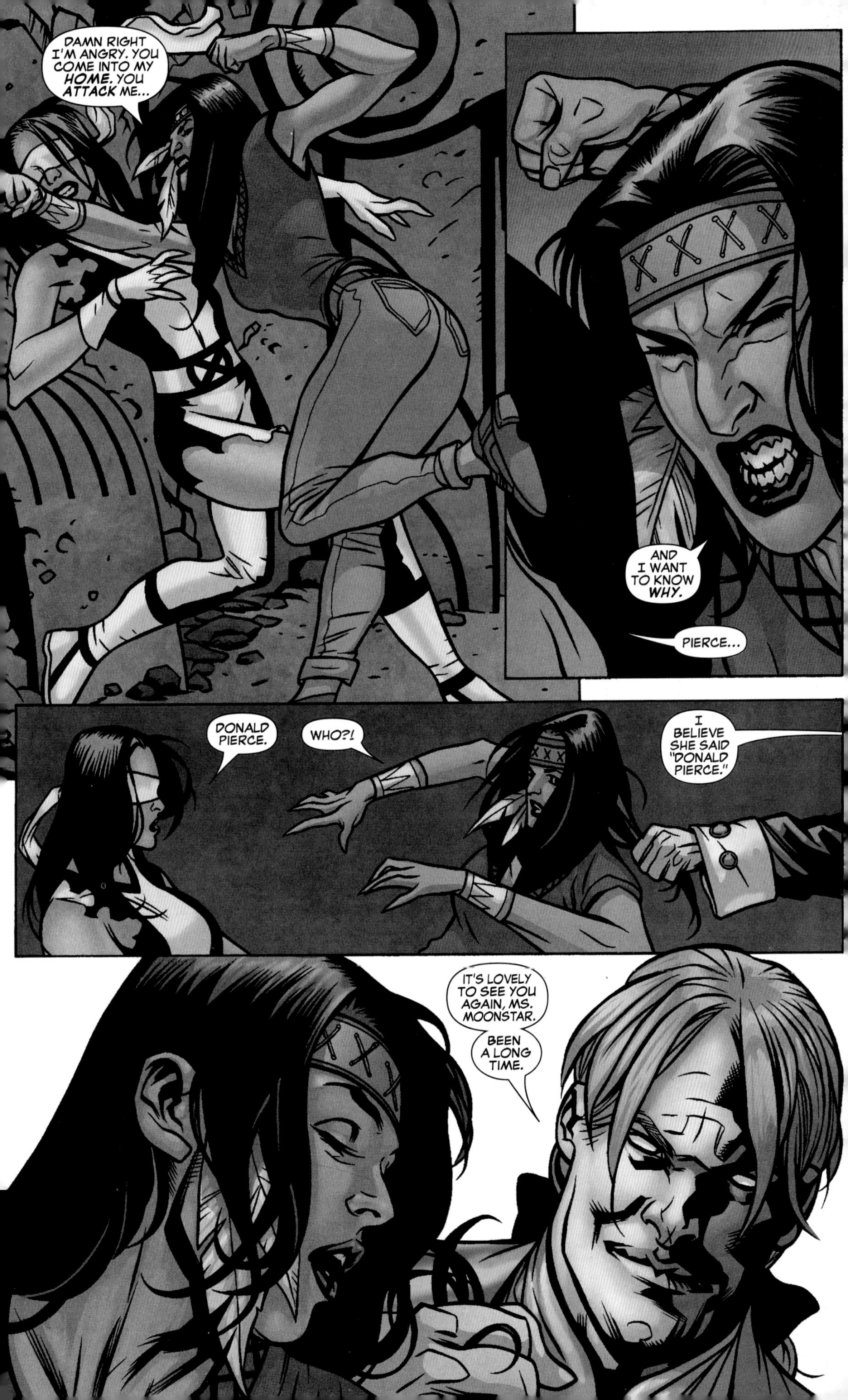
DAMN RIGHT I'M ANGRY. YOU COME INTO MY HOME. YOU ATTACK ME...
AND I WANT TO KNOW WHY.
PIERCE...
DONALD PIERCE.
WHO?!
I BELIEVE SHE SAID "DONALD PIERCE."
IT'S LOVELY TO SEE YOU AGAIN, MS. MOONSTAR.
BEEN A LONG TIME.

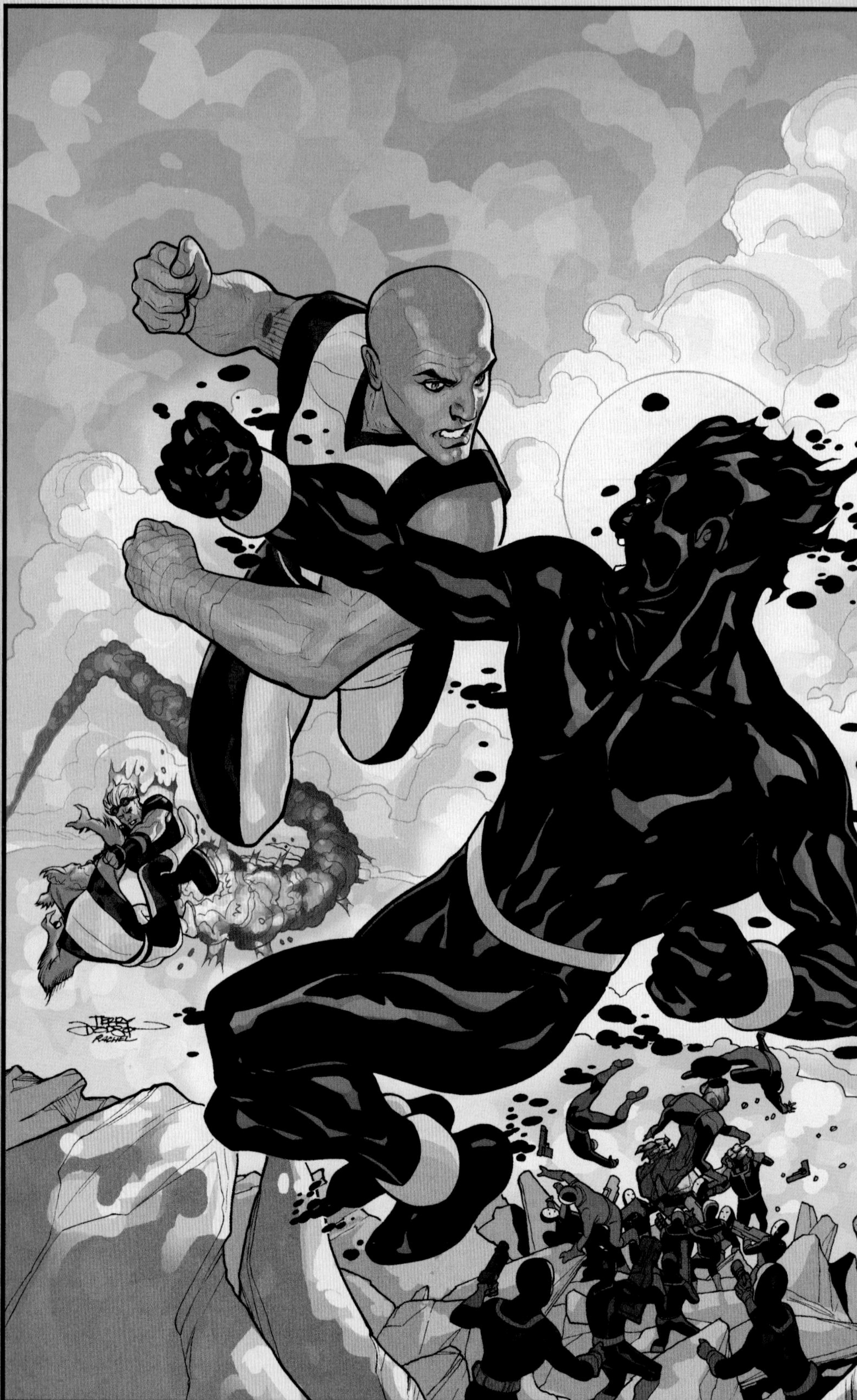

4

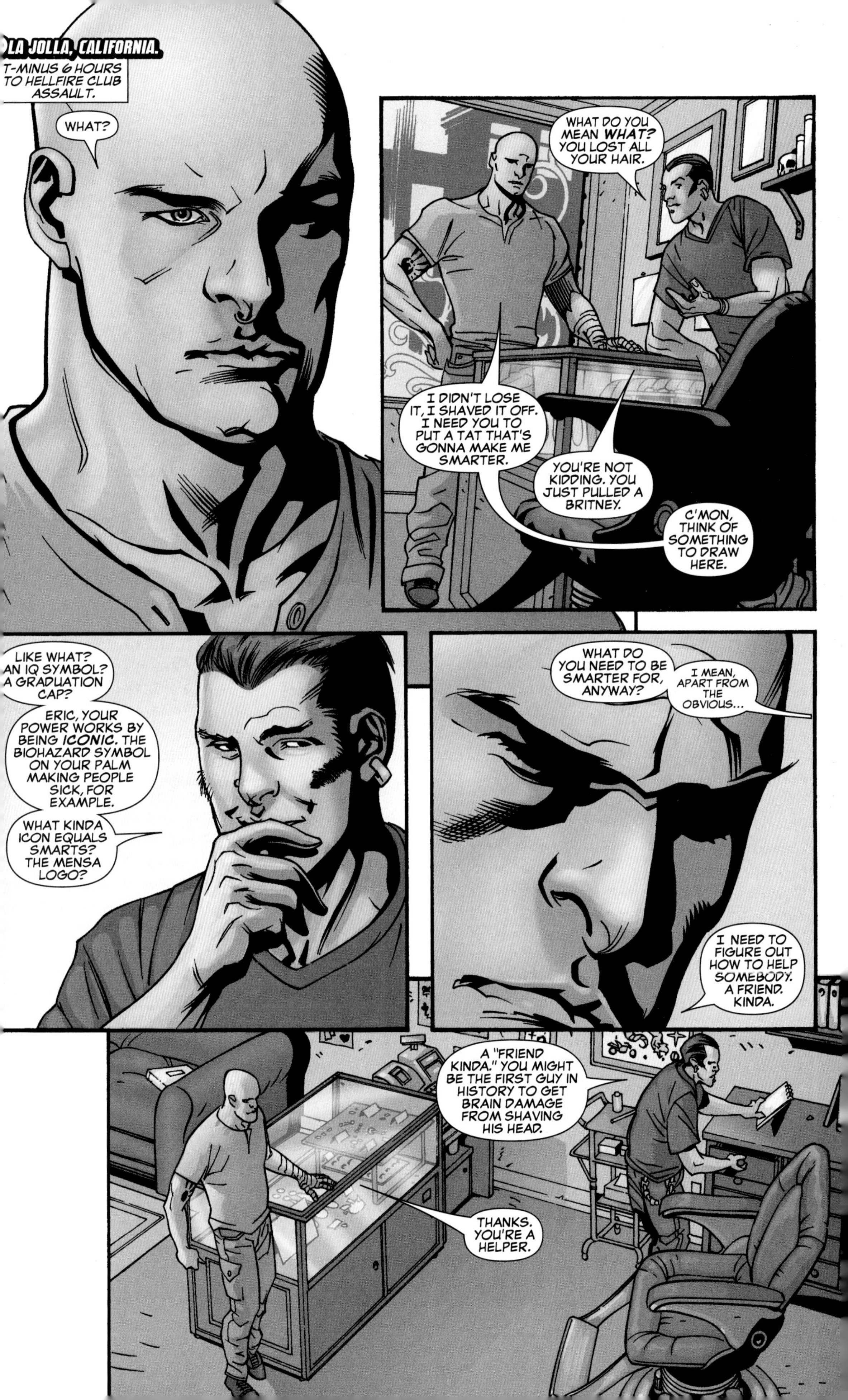
LA JOLLA, CALIFORNIA.
T-MINUS 6 HOURS TO HELLFIRE CLUB ASSAULT.
WHAT?
WHAT DO YOU MEAN WHAT? YOU LOST ALL YOUR HAIR.
I DIDN'T LOSE IT, I SHAVED IT OFF. I NEED YOU TO PUT A TAT THAT'S GONNA MAKE ME SMARTER.
YOU'RE NOT KIDDING. YOU JUST PULLED A BRITNEY.
C'MON, THINK OF SOMETHING TO DRAW HERE.
LIKE WHAT? AN IQ SYMBOL? A GRADUATION CAP?
ERIC, YOUR POWER WORKS BY BEING ICONIC. THE BIOHAZARD SYMBOL ON YOUR PALM MAKING PEOPLE SICK, FOR EXAMPLE.
WHAT KINDA ICON EQUALS SMARTS? THE MENSA LOGO?
WHAT DO YOU NEED TO BE SMARTER FOR, ANYWAY?
I MEAN, APART FROM THE OBVIOUS...
I NEED TO FIGURE OUT HOW TO HELP SOMEBODY. A FRIEND. KINDA.
A "FRIEND KINDA." YOU MIGHT BE THE FIRST GUY IN HISTORY TO GET BRAIN DAMAGE FROM SHAVING HIS HEAD.
THANKS. YOU'RE A HELPER.

LOOK, I DON'T KNOW WHAT KINDA TAT I COULD PUT ON YOU THAT'D MAKE YOU SMARTER...

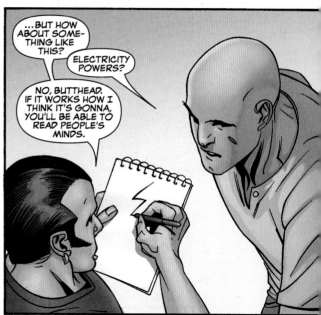

...BUT HOW ABOUT SOMETHING LIKE THIS?

ELECTRICITY POWERS?

NO, BUTTHEAD. IF IT WORKS HOW I THINK IT'S GONNA, YOU'LL BE ABLE TO READ PEOPLE'S MINDS.

CHECK THIS OUT HERE.

X-MEN

YOU WANT ME TO TATTOO MY HEAD BASED ON SOMETHING YOU SAW IN A COMIC BOOK?

WHAT THE HELL. IF IT LOOKS STUPID, I CAN ALWAYS GROW MY HAIR BACK TO COVER IT.

I THOUGHT YOU WERE KICKING IT IN NEW YORK THESE DAYS.

I TOOK A RIDE HERE. WHICH REMINDS ME: MAKE THIS FAST, 'CAUSE I'VE GOT ONE MORE THING I WANT YOU TO INK, AND...

...I'M KINDA DOUBLE-PARKED.

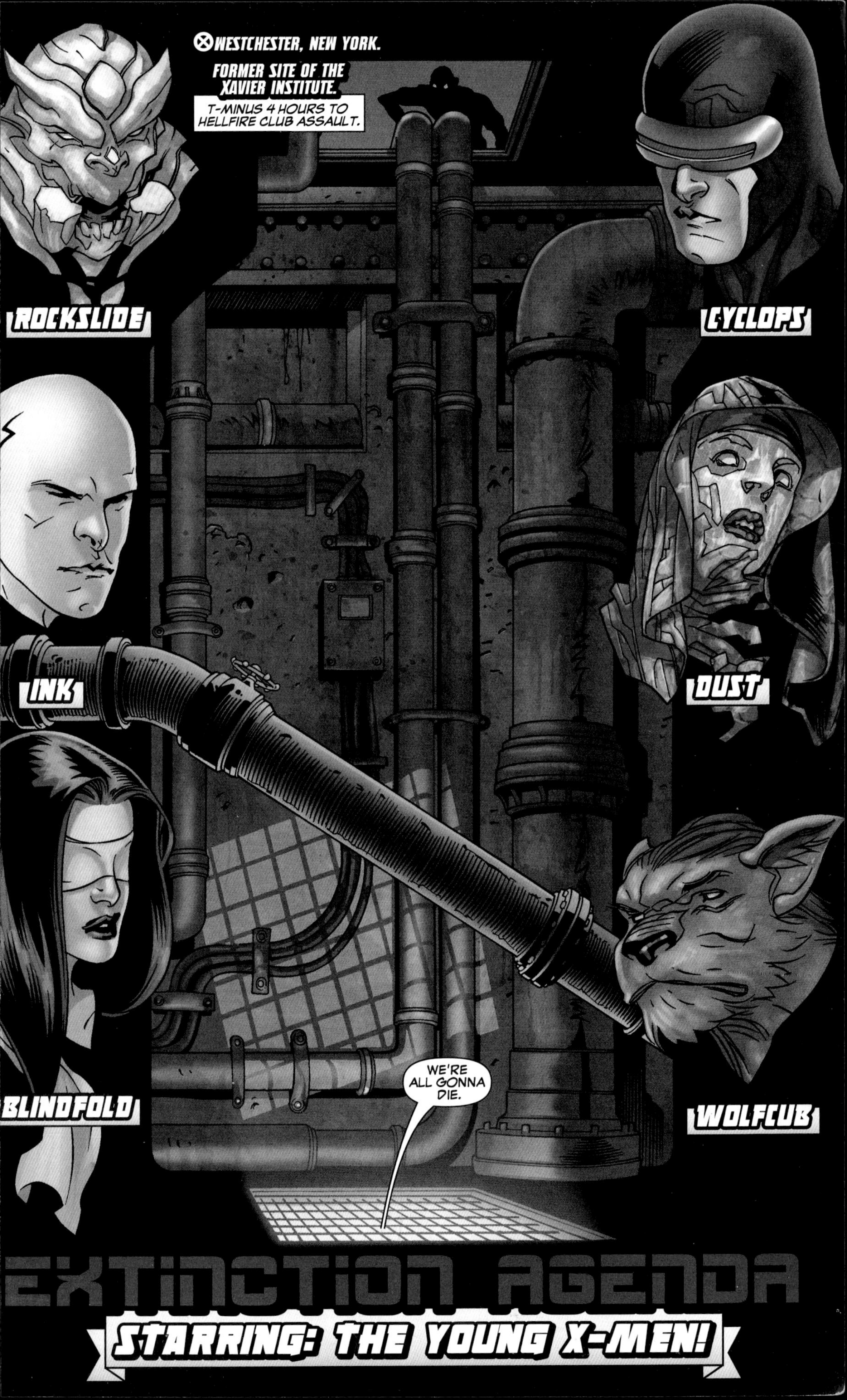

WESTCHESTER, NEW YORK.
FORMER SITE OF THE XAVIER INSTITUTE.
T-MINUS 4 HOURS TO HELLFIRE CLUB ASSAULT.
ROCKSLIDE
CYCLOPS
INK
DUST
BLINDFOLD
WOLFCUB
WE'RE ALL GONNA DIE.
EXTINCTION AGENDA
STARRING: THE YOUNG X-MEN!

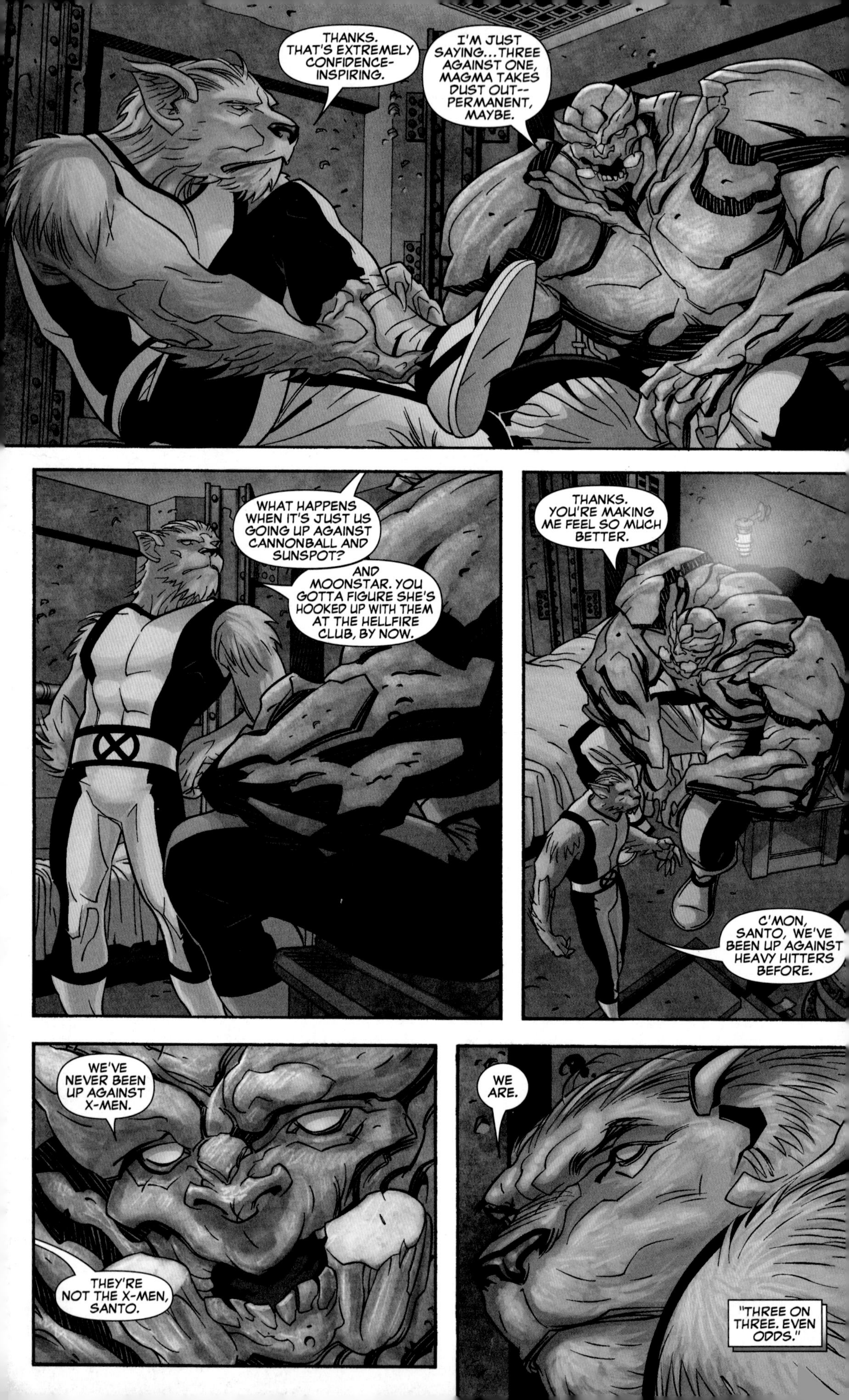
THANKS. THAT'S EXTREMELY CONFIDENCE-INSPIRING.
I'M JUST SAYING...THREE AGAINST ONE, MAGMA TAKES DUST OUT--PERMANENT, MAYBE.
WHAT HAPPENS WHEN IT'S JUST US GOING UP AGAINST CANNONBALL AND SUNSPOT?
AND MOONSTAR. YOU GOTTA FIGURE SHE'S HOOKED UP WITH THEM AT THE HELLFIRE CLUB, BY NOW.
THANKS. YOU'RE MAKING ME FEEL SO MUCH BETTER.
C'MON, SANTO, WE'VE BEEN UP AGAINST HEAVY HITTERS BEFORE.
WE'VE NEVER BEEN UP AGAINST X-MEN.
THEY'RE NOT THE X-MEN, SANTO.
WE ARE.
"THREE ON THREE. EVEN ODDS."

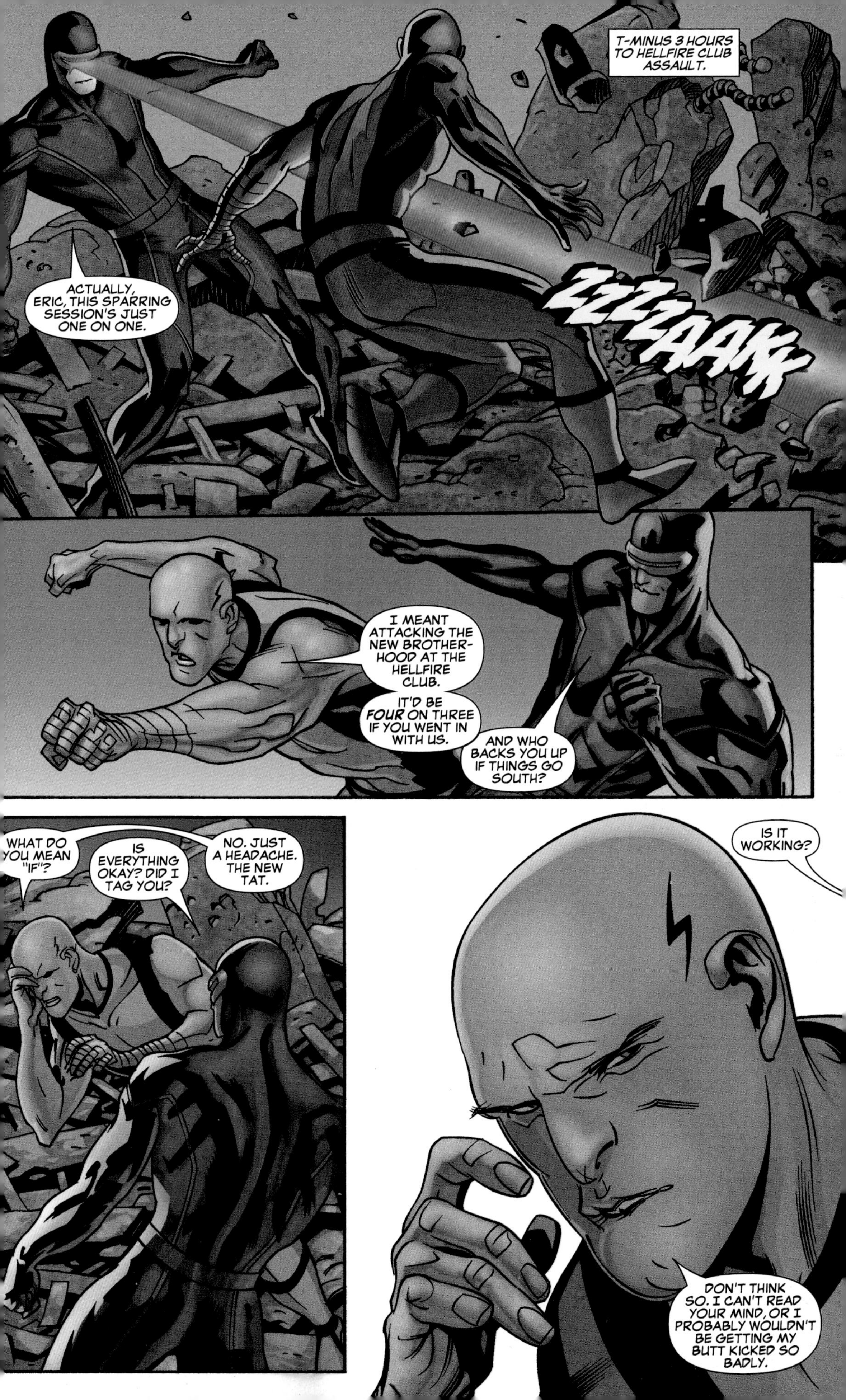

T-MINUS 3 HOURS TO HELLFIRE CLUB ASSAULT.
ACTUALLY, ERIC, THIS SPARRING SESSION'S JUST ONE ON ONE.
ZZZZAAKK
I MEANT ATTACKING THE NEW BROTHER-HOOD AT THE HELLFIRE CLUB.
IT'D BE FOUR ON THREE IF YOU WENT IN WITH US.
AND WHO BACKS YOU UP IF THINGS GO SOUTH?
WHAT DO YOU MEAN "IF"?
IS EVERYTHING OKAY? DID I TAG YOU?
NO. JUST A HEADACHE. THE NEW TAT.
IS IT WORKING?
DON'T THINK SO. I CAN'T READ YOUR MIND, OR I PROBABLY WOULDN'T BE GETTING MY BUTT KICKED SO BADLY.

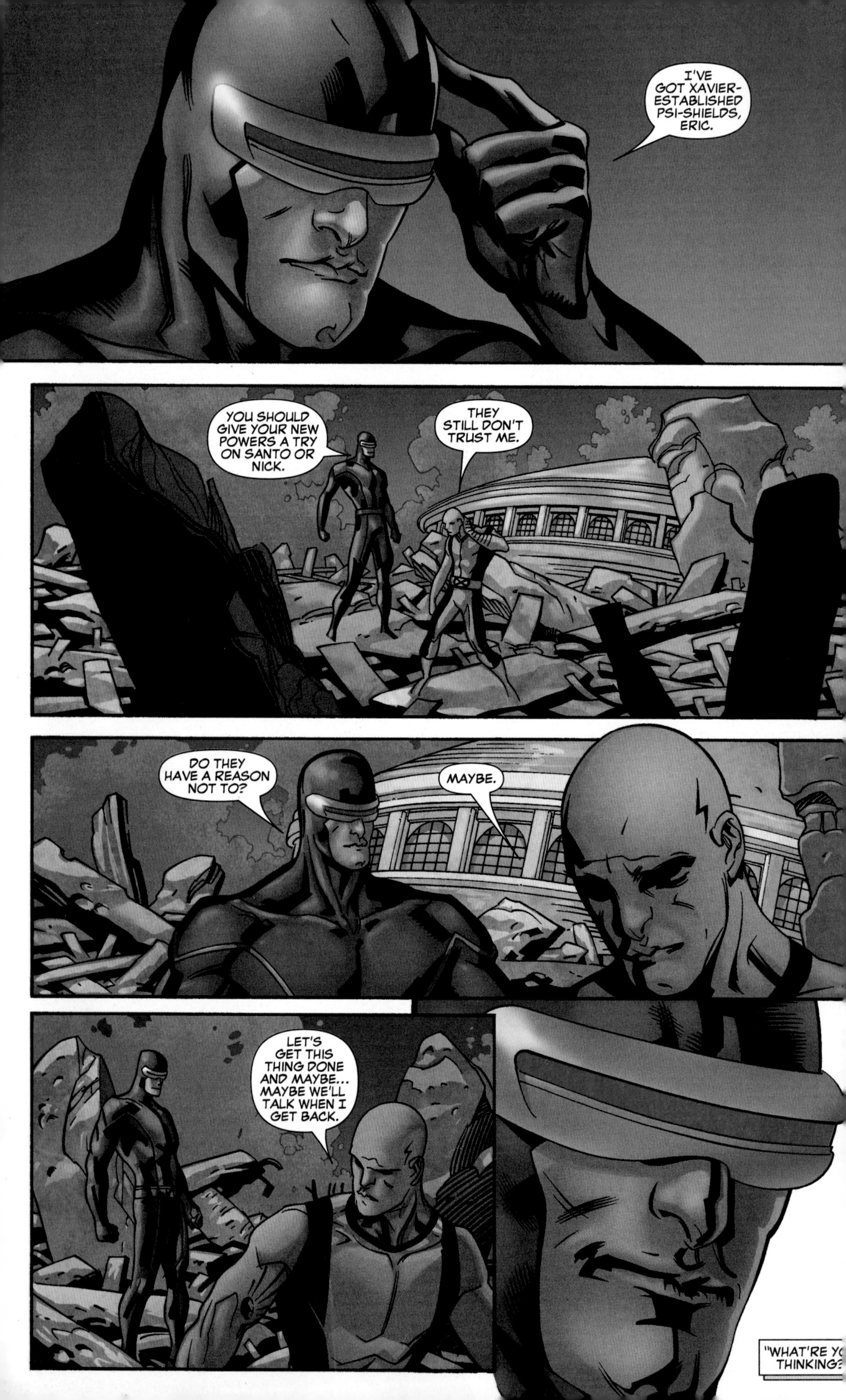
I'VE GOT XAVIER-ESTABLISHED PSI-SHIELDS, ERIC.
YOU SHOULD GIVE YOUR NEW POWERS A TRY ON SANTO OR NICK.
THEY STILL DON'T TRUST ME.
DO THEY HAVE A REASON NOT TO?
MAYBE.
LET'S GET THIS THING DONE AND MAYBE... MAYBE WE'LL TALK WHEN I GET BACK.
"WHAT'RE YO THINKING?

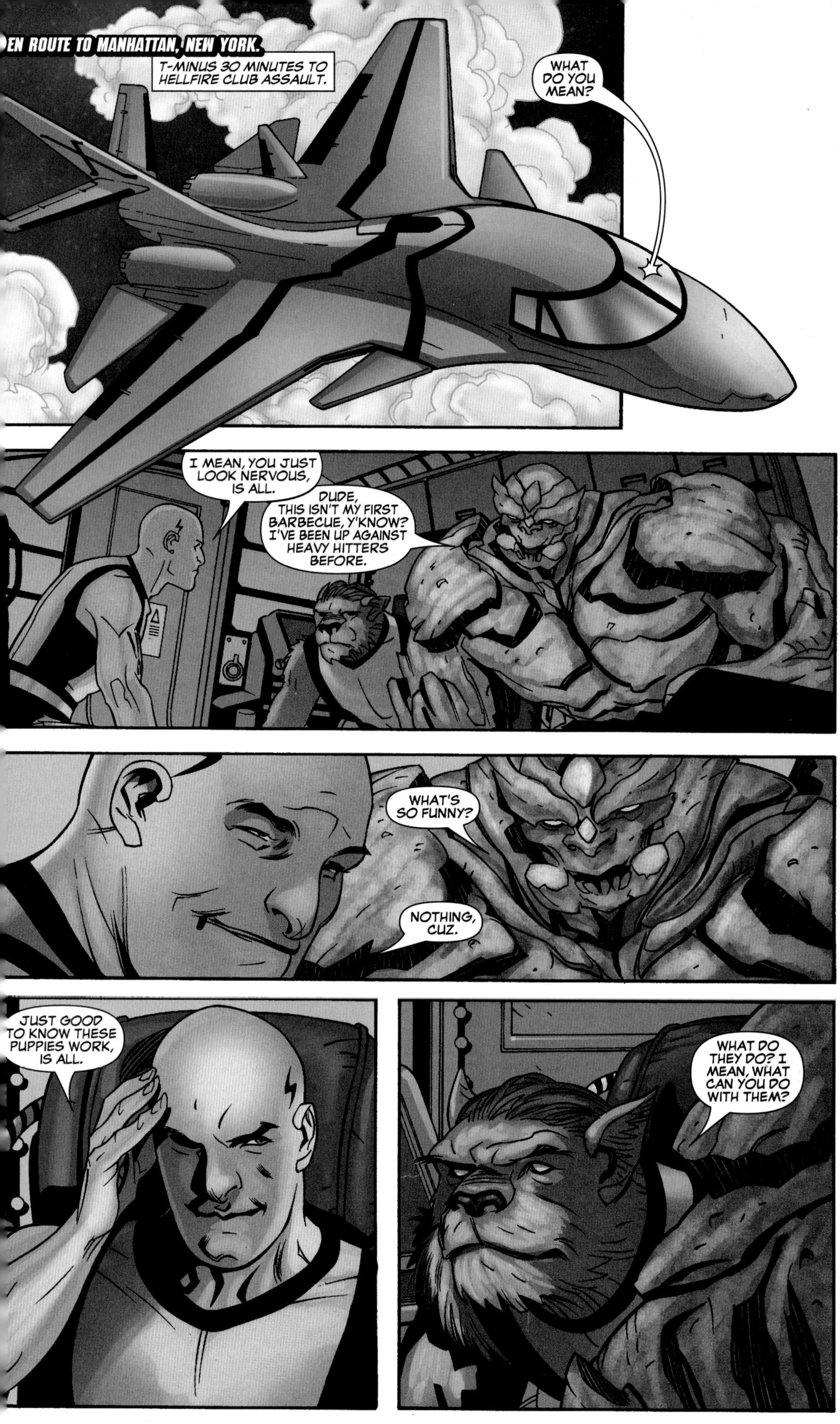
EN ROUTE TO MANHATTAN, NEW YORK.
T-MINUS 30 MINUTES TO HELLFIRE CLUB ASSAULT.
WHAT DO YOU MEAN?
I MEAN, YOU JUST LOOK NERVOUS, IS ALL.
DUDE, THIS ISN'T MY FIRST BARBECUE, Y'KNOW? I'VE BEEN UP AGAINST HEAVY HITTERS BEFORE.
WHAT'S SO FUNNY?
NOTHING, CUZ.
JUST GOOD TO KNOW THESE PUPPIES WORK, IS ALL.
WHAT DO THEY DO? I MEAN, WHAT CAN YOU DO WITH THEM?

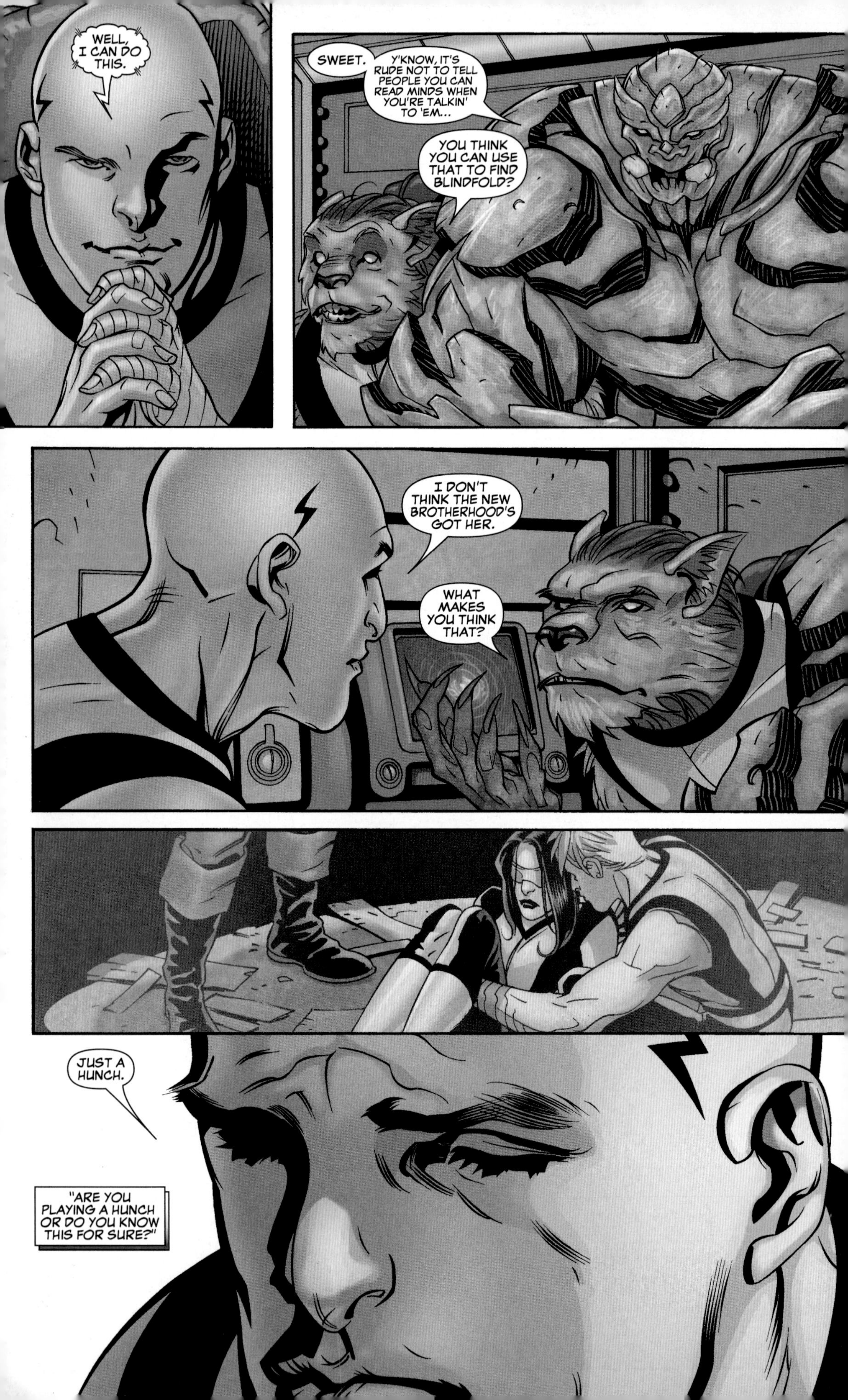
WELL, I CAN DO THIS.
SWEET.
Y'KNOW, IT'S RUDE NOT TO TELL PEOPLE YOU CAN READ MINDS WHEN YOU'RE TALKIN' TO 'EM...
YOU THINK YOU CAN USE THAT TO FIND BLINDFOLD?
I DON'T THINK THE NEW BROTHERHOOD'S GOT HER.
WHAT MAKES YOU THINK THAT?
JUST A HUNCH.
"ARE YOU PLAYING A HUNCH OR DO YOU KNOW THIS FOR SURE?"

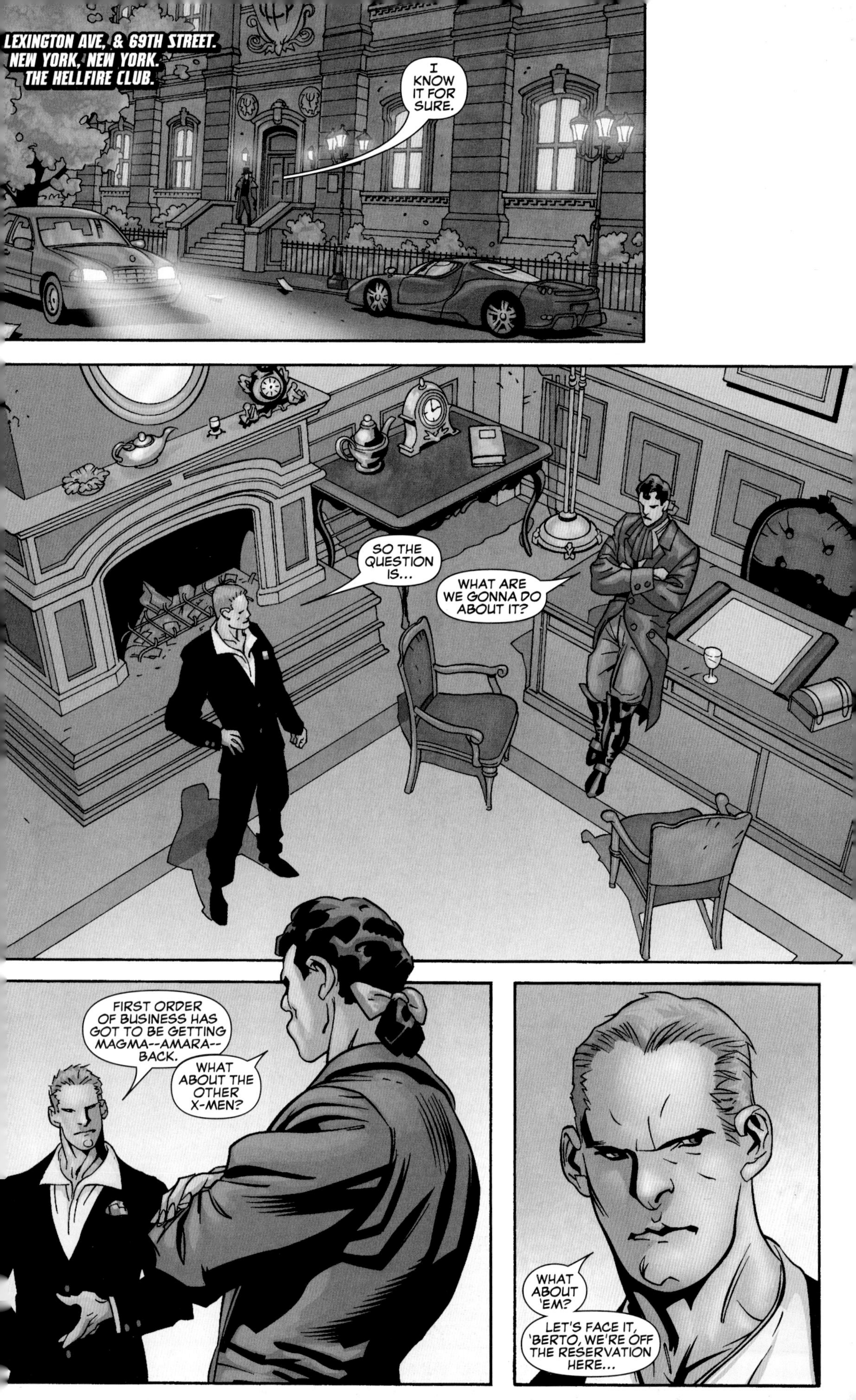

LEXINGTON AVE, & 69TH STREET. NEW YORK, NEW YORK. THE HELLFIRE CLUB.
I KNOW IT FOR SURE.
SO THE QUESTION IS...
WHAT ARE WE GONNA DO ABOUT IT?
FIRST ORDER OF BUSINESS HAS GOT TO BE GETTING MAGMA--AMARA--BACK.
WHAT ABOUT THE OTHER X-MEN?
WHAT ABOUT 'EM?
LET'S FACE IT, 'BERTO, WE'RE OFF THE RESERVATION HERE...

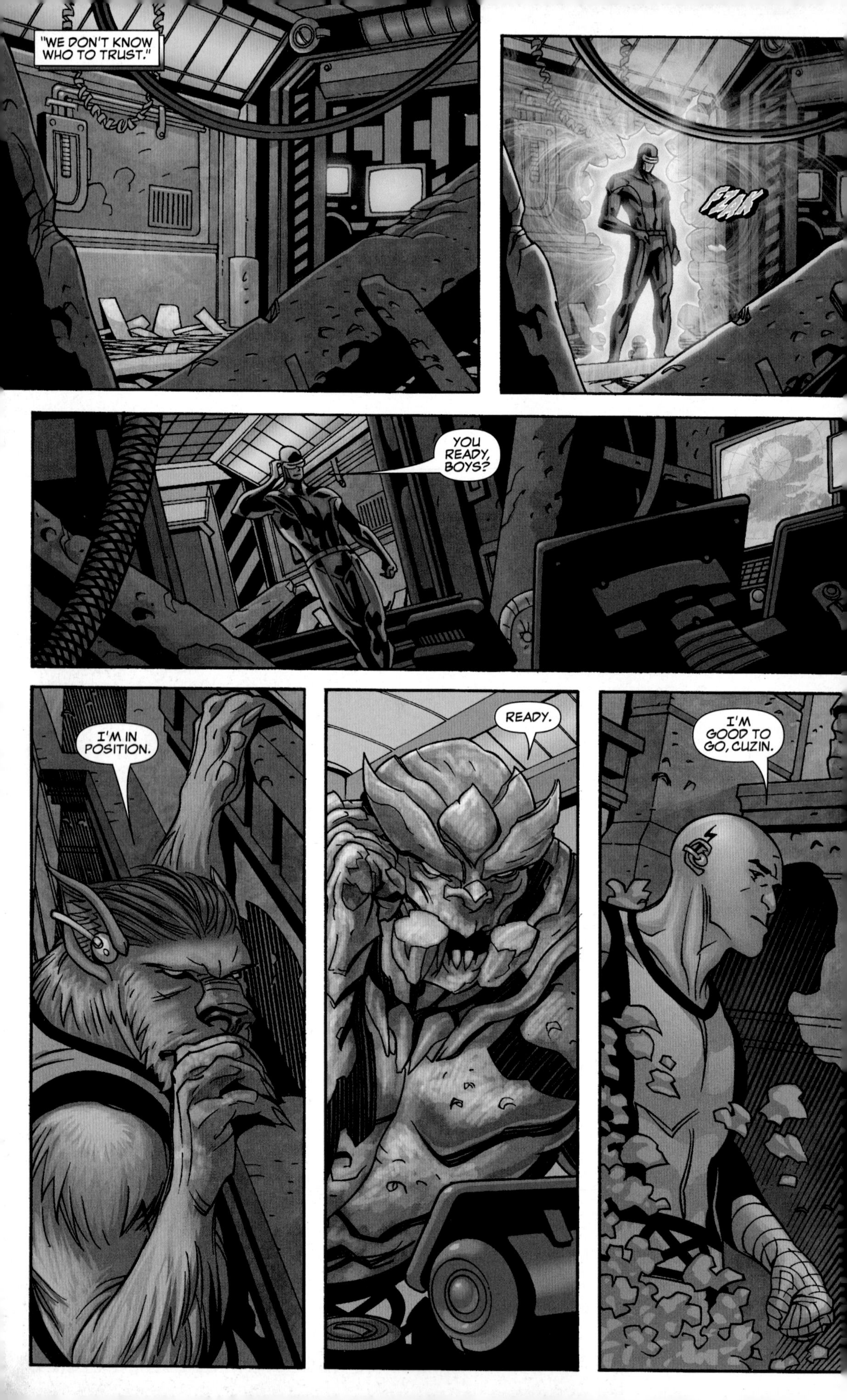
"WE DON'T KNOW WHO TO TRUST."
FZAK
YOU READY, BOYS?
I'M IN POSITION.
READY.
I'M GOOD TO GO, CUZIN.

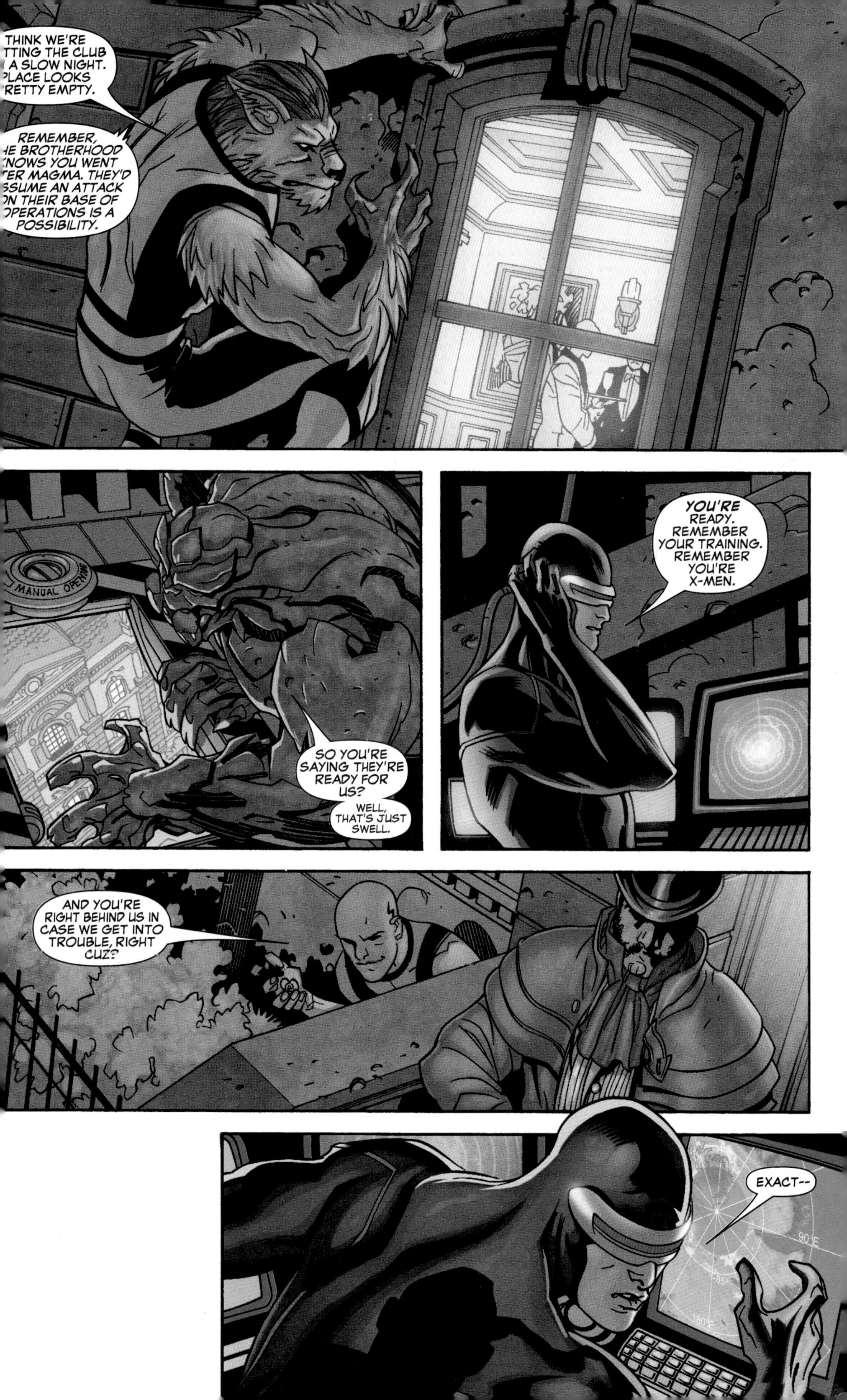
THINK WE'RE TTING THE CLUB A SLOW NIGHT. PLACE LOOKS RETTY EMPTY.
REMEMBER, HE BROTHERHOOD NOWS YOU WENT TER MAGMA. THEY'D SSUME AN ATTACK ON THEIR BASE OF OPERATIONS IS A POSSIBILITY.
MANUAL OPENING
SO YOU'RE SAYING THEY'RE READY FOR US?
WELL, THAT'S JUST SWELL.
YOU'RE READY. REMEMBER YOUR TRAINING. REMEMBER YOU'RE X-MEN.
AND YOU'RE RIGHT BEHIND US IN CASE WE GET INTO TROUBLE, RIGHT CUZ?
EXACT--
90°E
-85°
180°E

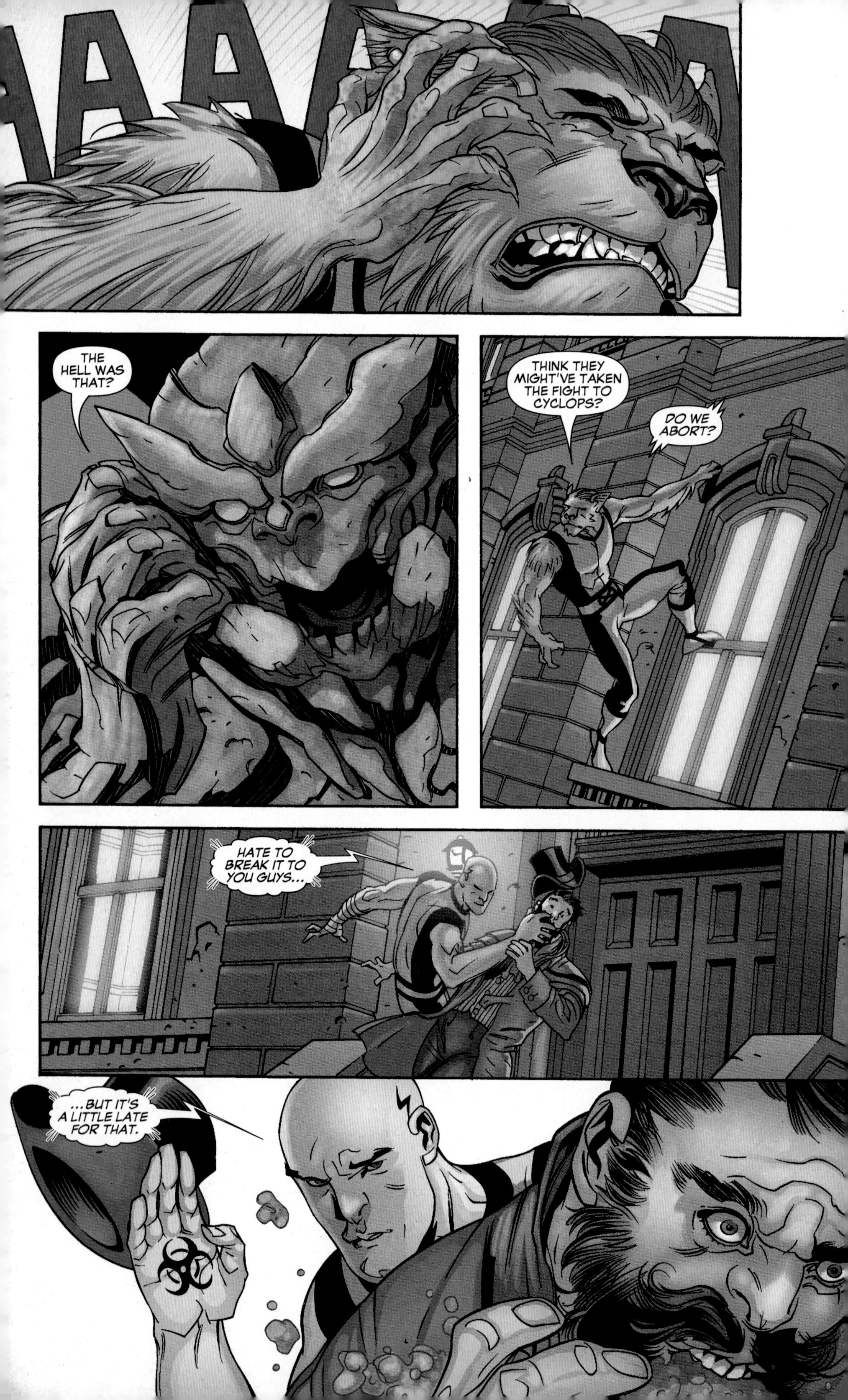
AAAAAA
THE HELL WAS THAT?
THINK THEY MIGHT'VE TAKEN THE FIGHT TO CYCLOPS?
DO WE ABORT?
HATE TO BREAK IT TO YOU GUYS...
...BUT IT'S A LITTLE LATE FOR THAT.

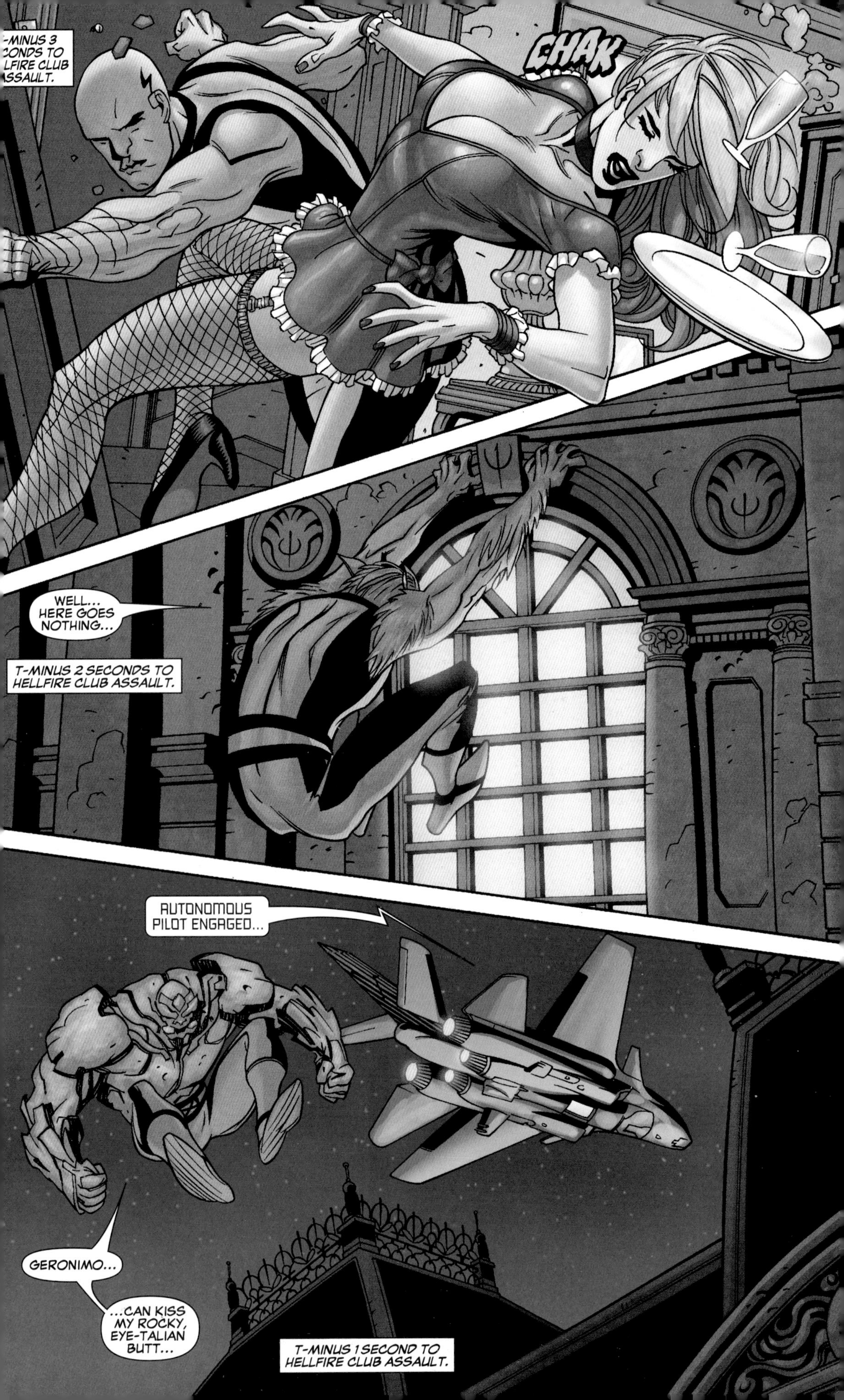

-MINUS 3
CONDS TO
LFIRE CLUB
SSAULT.
CHAK
WELL... HERE GOES NOTHING...
T-MINUS 2 SECONDS TO HELLFIRE CLUB ASSAULT.
AUTONOMOUS PILOT ENGAGED...
GERONIMO...
...CAN KISS MY ROCKY, EYE-TALIAN BUTT...
T-MINUS 1 SECOND TO HELLFIRE CLUB ASSAULT.

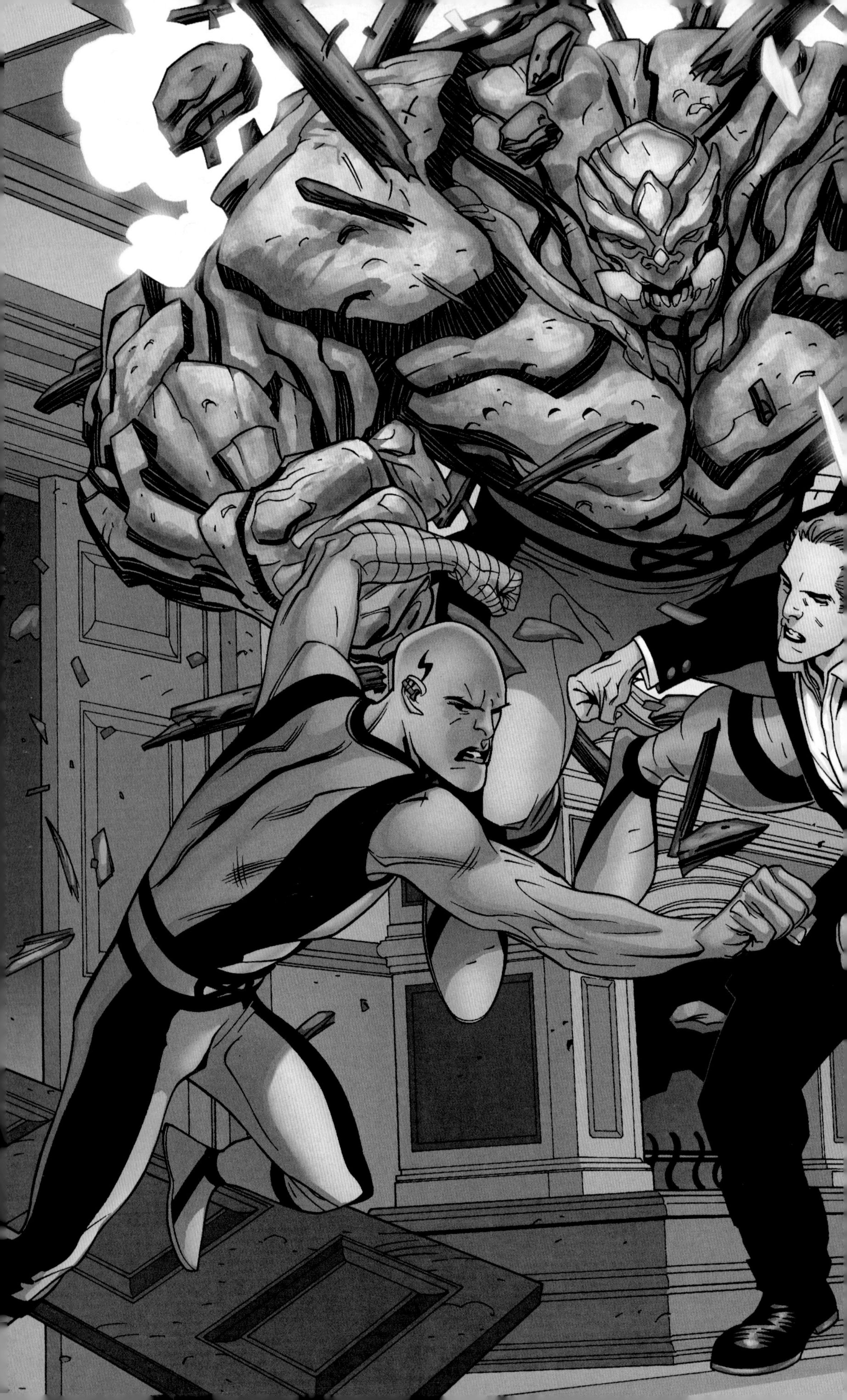

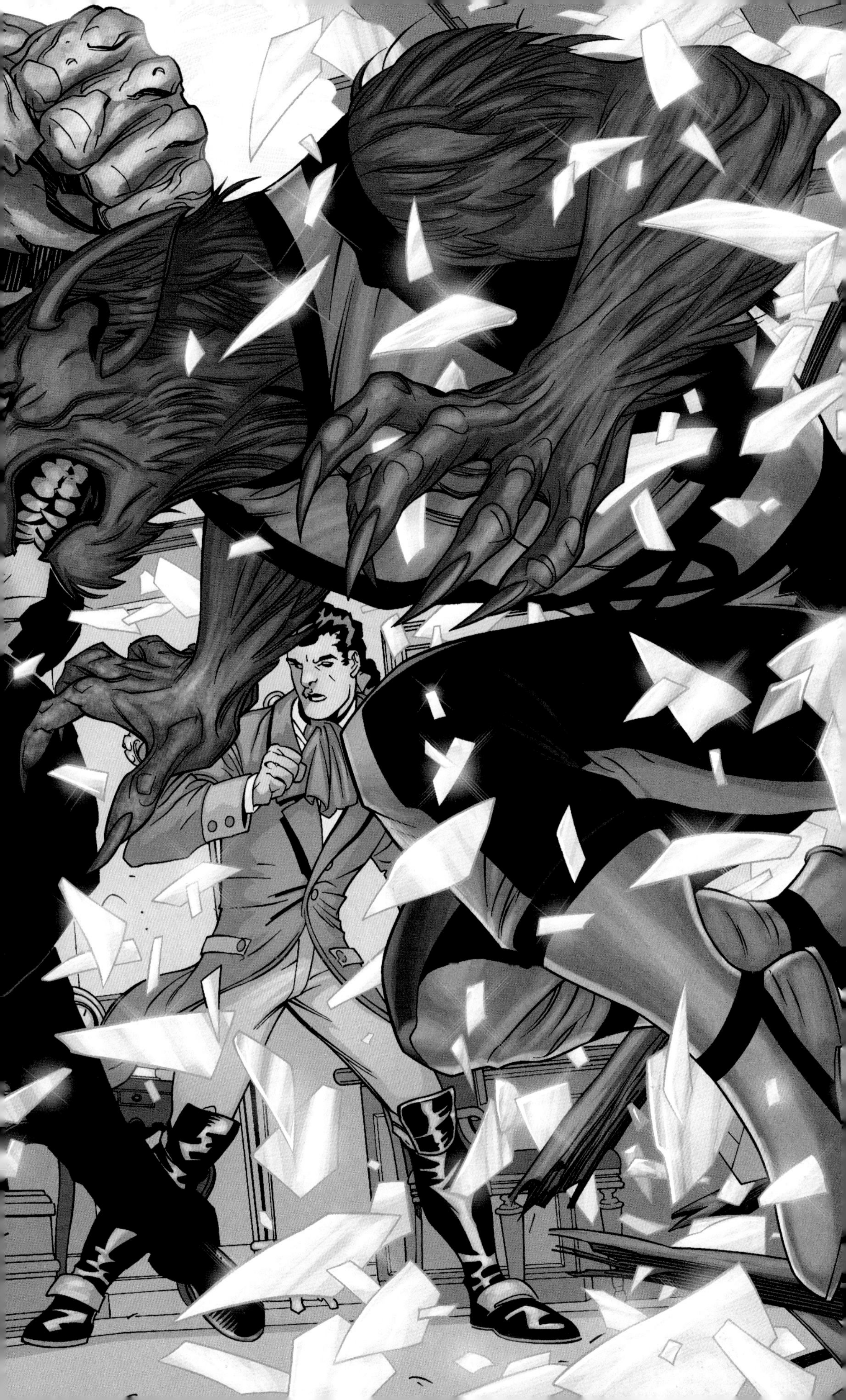

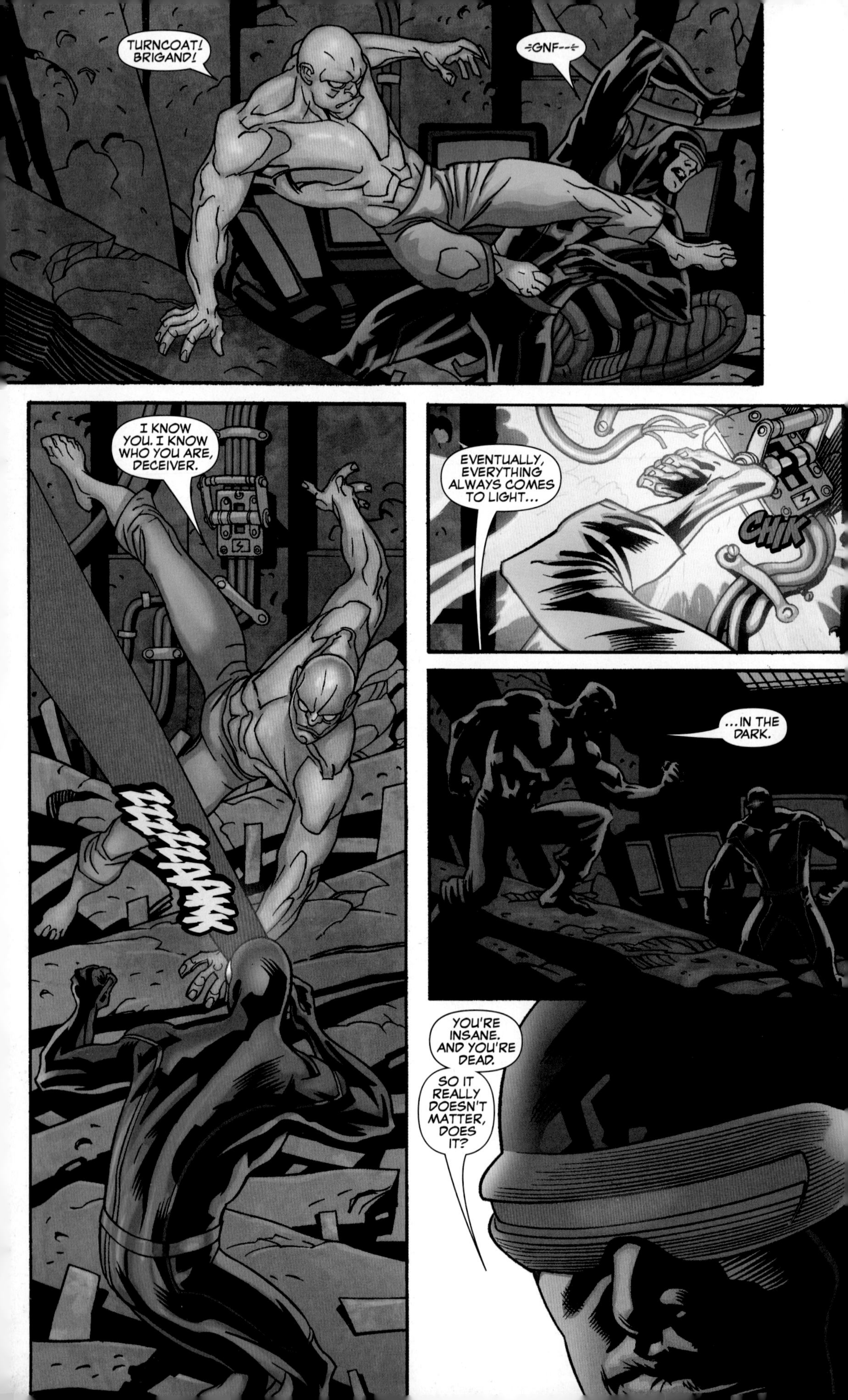
TURNCOAT! BRIGAND!
GNF--
I KNOW YOU. I KNOW WHO YOU ARE, DECEIVER.
CHIK
EVENTUALLY, EVERYTHING ALWAYS COMES TO LIGHT...
...IN THE DARK.
YOU'RE INSANE. AND YOU'RE DEAD.
SO IT REALLY DOESN'T MATTER, DOES IT?

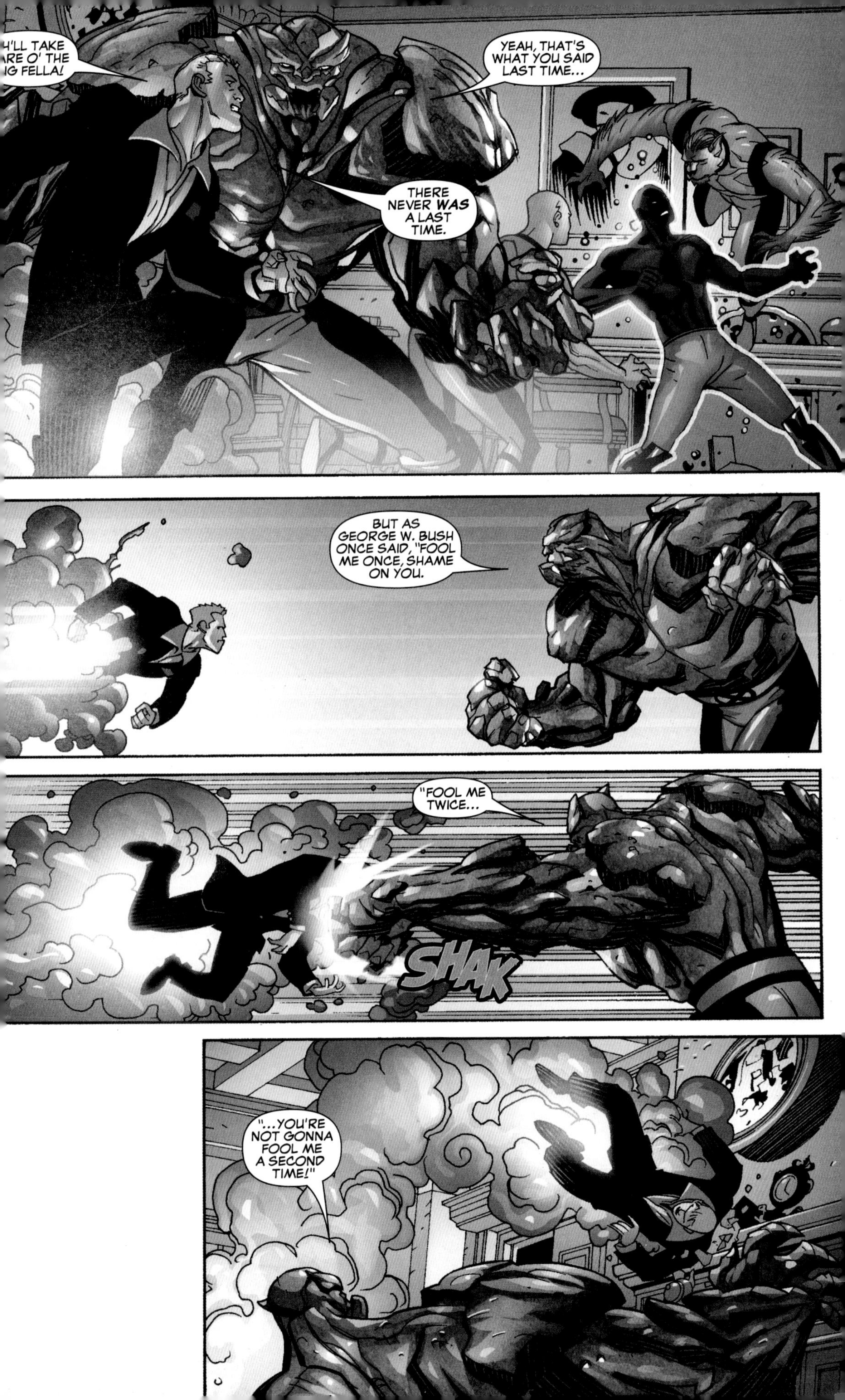
H'LL TAKE
ARE O' THE
IG FELLA!
YEAH, THAT'S WHAT YOU SAID LAST TIME...
THERE NEVER WAS A LAST TIME.
BUT AS GEORGE W. BUSH ONCE SAID, "FOOL ME ONCE, SHAME ON YOU.
"FOOL ME TWICE...
SHAK
"...YOU'RE NOT GONNA FOOL ME A SECOND TIME!"

"A SECOND TIME?" WHAT'RE YA TALKIN' ABOUT? YOU KIDS'VE GONE OFF YOUR NUT!

HE'S GOT PSI-SHIELDS. I CAN'T BREAK 'EM.

S'OKAY. WE'LL JUST ASK HIM WHERE THEY'RE KEEPIN' BLINDFOLD THE OLD FASHIONED WAY.

AND BY "OLD FASHIONED" I MEAN A HUMILIATING BEATDOWN.

WHO CALLS THEMSELVES EVIL MUTANTS, ANYWAY?

I MEAN, EVEN BIN LADEN DOESN'T CALL HIMSELF "EVIL."

THOUGH MAYBE HE DOES, I DUNNO...

EVIL? WHAT'RE YA TALKIN' ABOUT?

Y'ALL ARE THE FELLAS WHO'RE THE BAD GUYS HERE!

FOOOOOOOOO--

--GAH--

"WHAT D YOU THINK HAPPENIN HERE?"

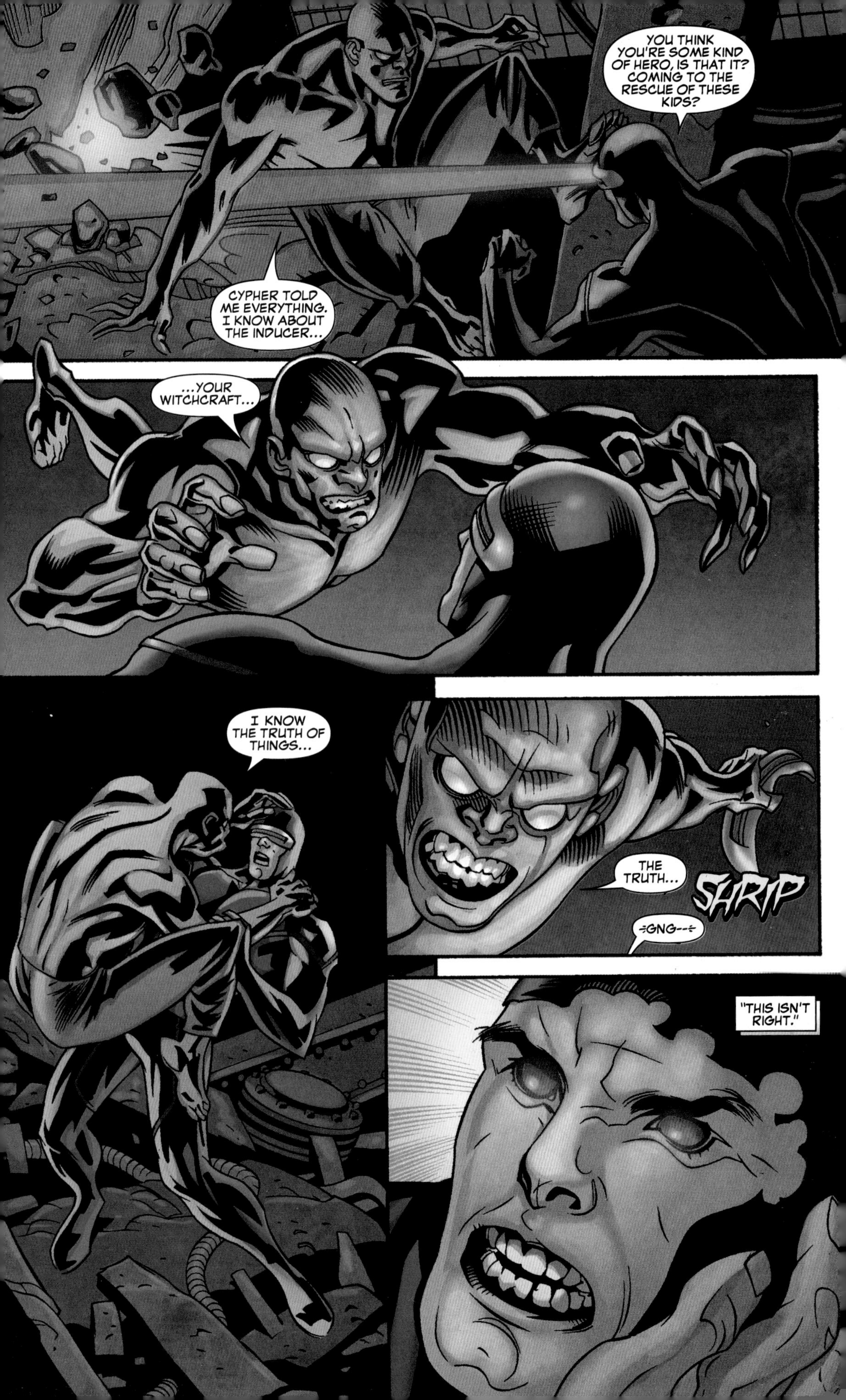
YOU THINK YOU'RE SOME KIND OF HERO, IS THAT IT? COMING TO THE RESCUE OF THESE KIDS?
CYPHER TOLD ME EVERYTHING. I KNOW ABOUT THE INDUCER...
...YOUR WITCHCRAFT...
I KNOW THE TRUTH OF THINGS...
THE TRUTH...
SHRIP
GNG
"THIS ISN'T RIGHT."

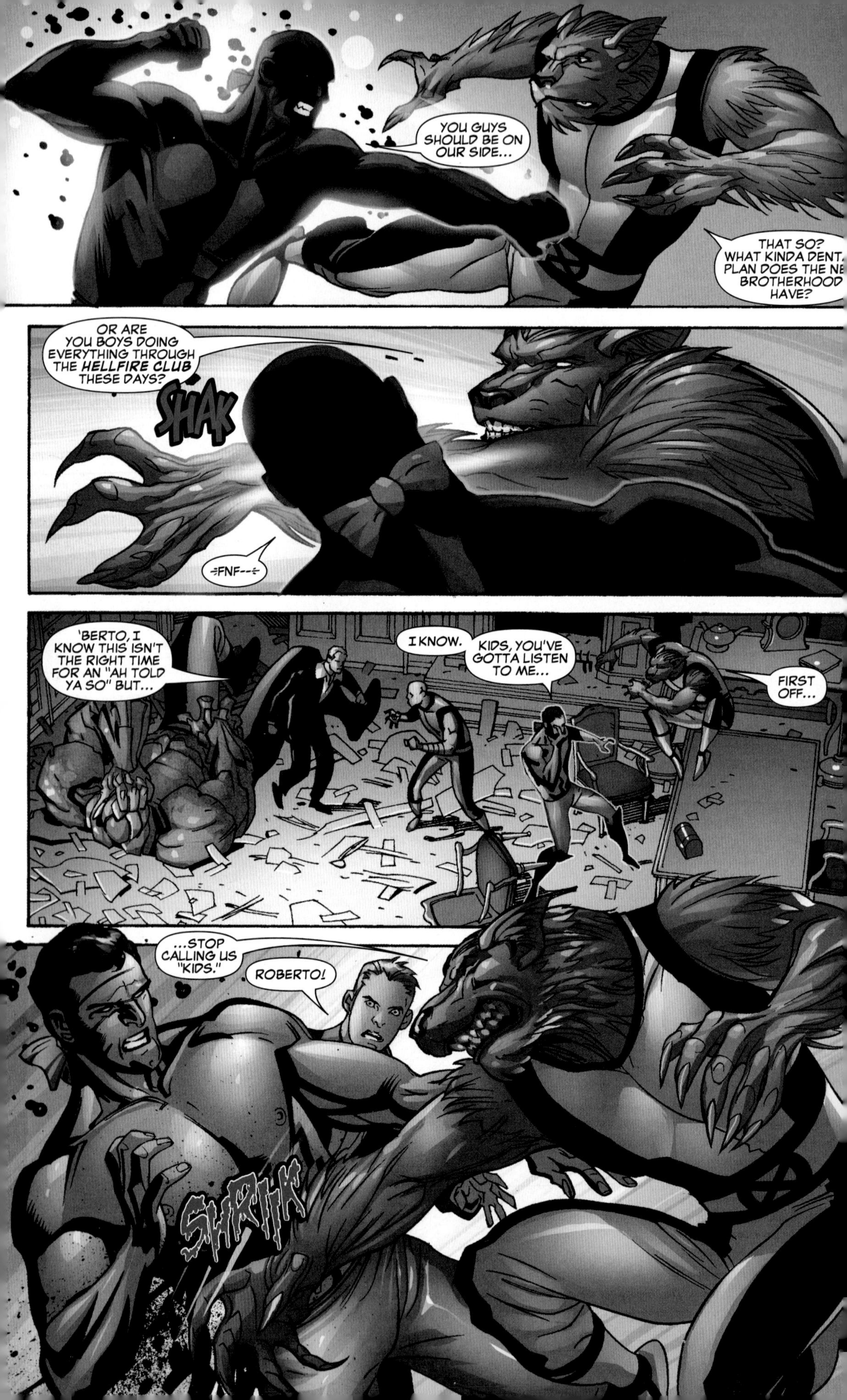

YOU GUYS SHOULD BE ON OUR SIDE...
THAT SO? WHAT KINDA DENT. PLAN DOES THE NE BROTHERHOOD HAVE?
OR ARE YOU BOYS DOING EVERYTHING THROUGH THE HELLFIRE CLUB THESE DAYS?
SHAK
FNF--
'BERTO, I KNOW THIS ISN'T THE RIGHT TIME FOR AN "AH TOLD YA SO" BUT...
I KNOW.
KIDS, YOU'VE GOTTA LISTEN TO ME...
FIRST OFF...
...STOP CALLING US "KIDS."
ROBERTO!
SHRIK

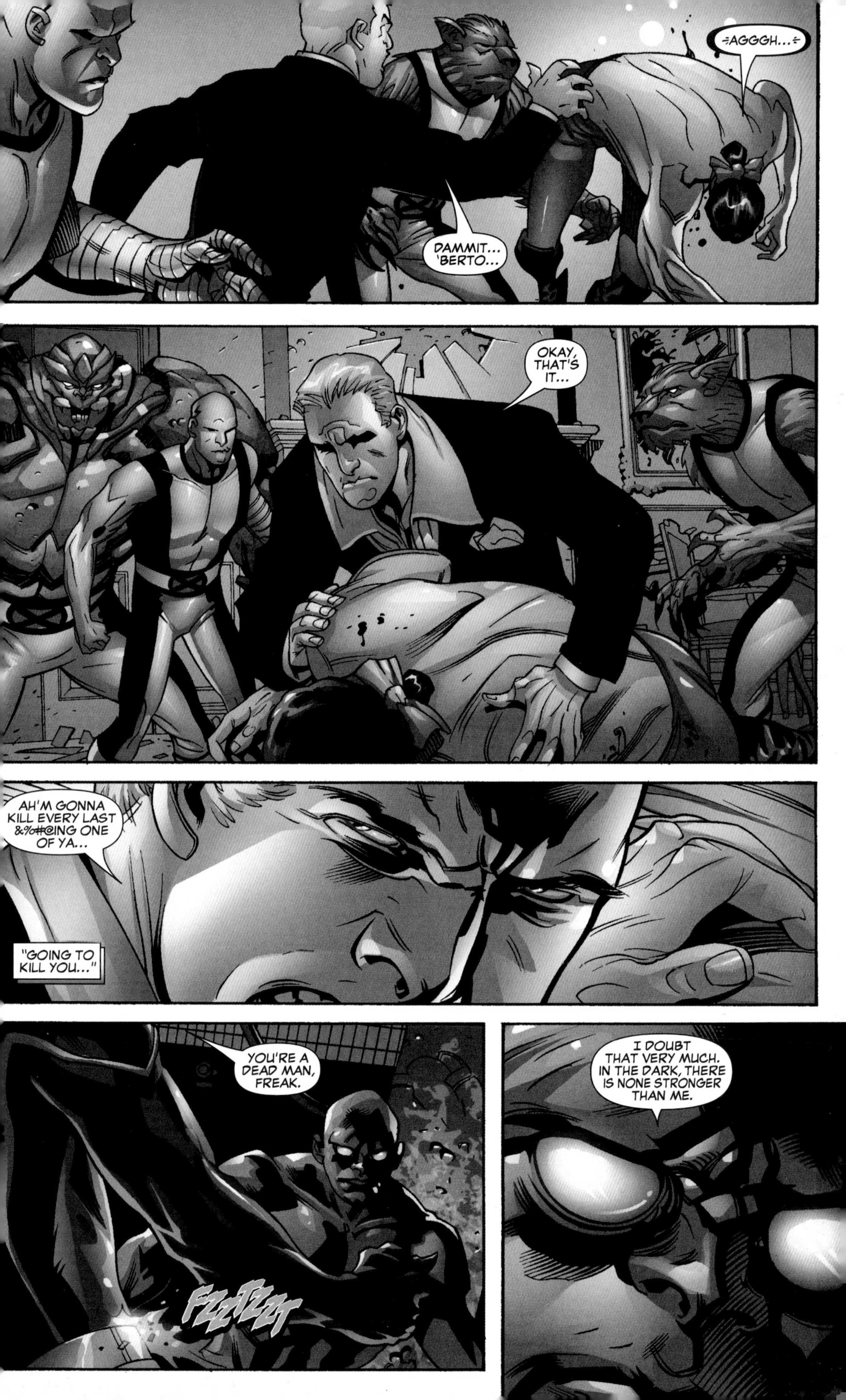
AGGGH...
DAMMIT... 'BERTO...
OKAY, THAT'S IT...
AH'M GONNA KILL EVERY LAST &%#@ING ONE OF YA...
"GOING TO KILL YOU..."
YOU'RE A DEAD MAN, FREAK.
FZZTZZT
I DOUBT THAT VERY MUCH. IN THE DARK, THERE IS NONE STRONGER THAN ME.

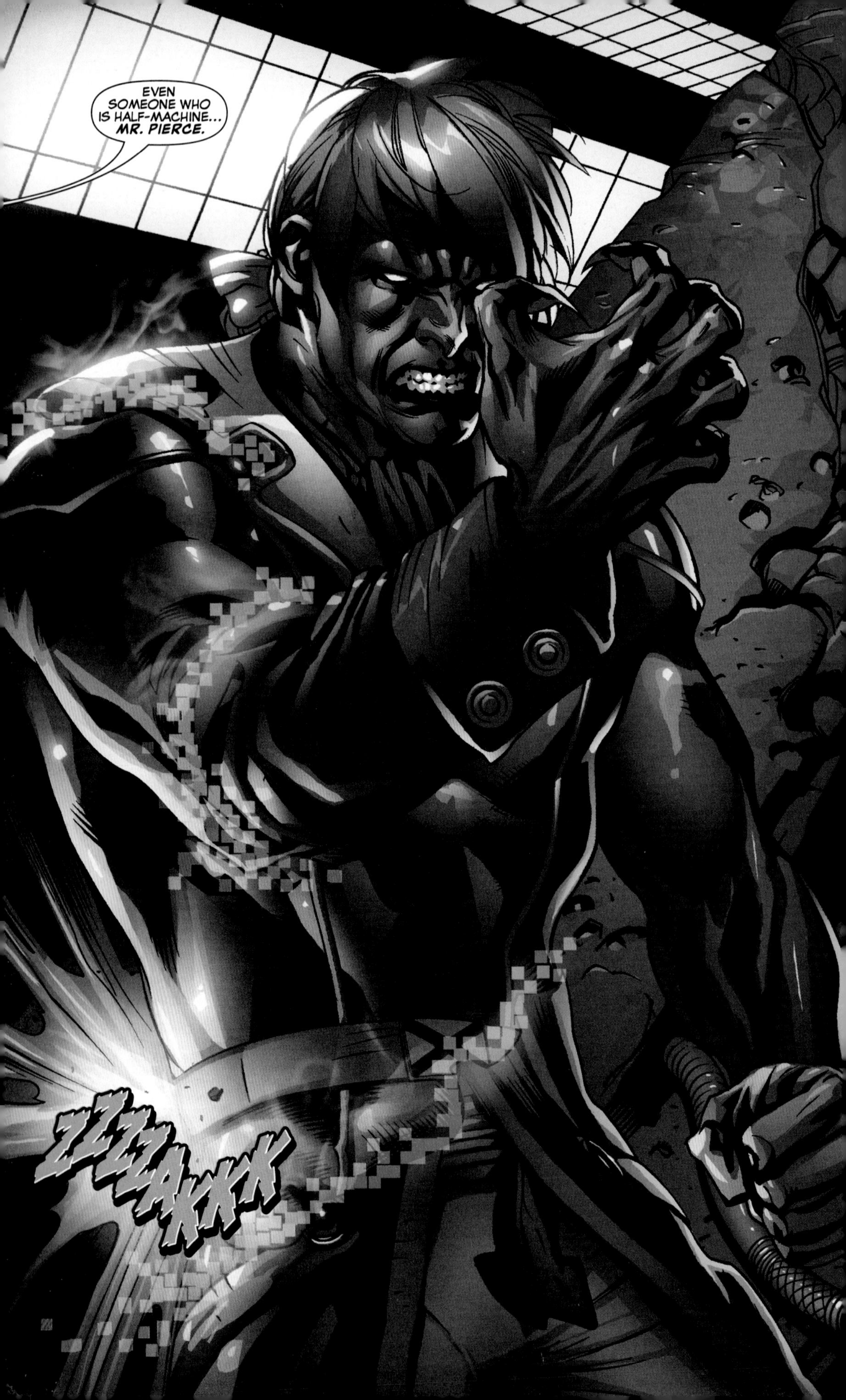
EVEN SOMEONE WHO IS HALF-MACHINE... MR. PIERCE.
ZZZZAKKKK

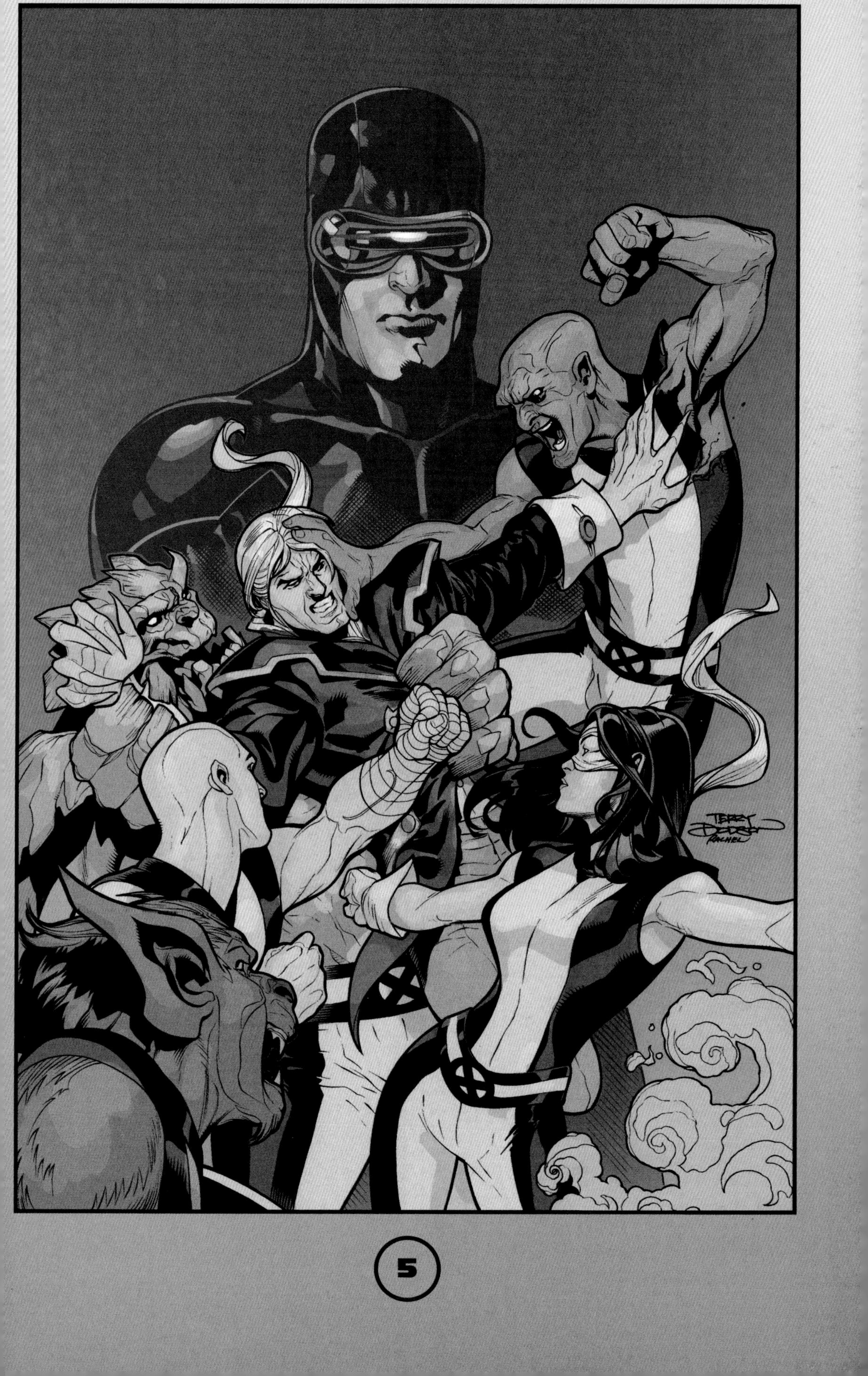
TERRY DODSON
RACHEL

5

SHHHHAAAAAAAAAAAAAASH

MUTANT PRESENCE DETECTED.

RRG--

≈GNF--≈

RESUMING PROGRAM FROM PREVIOUS ENDPOINT

BUT SHE JOINED THE X-MEN AFTER I DIED.

WHAT DEVILRY--?

QUERY RECEIVED. UNIT DESIGNATE "DANGER CAVE."

WHAT AN APPROPRIATE NAME.

LET ME SHOW YOU WHY.

FG--

SIMULACRUM GENERATED FROM BRIEFING FILES FOR EXERCISE, TRAINING AND RECREATIONAL PURPOSES.

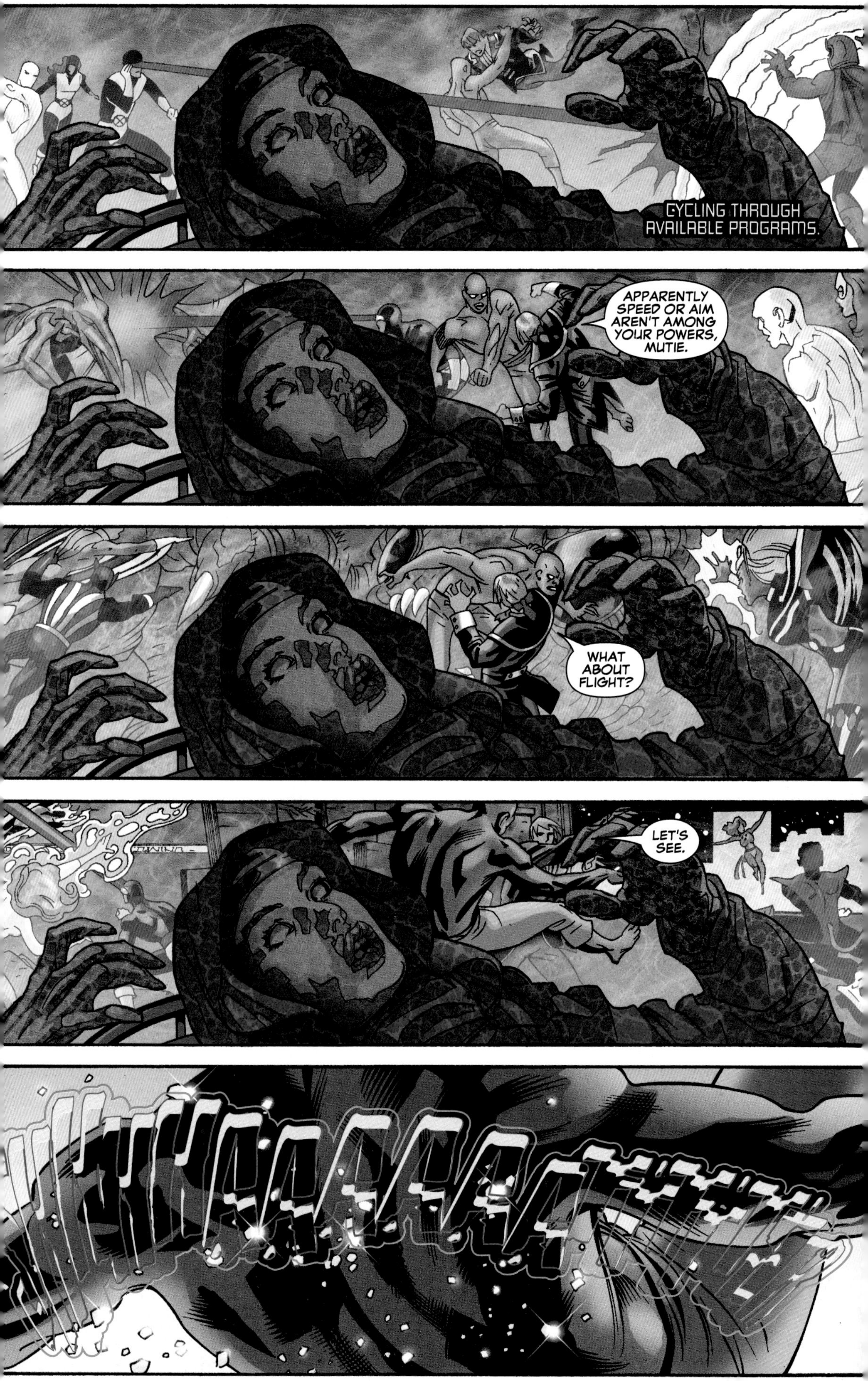
CYCLING THROUGH AVAILABLE PROGRAMS.
APPARENTLY SPEED OR AIM AREN'T AMONG YOUR POWERS, MUTIE.
WHAT ABOUT FLIGHT?
LET'S SEE.

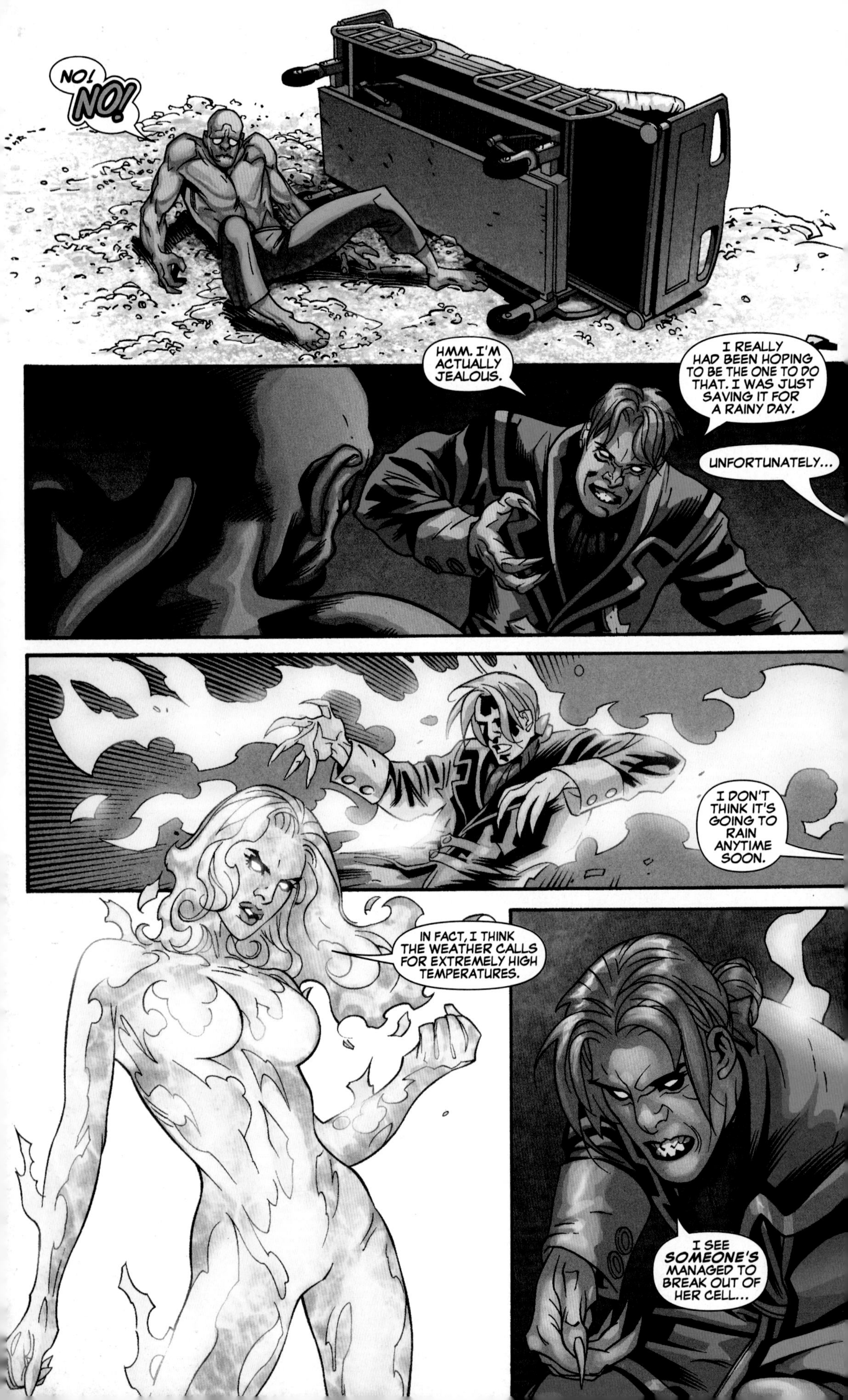
NO! NO!
HMM. I'M ACTUALLY JEALOUS.
I REALLY HAD BEEN HOPING TO BE THE ONE TO DO THAT. I WAS JUST SAVING IT FOR A RAINY DAY.
UNFORTUNATELY...
I DON'T THINK IT'S GOING TO RAIN ANYTIME SOON.
IN FACT, I THINK THE WEATHER CALLS FOR EXTREMELY HIGH TEMPERATURES.
I SEE SOMEONE'S MANAGED TO BREAK OUT OF HER CELL...

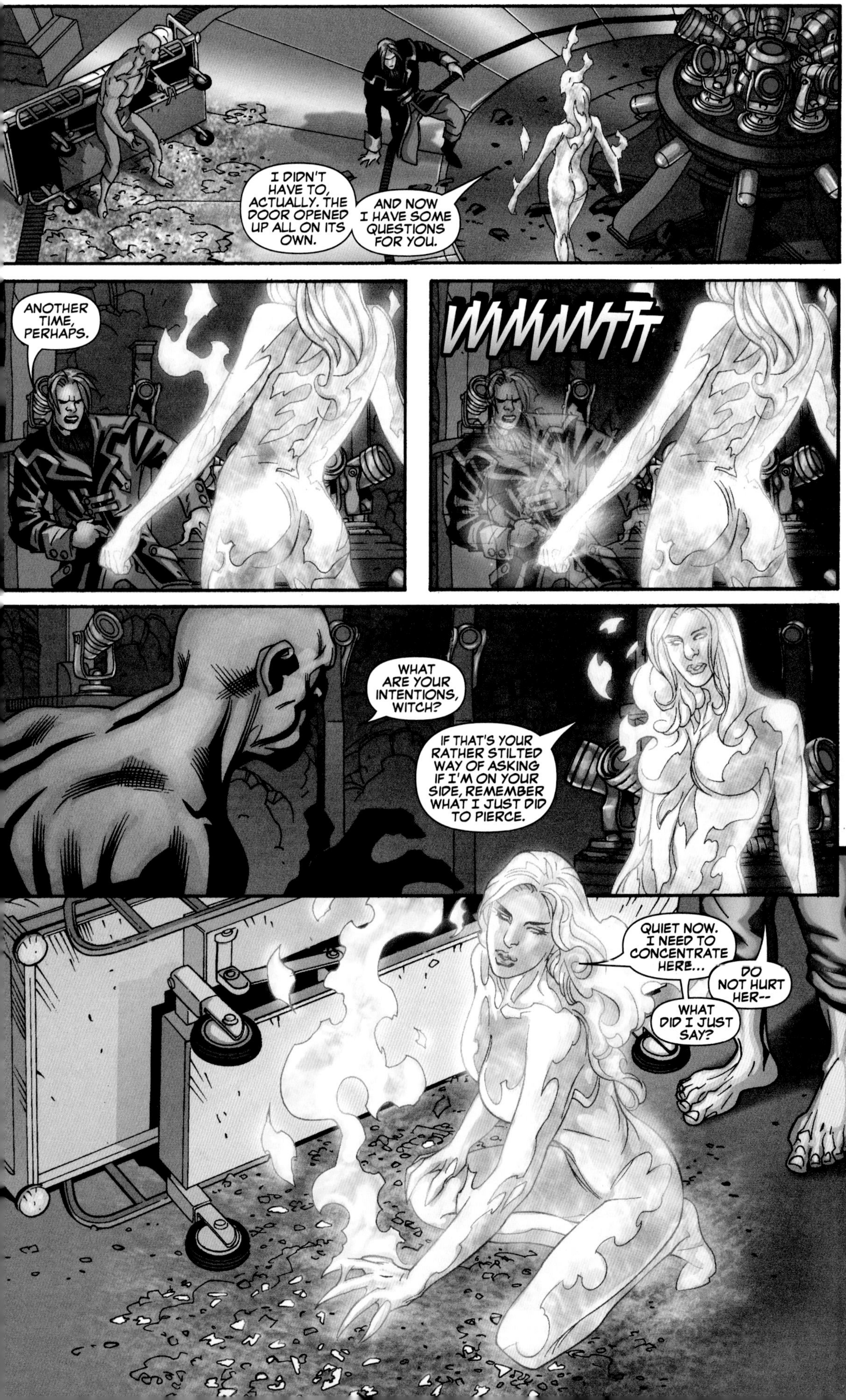
I DIDN'T HAVE TO, ACTUALLY. THE DOOR OPENED UP ALL ON ITS OWN.
AND NOW I HAVE SOME QUESTIONS FOR YOU.
ANOTHER TIME, PERHAPS.
VVVVVVVVTTT
WHAT ARE YOUR INTENTIONS, WITCH?
IF THAT'S YOUR RATHER STILTED WAY OF ASKING IF I'M ON YOUR SIDE, REMEMBER WHAT I JUST DID TO PIERCE.
QUIET NOW. I NEED TO CONCENTRATE HERE...
DO NOT HURT HER--
WHAT DID I JUST SAY?

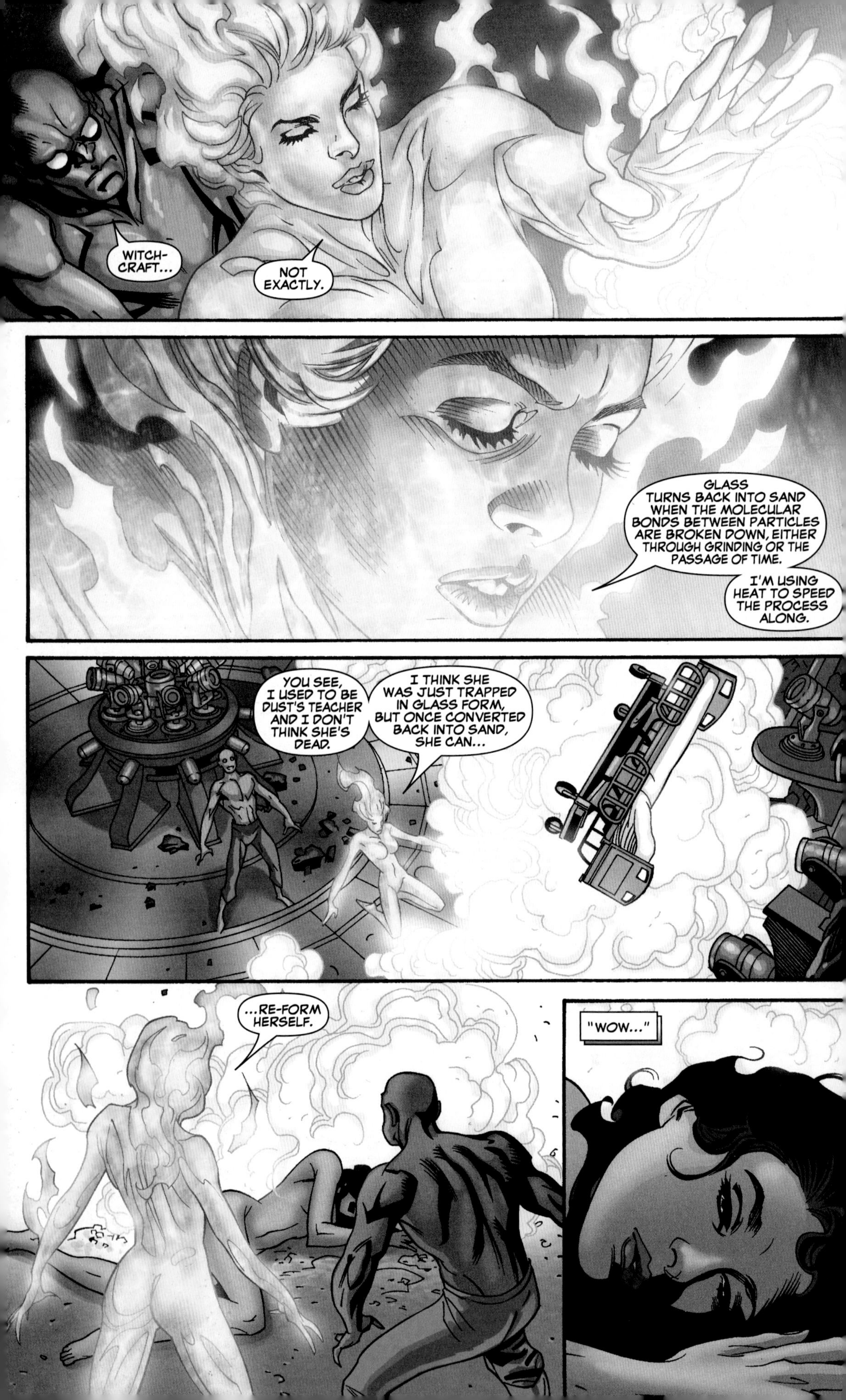
WITCH-CRAFT...
NOT EXACTLY.
GLASS TURNS BACK INTO SAND WHEN THE MOLECULAR BONDS BETWEEN PARTICLES ARE BROKEN DOWN, EITHER THROUGH GRINDING OR THE PASSAGE OF TIME.
I'M USING HEAT TO SPEED THE PROCESS ALONG.
YOU SEE, I USED TO BE DUST'S TEACHER AND I DON'T THINK SHE'S DEAD.
I THINK SHE WAS JUST TRAPPED IN GLASS FORM, BUT ONCE CONVERTED BACK INTO SAND, SHE CAN...
...RE-FORM HERSELF.
"WOW..."

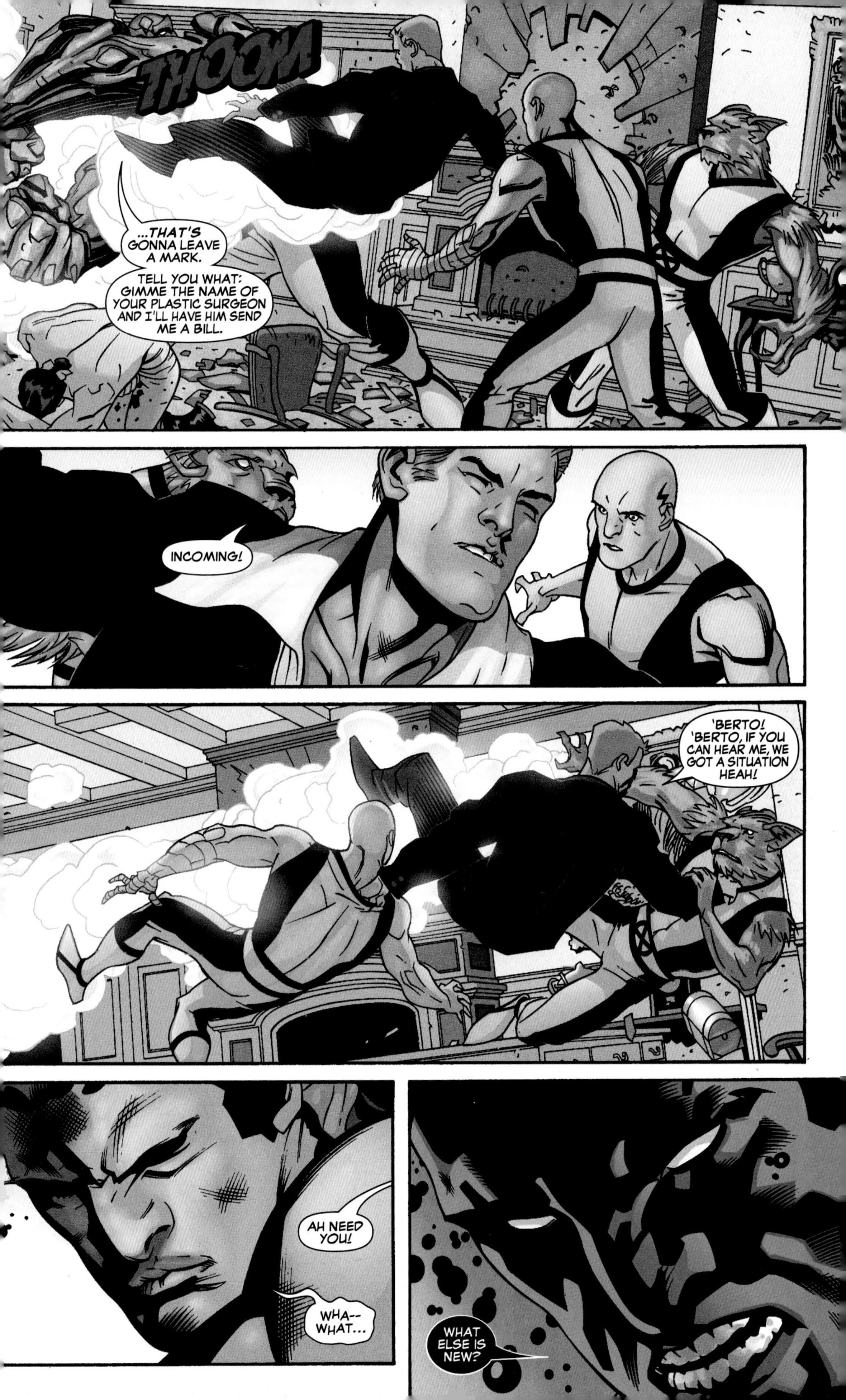
THOOM
...THAT'S GONNA LEAVE A MARK.
TELL YOU WHAT: GIMME THE NAME OF YOUR PLASTIC SURGEON AND I'LL HAVE HIM SEND ME A BILL.
INCOMING!
'BERTO! 'BERTO, IF YOU CAN HEAR ME, WE GOT A SITUATION HEAH!
AH NEED YOU!
WHA-- WHAT...
WHAT ELSE IS NEW?

PRETTY COCKY FOR THE FELLA WHO GOT US INTO THIS MESS TO BEGIN WITH.

HE'S GOING TO BE THROWING I-TOLDJA-SO'S AT ME 'TIL THE END OF TIME.

YOU HAVE ANY IDEA HO ANGRY THA MAKES ME?

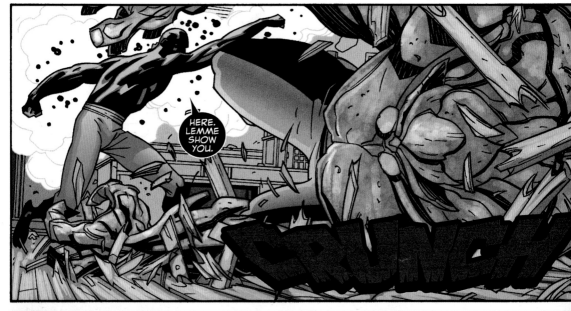

HERE. LEMME SHOW YOU.

CRUNCH

NICE TRY, BUT AH'M PRETTY MUCH INVULNERABLE WHEN AH'M BLASTIN'.

YOU FELLAS WOULDN'T HAPPEN TA BE INVULNERABLE, TOO, WOULDJA?

SAY IF I DROPP YOU FROM THOUSA FEET?

"THEY'RE GC TO KILL THE

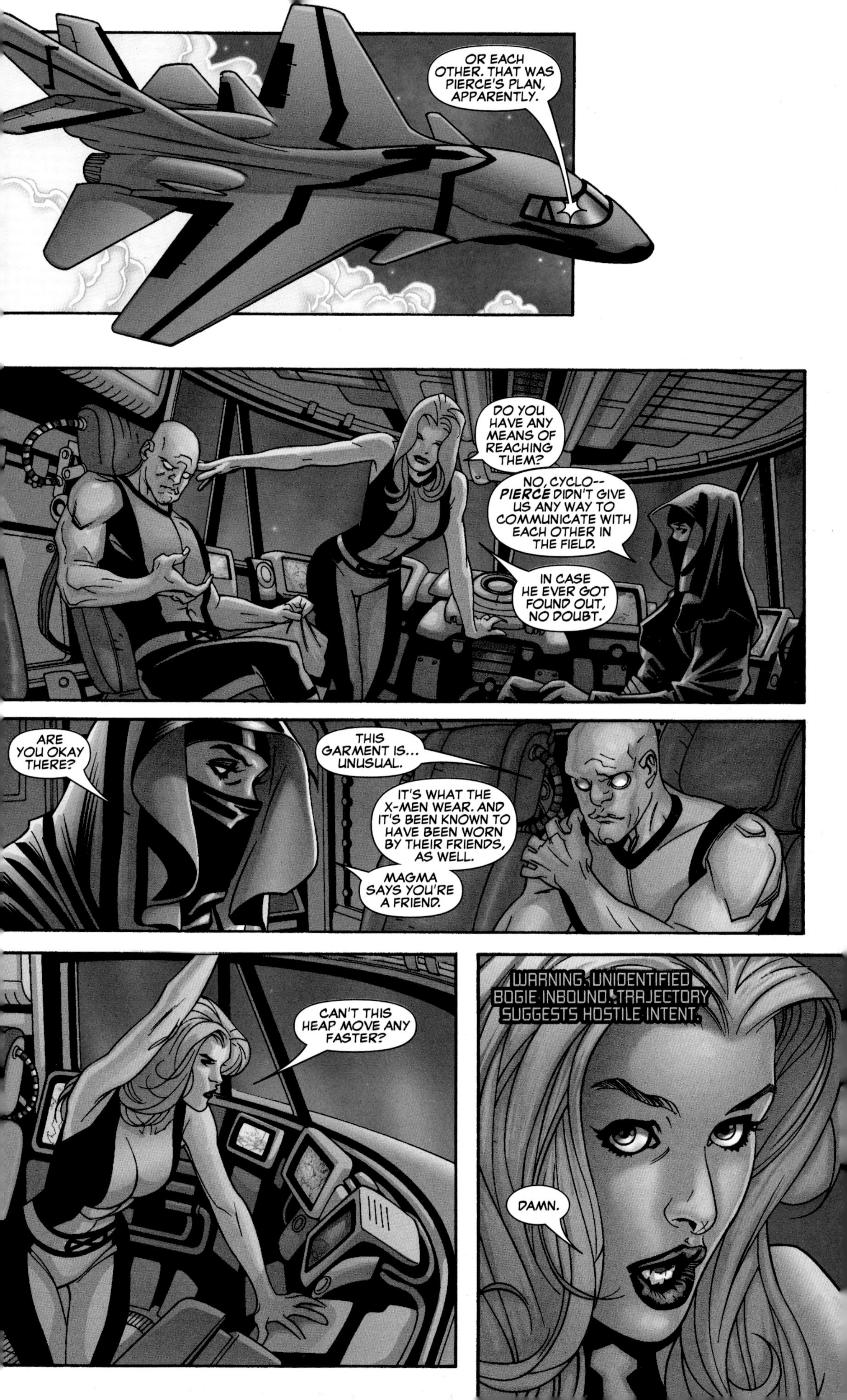
OR EACH OTHER. THAT WAS PIERCE'S PLAN, APPARENTLY.
DO YOU HAVE ANY MEANS OF REACHING THEM?
NO, CYCLO-- PIERCE DIDN'T GIVE US ANY WAY TO COMMUNICATE WITH EACH OTHER IN THE FIELD.
IN CASE HE EVER GOT FOUND OUT, NO DOUBT.
ARE YOU OKAY THERE?
THIS GARMENT IS... UNUSUAL.
IT'S WHAT THE X-MEN WEAR. AND IT'S BEEN KNOWN TO HAVE BEEN WORN BY THEIR FRIENDS, AS WELL.
MAGMA SAYS YOU'RE A FRIEND.
CAN'T THIS HEAP MOVE ANY FASTER?
WARNING. UNIDENTIFIED BOGIE INBOUND. TRAJECTORY SUGGESTS HOSTILE INTENT.
DAMN.

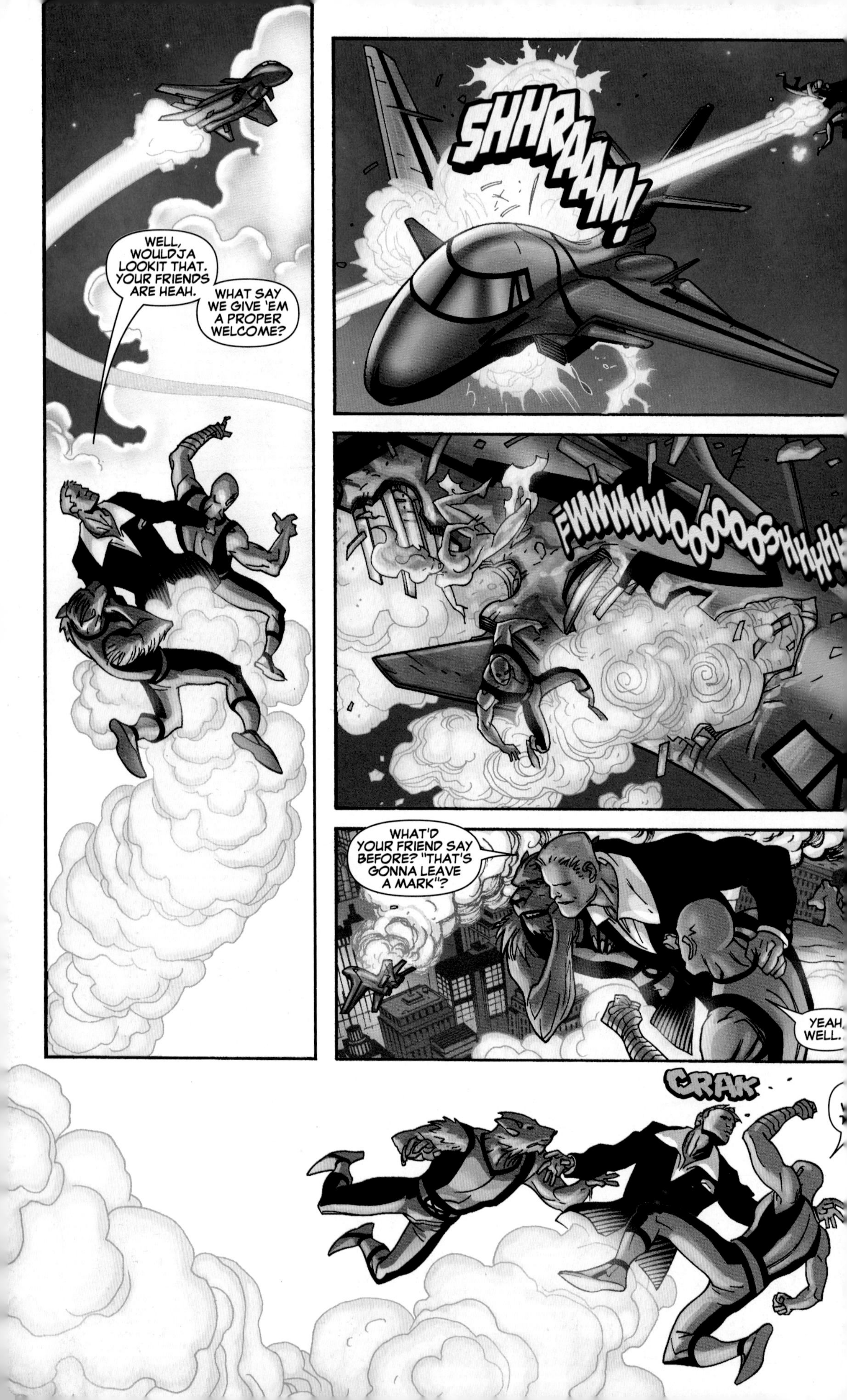
WELL, WOULDJA LOOKIT THAT. YOUR FRIENDS ARE HEAH.
WHAT SAY WE GIVE 'EM A PROPER WELCOME?
SHHRAAAM!
FWWWWWWOOOOOSHHHH
WHAT'D YOUR FRIEND SAY BEFORE? "THAT'S GONNA LEAVE A MARK"?
YEAH, WELL.
CRAK

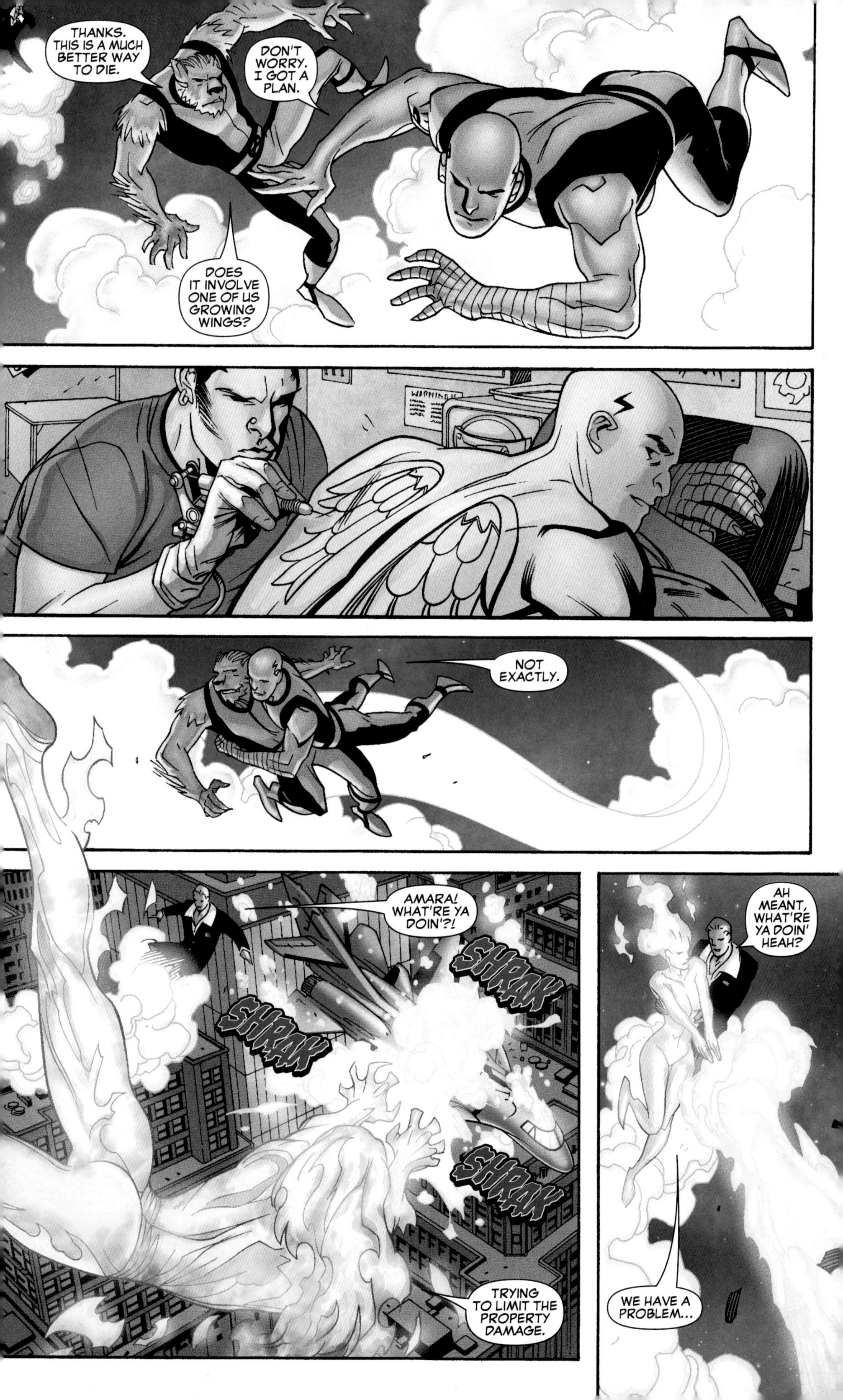
THANKS. THIS IS A MUCH BETTER WAY TO DIE.
DON'T WORRY. I GOT A PLAN.
DOES IT INVOLVE ONE OF US GROWING WINGS?
NOT EXACTLY.
AMARA! WHAT'RE YA DOIN'?!
SHRAK
SHRAK
SHRAK
SHRAK
TRYING TO LIMIT THE PROPERTY DAMAGE.
AH MEANT, WHAT'RE YA DOIN' HEAH?
WE HAVE A PROBLEM...

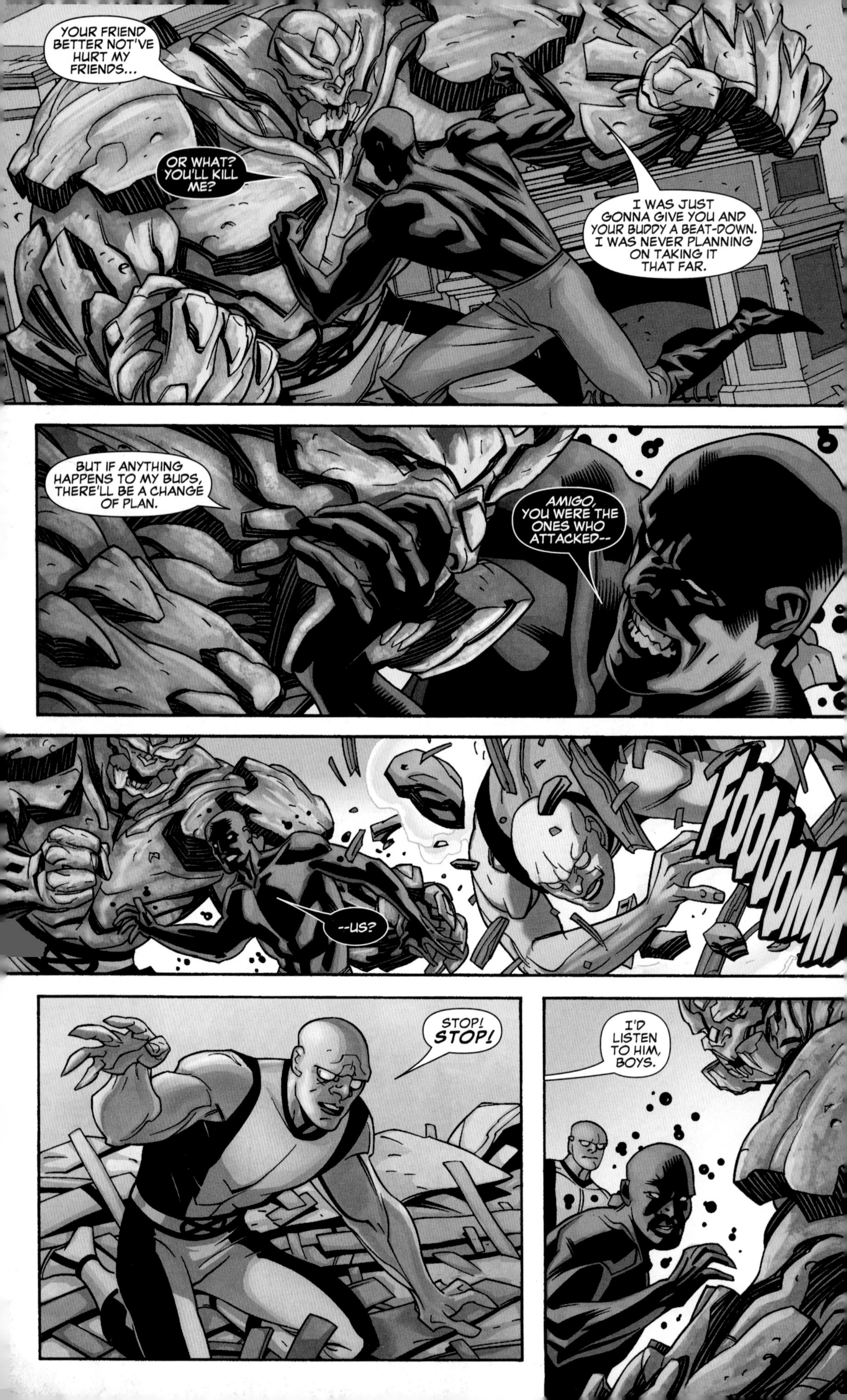
YOUR FRIEND BETTER NOT'VE HURT MY FRIENDS...
OR WHAT? YOU'LL KILL ME?
I WAS JUST GONNA GIVE YOU AND YOUR BUDDY A BEAT-DOWN. I WAS NEVER PLANNING ON TAKING IT THAT FAR.
BUT IF ANYTHING HAPPENS TO MY BUDS, THERE'LL BE A CHANGE OF PLAN.
AMIGO, YOU WERE THE ONES WHO ATTACKED--
--US?
FOOOOMM
STOP! STOP!
I'D LISTEN TO HIM, BOYS.

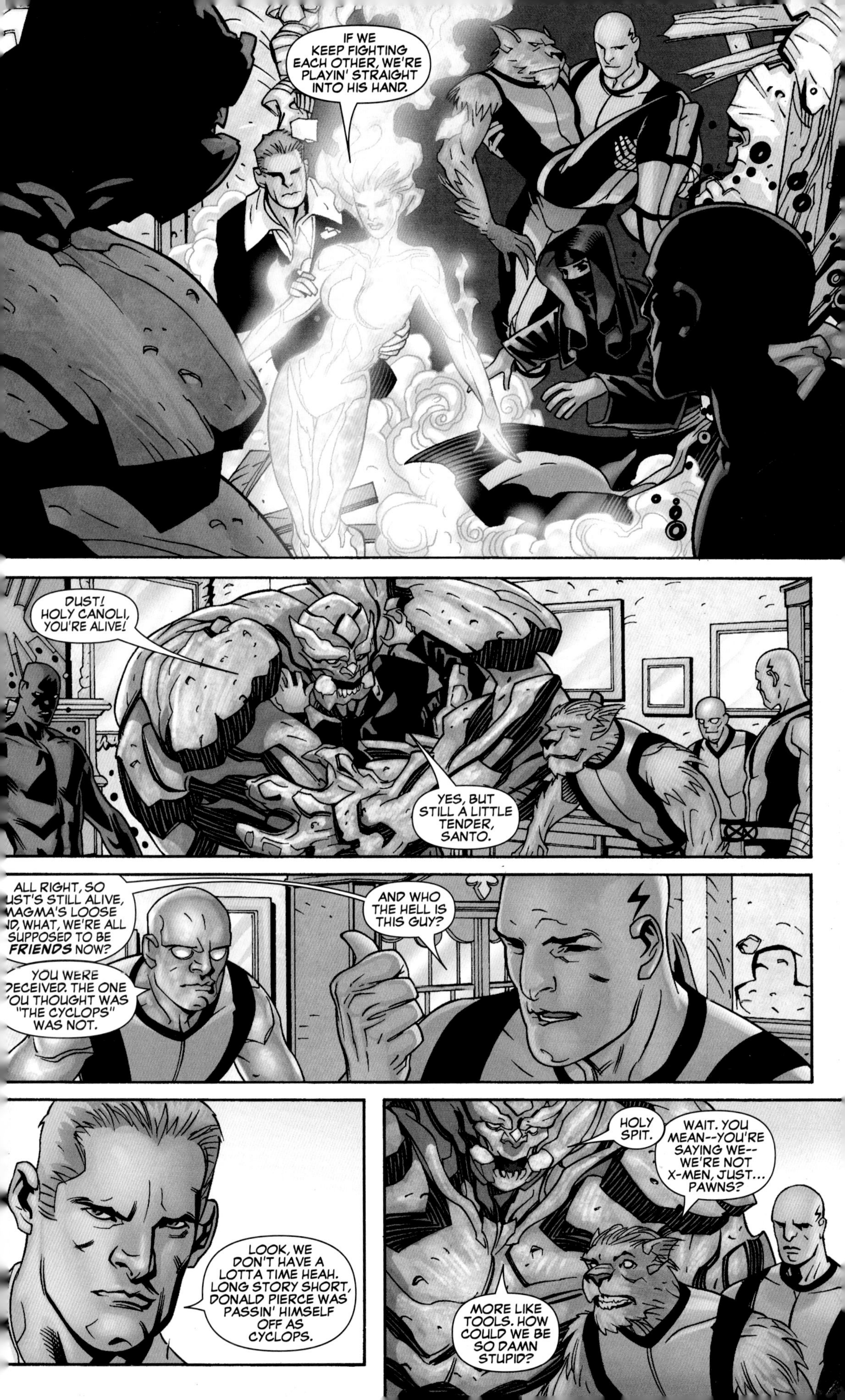
IF WE KEEP FIGHTING EACH OTHER, WE'RE PLAYIN' STRAIGHT INTO HIS HAND.
DUST! HOLY CANOLI, YOU'RE ALIVE!
YES, BUT STILL A LITTLE TENDER, SANTO.
ALL RIGHT, SO UST'S STILL ALIVE, MAGMA'S LOOSE ID, WHAT, WE'RE ALL SUPPOSED TO BE FRIENDS NOW?
AND WHO THE HELL IS THIS GUY?
YOU WERE DECEIVED. THE ONE 'OU THOUGHT WAS "THE CYCLOPS" WAS NOT.
LOOK, WE DON'T HAVE A LOTTA TIME HEAH. LONG STORY SHORT, DONALD PIERCE WAS PASSIN' HIMSELF OFF AS CYCLOPS.
HOLY SPIT.
WAIT. YOU MEAN--YOU'RE SAYING WE-- WE'RE NOT X-MEN, JUST... PAWNS?
MORE LIKE TOOLS. HOW COULD WE BE SO DAMN STUPID?

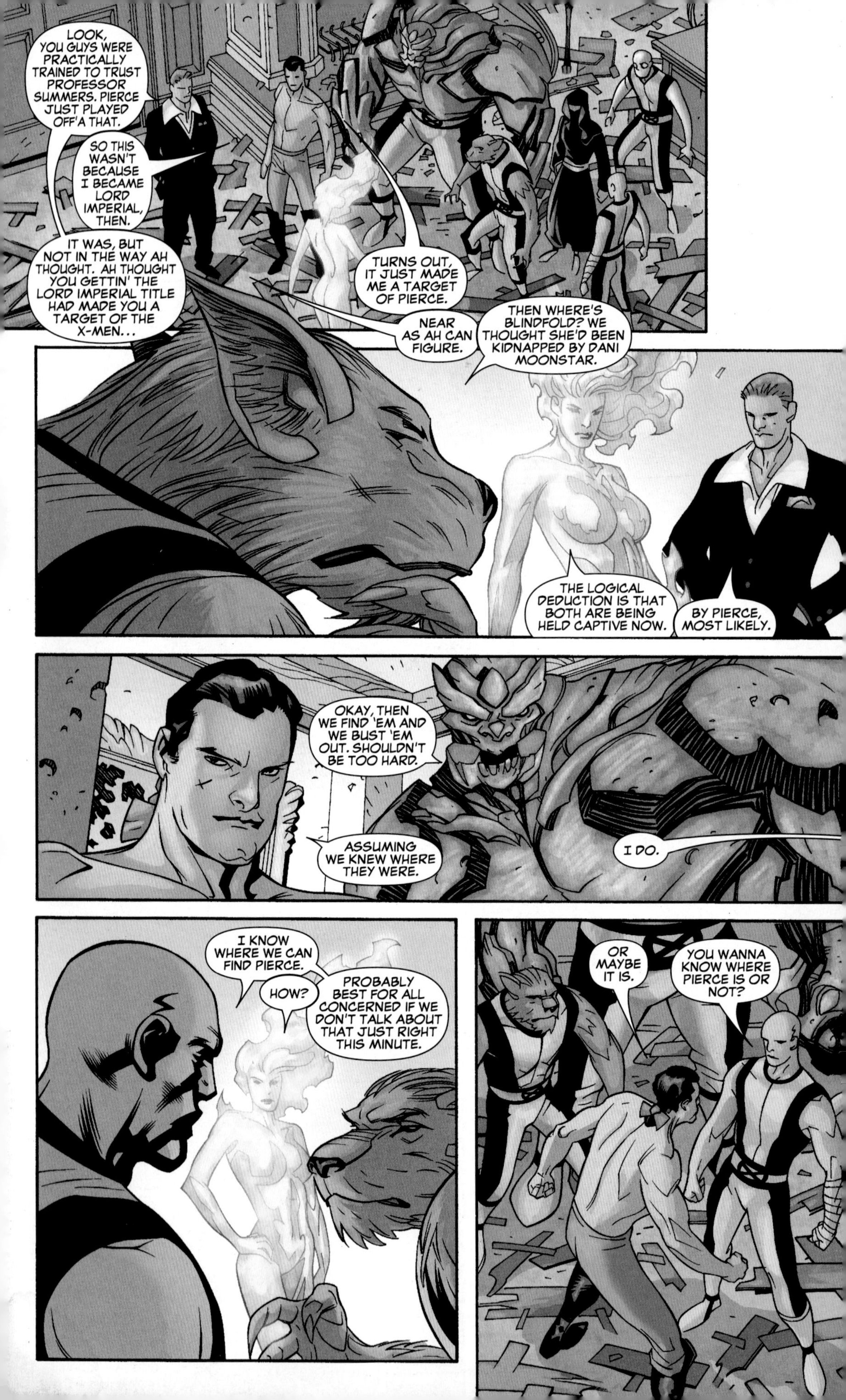

LOOK, YOU GUYS WERE PRACTICALLY TRAINED TO TRUST PROFESSOR SUMMERS. PIERCE JUST PLAYED OFF'A THAT.
SO THIS WASN'T BECAUSE I BECAME LORD IMPERIAL, THEN.
IT WAS, BUT NOT IN THE WAY AH THOUGHT. AH THOUGHT YOU GETTIN' THE LORD IMPERIAL TITLE HAD MADE YOU A TARGET OF THE X-MEN...
TURNS OUT, IT JUST MADE ME A TARGET OF PIERCE.
NEAR AS AH CAN FIGURE.
THEN WHERE'S BLINDFOLD? WE THOUGHT SHE'D BEEN KIDNAPPED BY DANI MOONSTAR.
THE LOGICAL DEDUCTION IS THAT BOTH ARE BEING HELD CAPTIVE NOW.
BY PIERCE, MOST LIKELY.
OKAY, THEN WE FIND 'EM AND WE BUST 'EM OUT. SHOULDN'T BE TOO HARD.
ASSUMING WE KNEW WHERE THEY WERE.
I DO.
I KNOW WHERE WE CAN FIND PIERCE.
HOW?
PROBABLY BEST FOR ALL CONCERNED IF WE DON'T TALK ABOUT THAT JUST RIGHT THIS MINUTE.
OR MAYBE IT IS.
YOU WANNA KNOW WHERE PIERCE IS OR NOT?

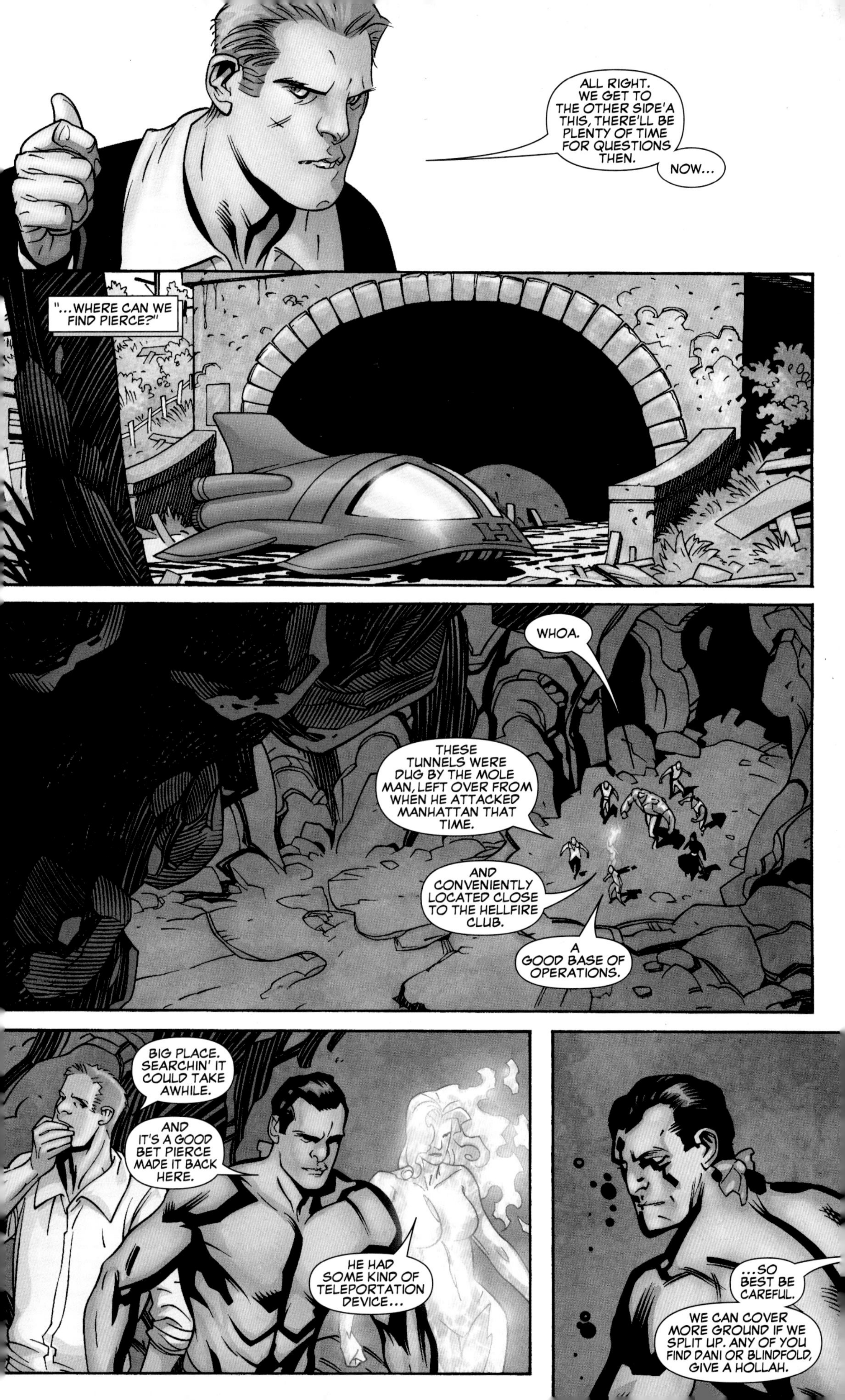

ALL RIGHT. WE GET TO THE OTHER SIDE'A THIS, THERE'LL BE PLENTY OF TIME FOR QUESTIONS THEN.
NOW...
"...WHERE CAN WE FIND PIERCE?"
WHOA.
THESE TUNNELS WERE DUG BY THE MOLE MAN, LEFT OVER FROM WHEN HE ATTACKED MANHATTAN THAT TIME.
AND CONVENIENTLY LOCATED CLOSE TO THE HELLFIRE CLUB.
A GOOD BASE OF OPERATIONS.
BIG PLACE. SEARCHIN' IT COULD TAKE AWHILE.
AND IT'S A GOOD BET PIERCE MADE IT BACK HERE.
HE HAD SOME KIND OF TELEPORTATION DEVICE...
...SO BEST BE CAREFUL.
WE CAN COVER MORE GROUND IF WE SPLIT UP. ANY OF YOU FIND DANI OR BLINDFOLD, GIVE A HOLLAH.

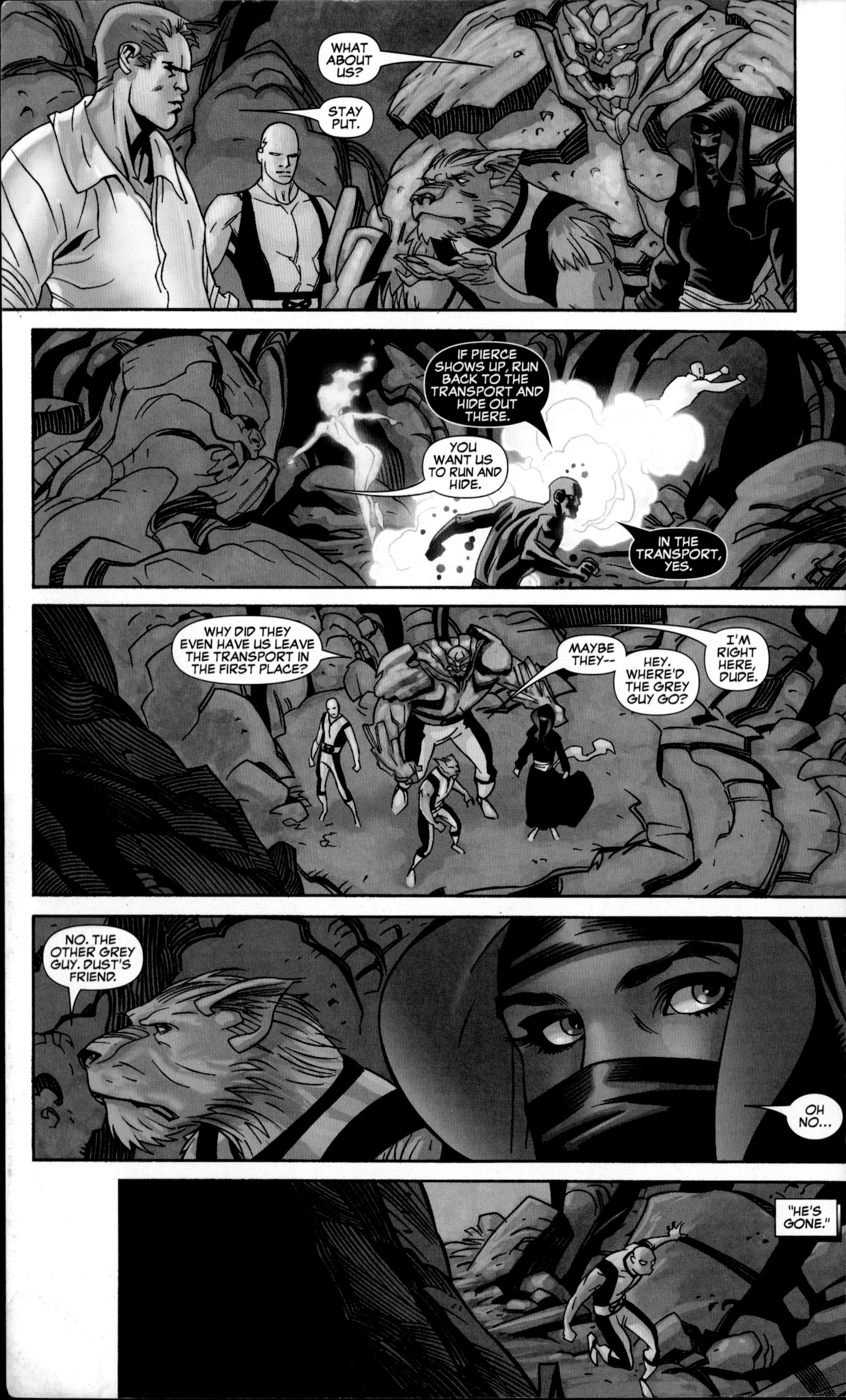
WHAT ABOUT US?
STAY PUT.
IF PIERCE SHOWS UP, RUN BACK TO THE TRANSPORT AND HIDE OUT THERE.
YOU WANT US TO RUN AND HIDE.
IN THE TRANSPORT, YES.
WHY DID THEY EVEN HAVE US LEAVE THE TRANSPORT IN THE FIRST PLACE?
MAYBE THEY--
HEY. WHERE'D THE GREY GUY GO?
I'M RIGHT HERE, DUDE.
NO. THE OTHER GREY GUY. DUST'S FRIEND.
OH NO...
"HE'S GONE."

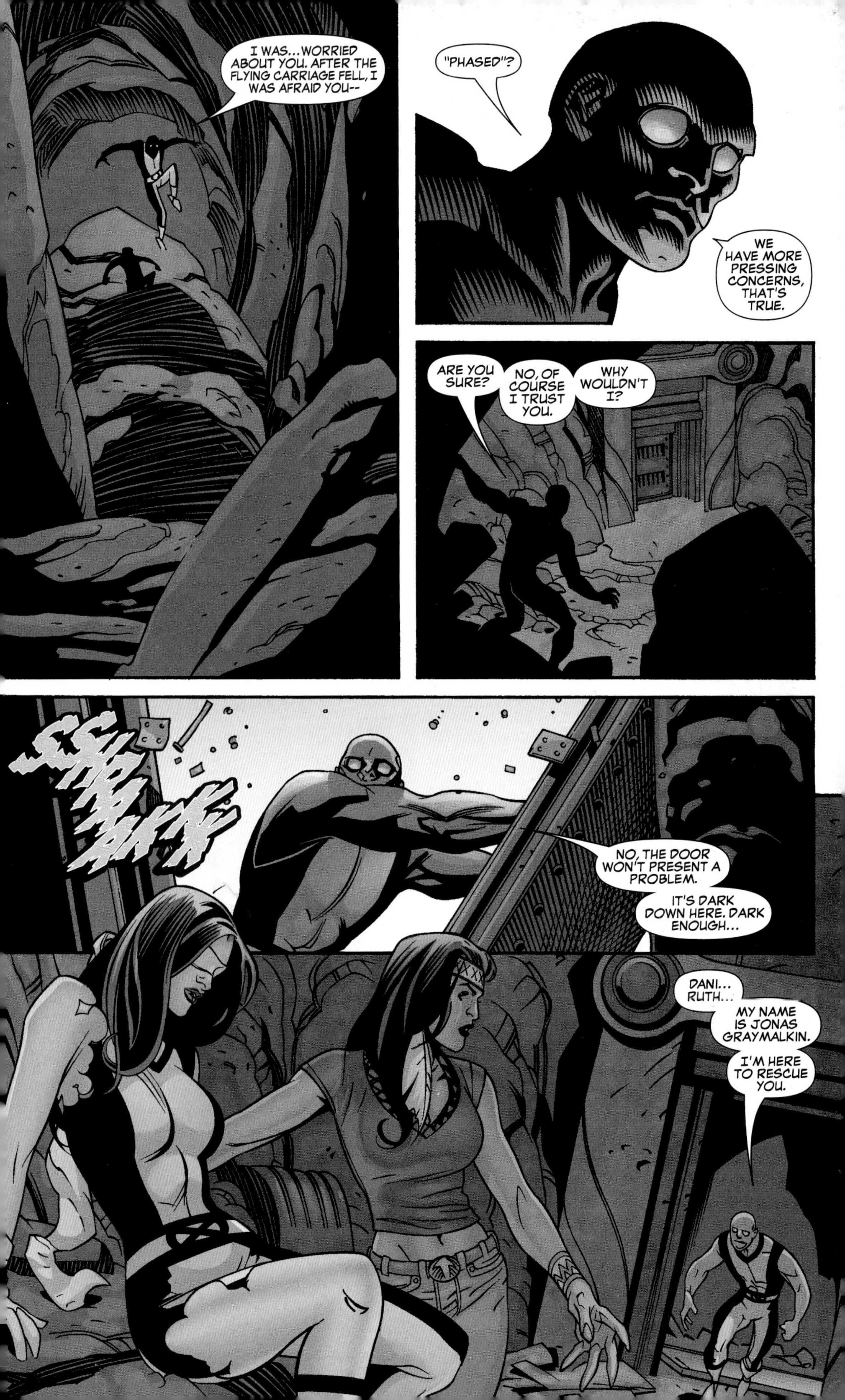

I WAS...WORRIED ABOUT YOU. AFTER THE FLYING CARRIAGE FELL, I WAS AFRAID YOU--
"PHASED"?
WE HAVE MORE PRESSING CONCERNS, THAT'S TRUE.
ARE YOU SURE?
NO, OF COURSE I TRUST YOU.
WHY WOULDN'T I?
NO, THE DOOR WON'T PRESENT A PROBLEM.
IT'S DARK DOWN HERE. DARK ENOUGH...
DANI... RUTH...
MY NAME IS JONAS GRAYMALKIN.
I'M HERE TO RESCUE YOU.

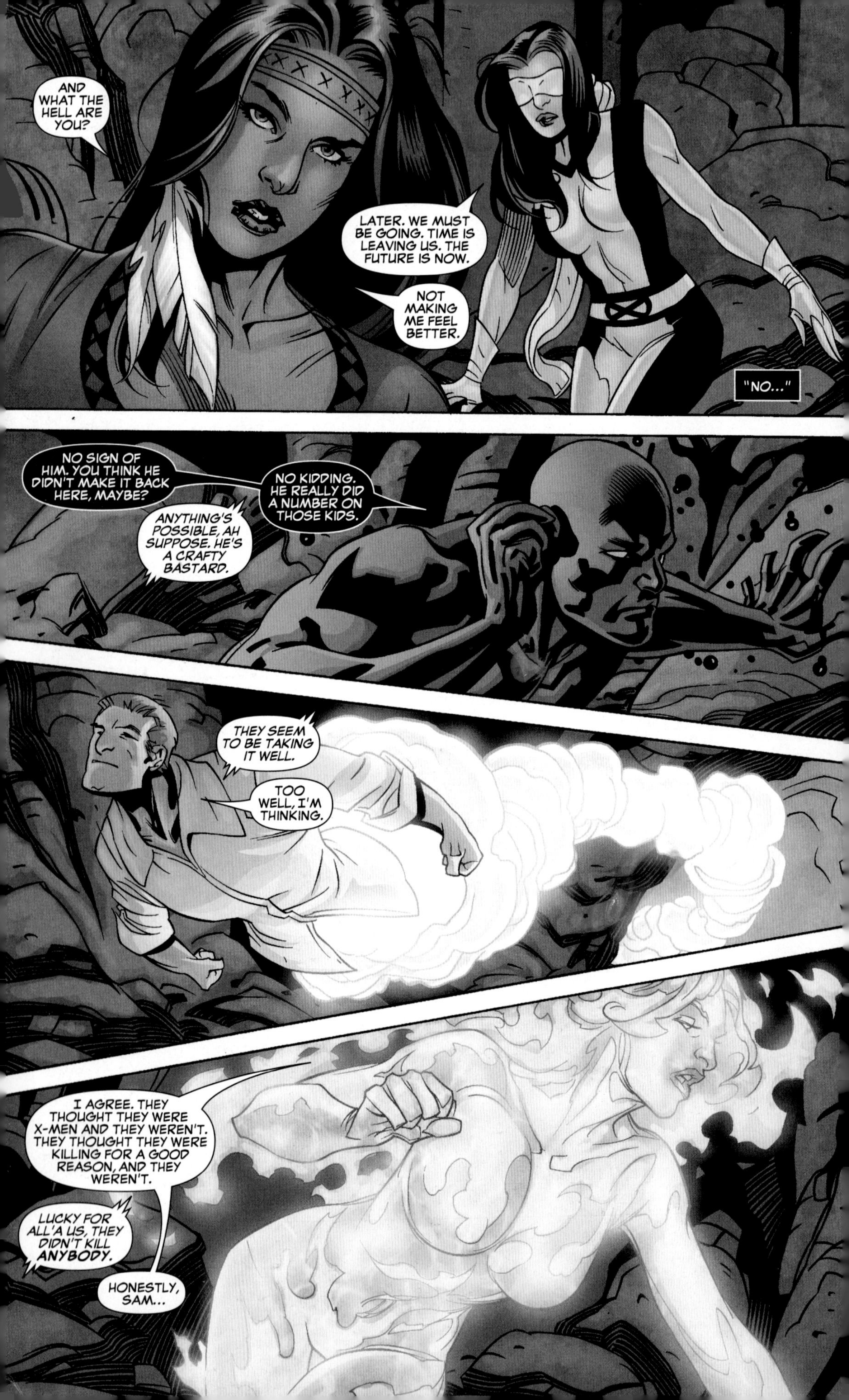
AND WHAT THE HELL ARE YOU?
LATER. WE MUST BE GOING. TIME IS LEAVING US. THE FUTURE IS NOW.
NOT MAKING ME FEEL BETTER.
"NO..."
NO SIGN OF HIM. YOU THINK HE DIDN'T MAKE IT BACK HERE, MAYBE?
ANYTHING'S POSSIBLE, AH SUPPOSE. HE'S A CRAFTY BASTARD.
NO KIDDING. HE REALLY DID A NUMBER ON THOSE KIDS.
THEY SEEM TO BE TAKING IT WELL.
TOO WELL, I'M THINKING.
I AGREE. THEY THOUGHT THEY WERE X-MEN AND THEY WEREN'T. THEY THOUGHT THEY WERE KILLING FOR A GOOD REASON, AND THEY WEREN'T.
LUCKY FOR ALL'A US, THEY DIDN'T KILL ANYBODY.
HONESTLY, SAM...

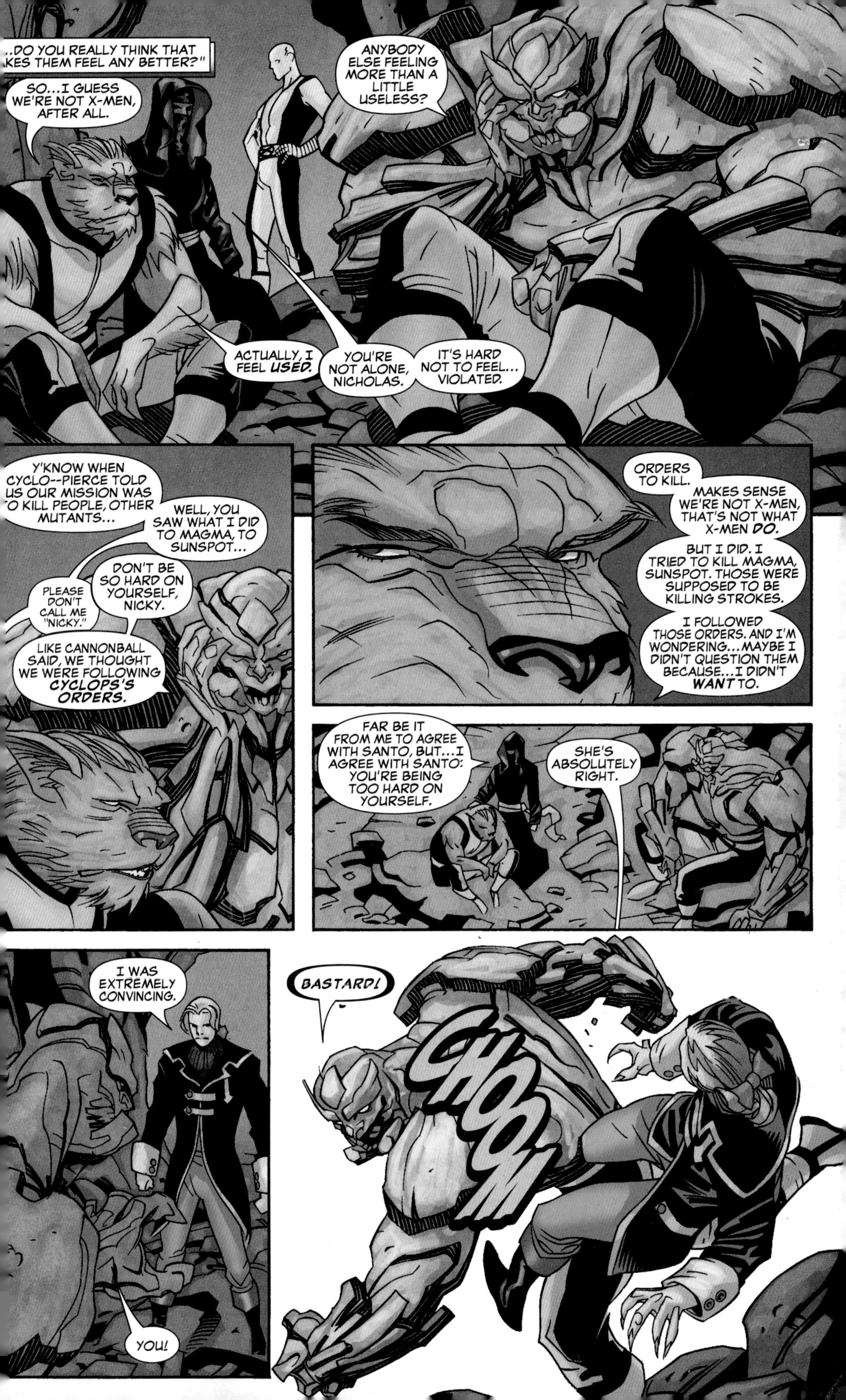
..DO YOU REALLY THINK THAT
AKES THEM FEEL ANY BETTER?"
SO...I GUESS WE'RE NOT X-MEN, AFTER ALL.
ANYBODY ELSE FEELING MORE THAN A LITTLE USELESS?
ACTUALLY, I FEEL USED.
YOU'RE NOT ALONE, NICHOLAS.
IT'S HARD NOT TO FEEL... VIOLATED.
Y'KNOW WHEN CYCLO--PIERCE TOLD US OUR MISSION WAS TO KILL PEOPLE, OTHER MUTANTS...
WELL, YOU SAW WHAT I DID TO MAGMA, TO SUNSPOT...
DON'T BE SO HARD ON YOURSELF, NICKY.
PLEASE DON'T CALL ME "NICKY."
LIKE CANNONBALL SAID, WE THOUGHT WE WERE FOLLOWING CYCLOPS'S ORDERS.
ORDERS TO KILL.
MAKES SENSE WE'RE NOT X-MEN, THAT'S NOT WHAT X-MEN DO.
BUT I DID. I TRIED TO KILL MAGMA, SUNSPOT. THOSE WERE SUPPOSED TO BE KILLING STROKES.
I FOLLOWED THOSE ORDERS. AND I'M WONDERING...MAYBE I DIDN'T QUESTION THEM BECAUSE...I DIDN'T WANT TO.
FAR BE IT FROM ME TO AGREE WITH SANTO, BUT...I AGREE WITH SANTO: YOU'RE BEING TOO HARD ON YOURSELF.
SHE'S ABSOLUTELY RIGHT.
I WAS EXTREMELY CONVINCING.
YOU!
BASTARD!
CHOOM

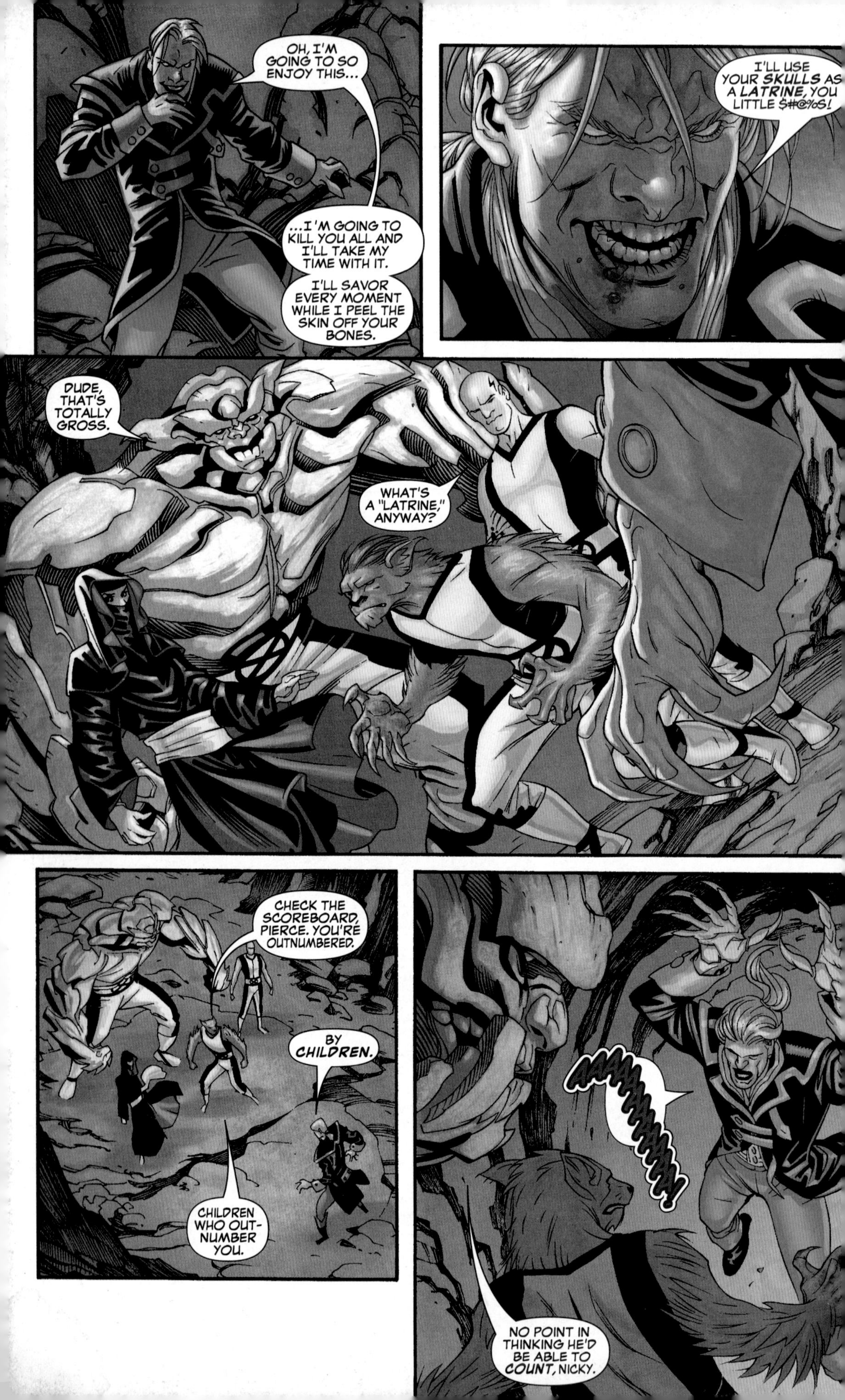
OH, I'M GOING TO SO ENJOY THIS...
...I'M GOING TO KILL YOU ALL AND I'LL TAKE MY TIME WITH IT.
I'LL SAVOR EVERY MOMENT WHILE I PEEL THE SKIN OFF YOUR BONES.
I'LL USE YOUR SKULLS AS A LATRINE, YOU LITTLE $#@%S!
DUDE, THAT'S TOTALLY GROSS.
WHAT'S A "LATRINE," ANYWAY?
CHECK THE SCOREBOARD, PIERCE. YOU'RE OUTNUMBERED.
BY CHILDREN.
CHILDREN WHO OUT-NUMBER YOU.
AAAAAAAAAAH!
NO POINT IN THINKING HE'D BE ABLE TO COUNT, NICKY.

AAAAAAAAAAAAAAAAAAAAAAAAAAAAAAA!

OH NO...IT'S HAPPENING...

WHAT'S HAPPENING? WHAT THE HELL'S GOING ON?

HURRY...

FFFFOOOOOOOOOOOOMMMM

THAT SOUNDS LIKE DUST...

IT WAS, YES. SHE JUST PULLED OFF DONALD PIERCE'S FACE.

AAAAGHH!

PARDON, FASTER--

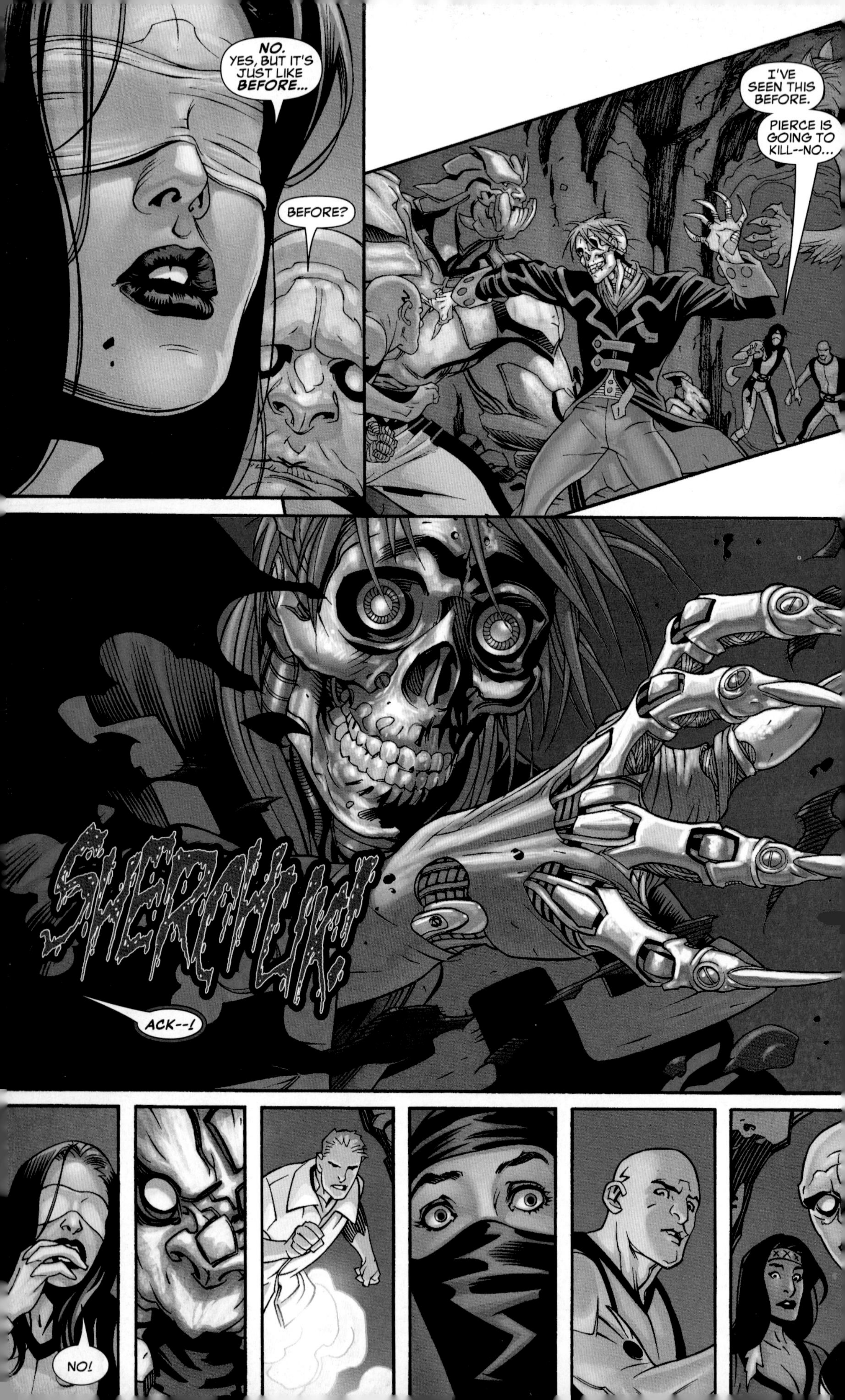
NO. YES, BUT IT'S JUST LIKE BEFORE...
BEFORE?
I'VE SEEN THIS BEFORE.
PIERCE IS GOING TO KILL--NO...
SHCRONK!
ACK--!
NO!

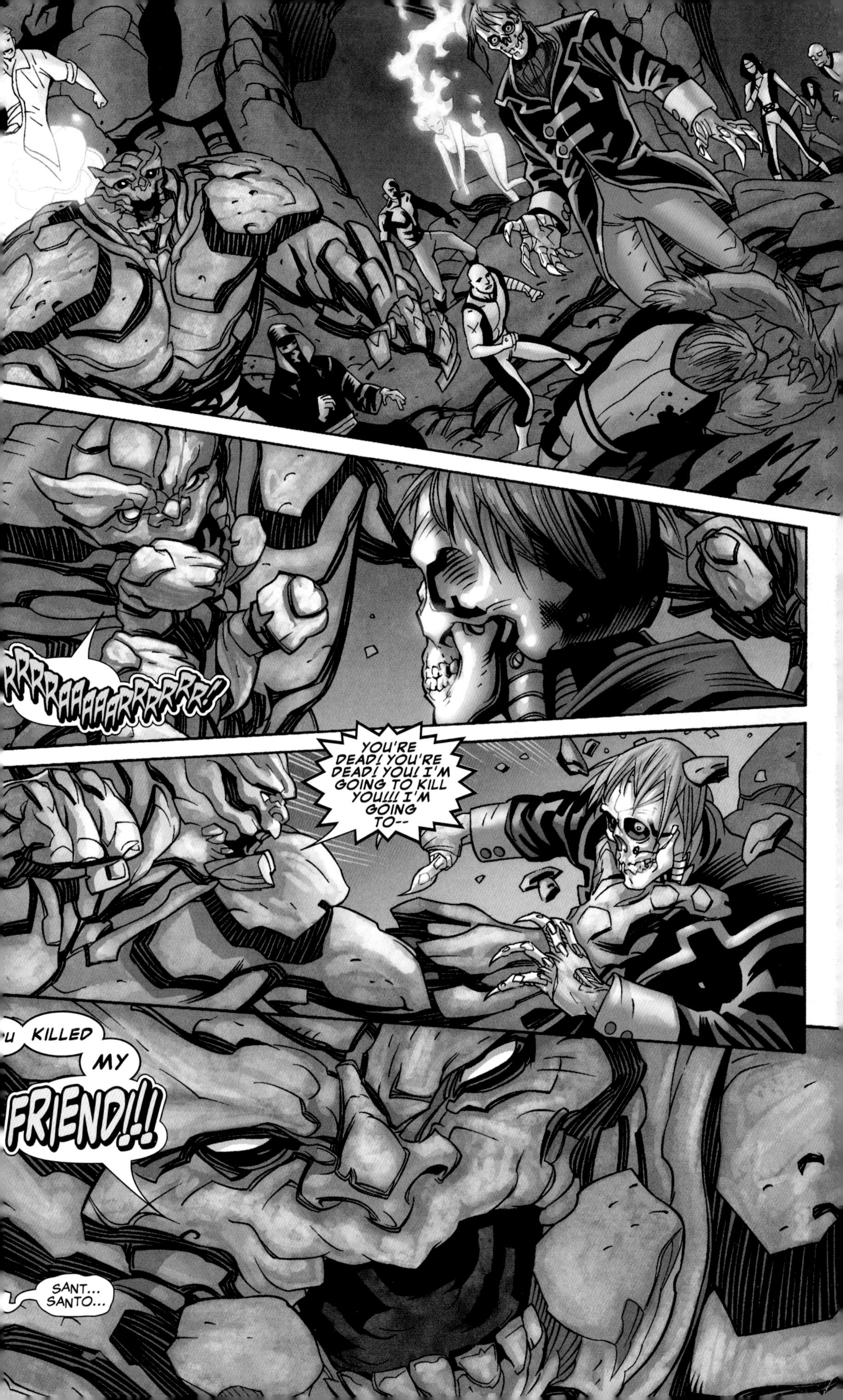
RRRRAAAAARRRRR!
YOU'RE DEAD! YOU'RE DEAD! YOU! I'M GOING TO KILL YOU!!! I'M GOING TO--
KILLED
MY
FRIEND!!!
SANT... SANTO...

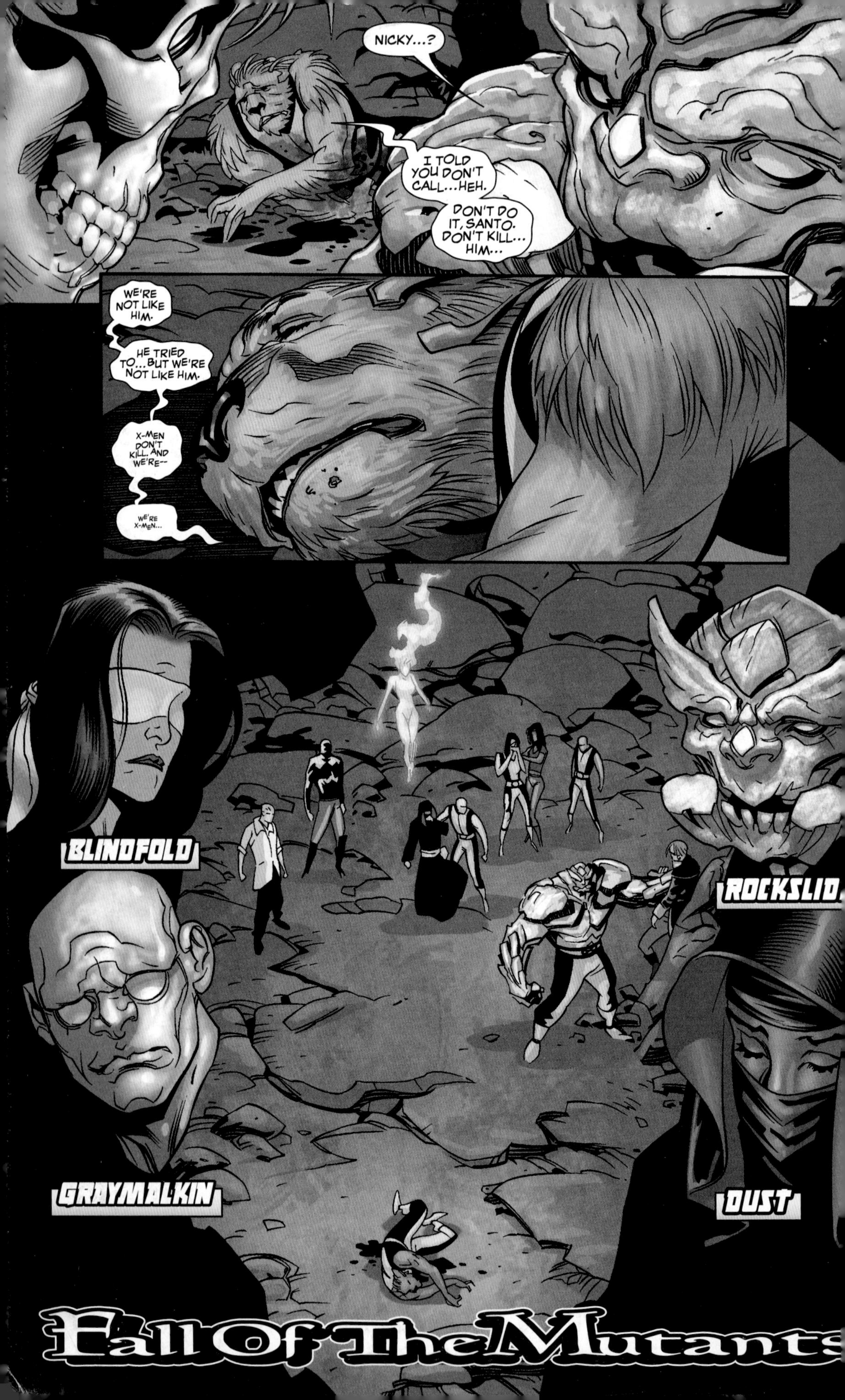
NICKY...?
I TOLD YOU DON'T CALL...HEH.
DON'T DO IT, SANTO. DON'T KILL... HIM...
WE'RE NOT LIKE HIM.
HE TRIED TO...BUT WE'RE NOT LIKE HIM.
X-MEN DON'T KILL. AND WE'RE--
WE'RE X-MEN...
BLINDFOLD
ROCKSLID
GRAYMALKIN
DUST
Fall Of The Mutants

CHARACTER & JET SKETCHES BY YANICK PAQUETTE

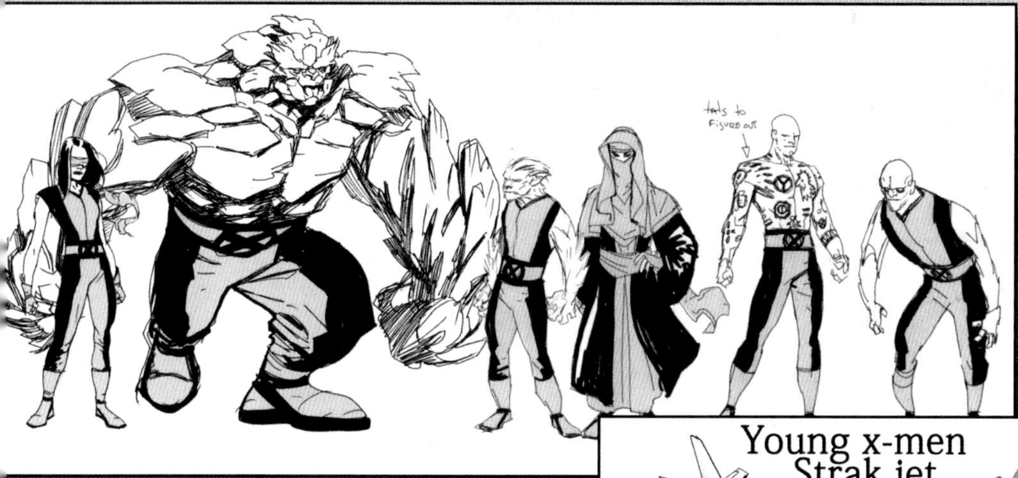
tats to
figure out

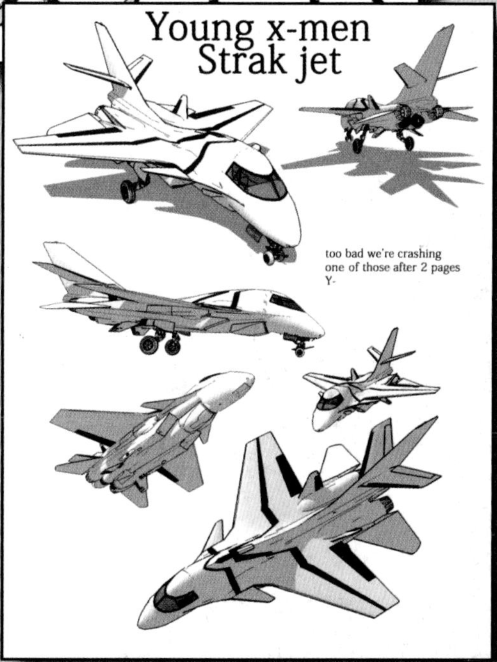
Young x-men
Strak jet
too bad we're crashing
one of those after 2 pages
Y-

COVER SKETCHES BY TERRY DODSON

ISSUE #1 SKETCHES

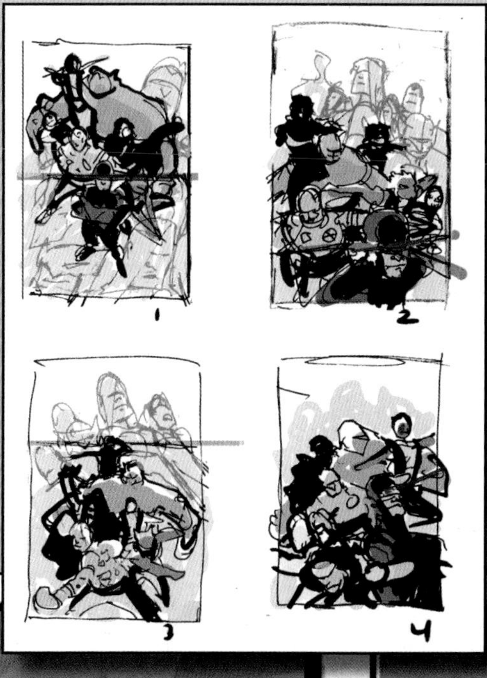

ISSUE #2 SKETCHES

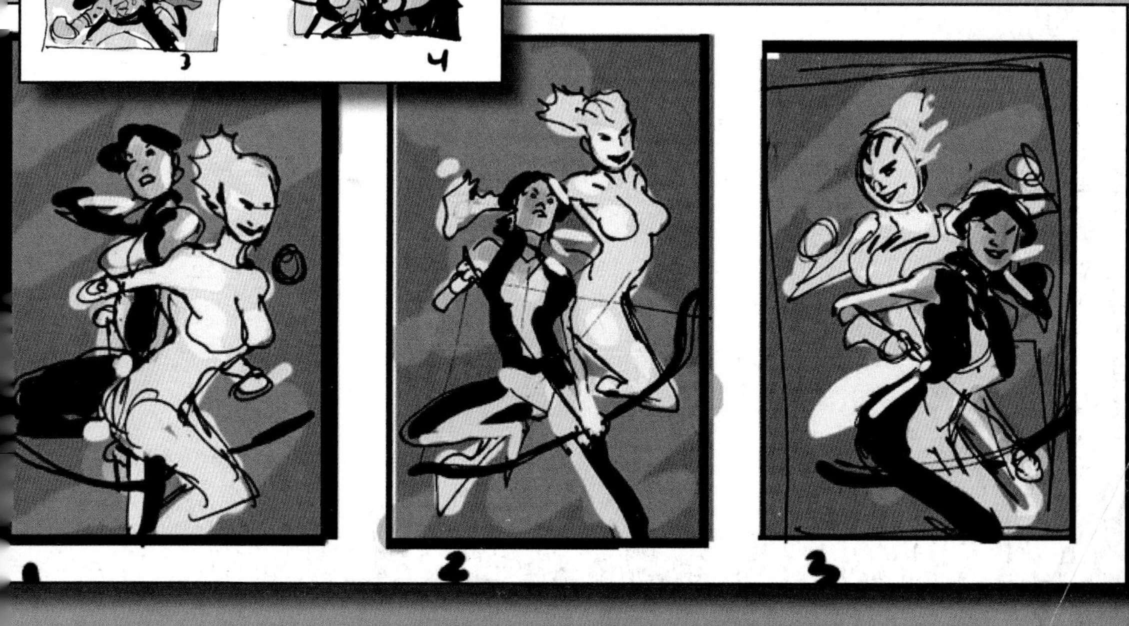

DEDICATED TO STÉPHANE PERU

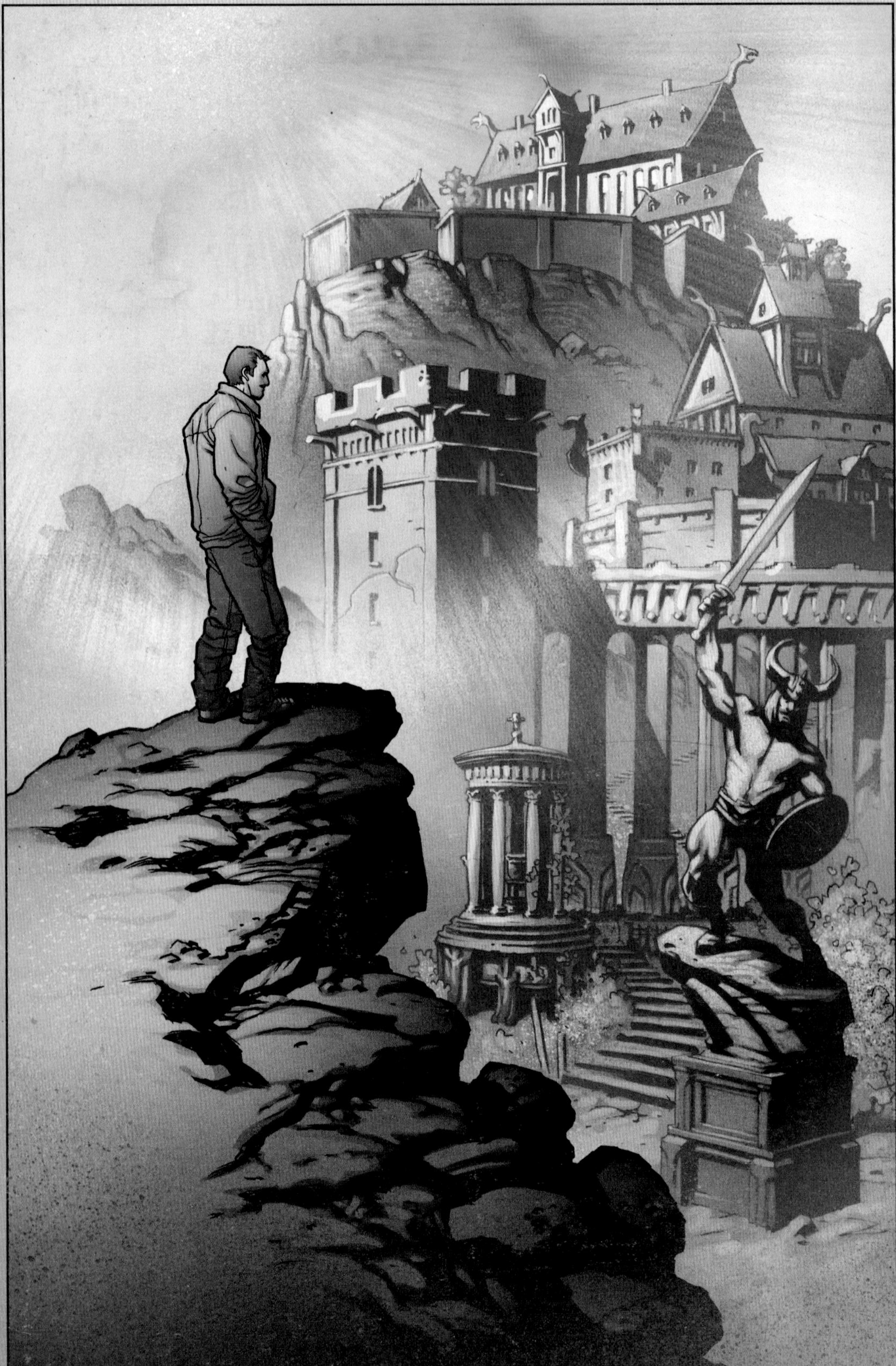

BY YANICK PAQUETTE & RICHARD ISANOVE